IMAGES
of America

THE RINES FAMILY LEGACY

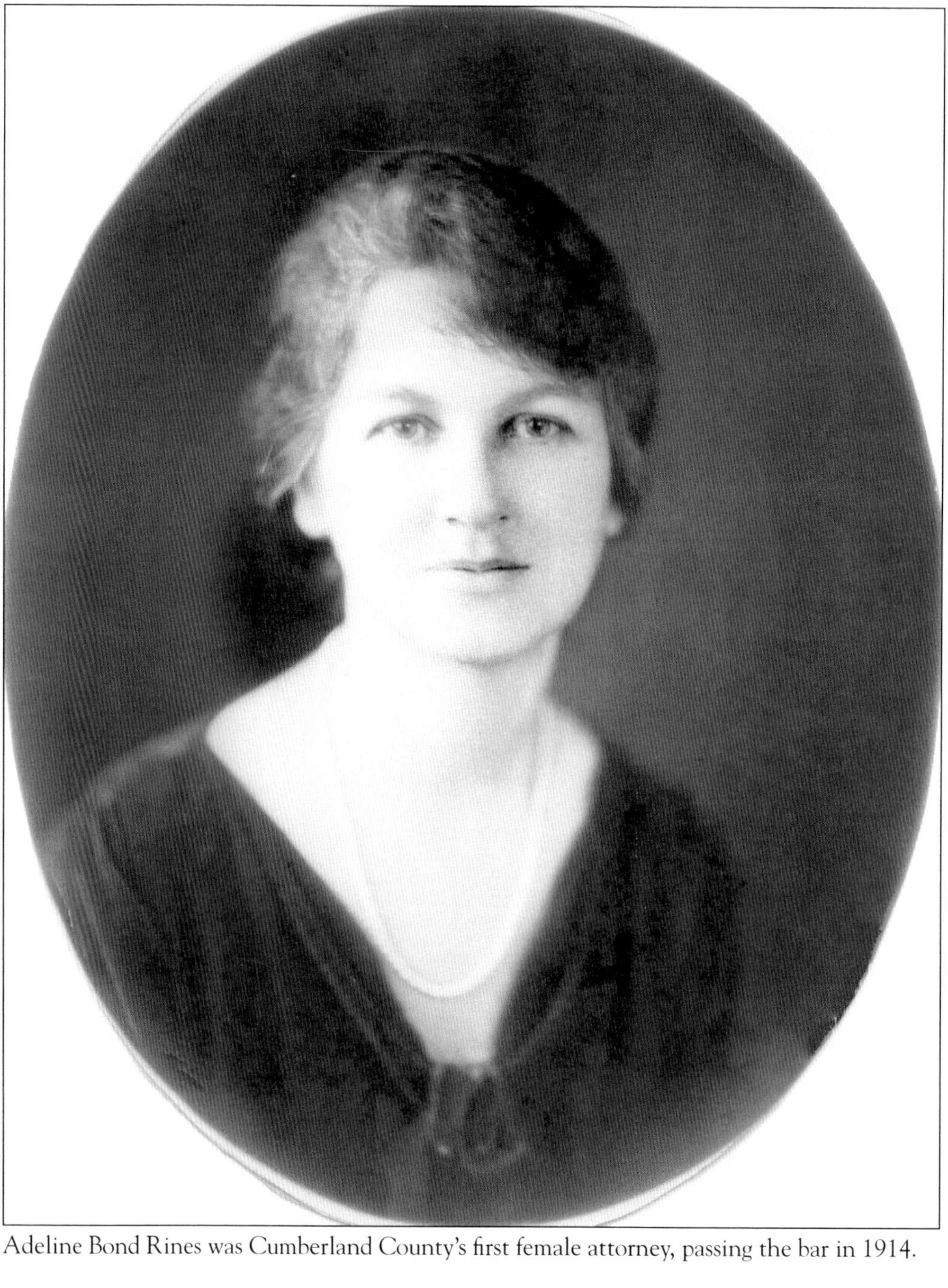

Adeline Bond Rines was Cumberland County's first female attorney, passing the bar in 1914.

IMAGES
of America

THE RINES FAMILY LEGACY

Frederic L. Thompson

ARCADIA

ISBN 0-7385-3882-5

Published by Arcadia Publishing
Charleston SC, Chicago IL, Portsmouth NH, San Francisco CA

Printed in Great Britain

Library of Congress Catalog Card Number: 2005926756

For all general information contact Arcadia Publishing at:
Telephone 843-853-2070
Fax 843-853-0044
E-mail sales@arcadiapublishing.com
For customer service and orders:
Toll-Free 1-888-313-2665

Visit us on the internet at http://www.arcadiapublishing.com

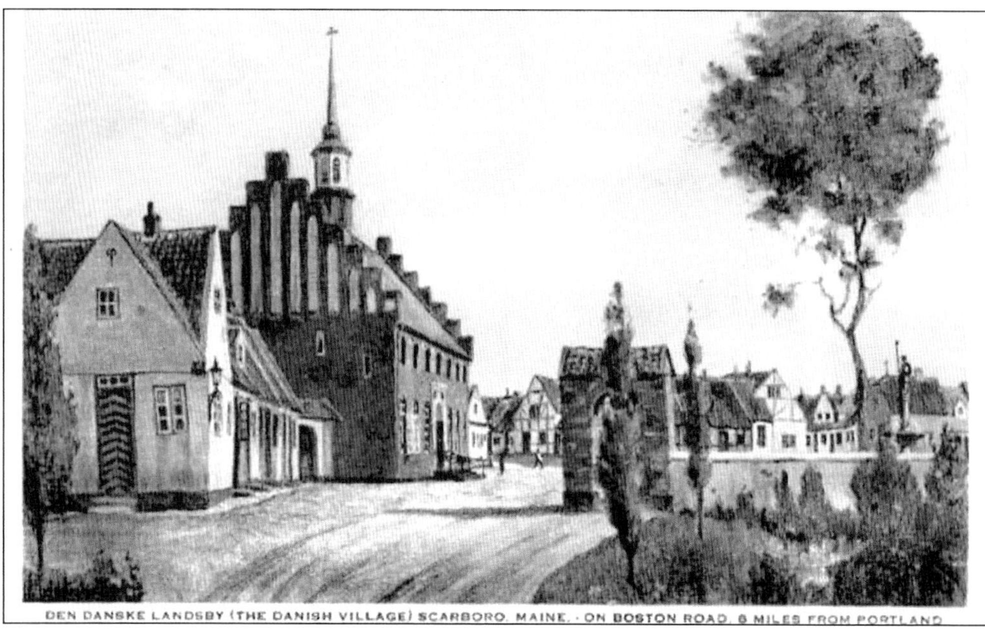

This illustrated postcard of the Danish Village dates from 1930.

CONTENTS

Acknowledgments

I would like to thank the following people for their help and advice: Nick Noyes, Bill Barry and Richard D'Abate at the Maine Historical Society; Hilary Bassett at Landmarks; Steve Thaxton, Bob Bettencourt, and Fred Nutter at WCSH6; Suzanne Goucher and the Maine Association of Broadcasters; Earle Shuttleworth at the Maine Historic Preservation Commission; Todd Reynolds of the City of Portland; Kathleen Pacella at the Eastland Park Hotel; Peggy Fuller of Good Works; Ed Brouder, Man from Mars Productions; Bernard, Dale, and Mathew Rines; Paul Tulley; Randy Henry; Dr. Philip P. Thompson Jr.; Nathaniel Thompson; Roland Sharrillo; Joseph Delafield; Britta Pejic; and Quinby Thompson.

INTRODUCTION

There is little doubt that the Rines family has left an indelible stamp on Maine. But who were they and what exactly was it that they did? This book provides some answers to these questions.

The four Rines brothers who arrived in Portland in the 1870s were born in Athens, Maine. They opened Portland's first department store in 1883, a store that would redefine Portland's retail shopping district. By the 1900s, they were one of Portland's largest landholders, owning great stretches of Congress Street. By the 1930s, the Rines family hotels and apartments had over 1,000 rooms in Portland and would employ hundreds during the darkest days of the Great Depression.

Henry Rines built Maine and New Hampshire's first commercial radio stations, WCSH and WFEA respectively. He would subsequently string a line of radio stations over most of northern New England. By the 1940s, his family owned and operated the largest hotel complex in New England, the Eastland and Congress Square hotels, with over 750 rooms. In 1927, NBC radio was brought to Maine and by 1990 the Rines stations were the oldest NBC affiliates in the country still under the same ownership. The First Radio Parish Church, brainchild of Henry Rines in 1926, is still the oldest continuous religious broadcast in the United States, seen daily on WCSH6 and WLBZ2. Rines' Danish Village in Scarborough was a re-created, medieval Danish town located on the edge of the Scarborough Marsh in the 1930s and 1940s, and considered by National Geographic Magazine to be one of America's first motels. During World War II, the Rines family utilized every bit of available space in their hotels to house service men and women and at times had dozens camping out in the lobby of the Eastland Hotel. Each room of the Eastland Hotel was built with three faucets for hot, cold, and ice water. Every room had a radio, all tuned to WCSH. The Eastland was the first hotel in America to have radios in every room.

The Rines family women were extraordinary individuals. Adeline Bond Rines was the first female attorney in Cumberland County, passing the bar in 1914. The main dining room at the Eastland Park Hotel carries her name today. The Portland Public Library's Rines Room was given by the family to the city in her honor. An award given annually by the Greater Portland United Way and WCSH6 recognizes Adeline's daughter, Mary Rines Thompson, posthumously. During her illustrious life she received the highest honors given by St. Joseph's College, Westbrook College of the University of New England, and Smith College. She sat on many boards, often as the only woman, and Portland's YWCA gave her the prestigious TWIN Award Emerita. In the 1970s and 1980s, she was one of only a few females to run a major media company in the

United States.

The Rines family has been a generous supporter of many of Portland's community institutions, leading the campaign to bring the Children's Museum of Maine and its world-class camera obscura to downtown Portland. The Rines/Thompson Fund of the Maine Community Foundation gives more than $100,000 annually to Portland charitable and civic organizations. The Rines family television stations have won many national awards and accolades, often chosen ahead of the largest television stations in the country. And as longtime broadcasters, the family has accumulated some of the industry's oldest and most unique memorabilia including the world's oldest television camera and the only original NBC chimes known to exist. Many of the Maine Broadcasting System personnel were recognized nationally for their talents. The founder of the National Radio and Television News Director's Association was the news director of WCSH Radio at the time. Jean Murray, a Rines company employee, was Maine's first female news correspondent. The accomplishments go on. I hope this book will give readers some insight into this singularly unique and industrious Maine family.

One

FOUR BROTHERS AND ONE TRANSCENDENT MOMENT

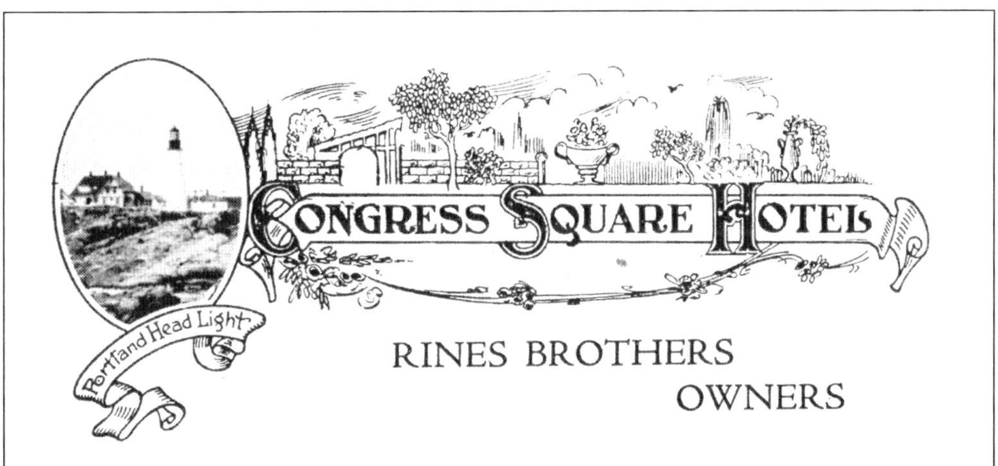

The four Rines brothers arrived in Portland in the 1870s from Athens, Maine, by way of Bangor. Their business enterprises over the next 40 years would change the face of downtown Portland forever.

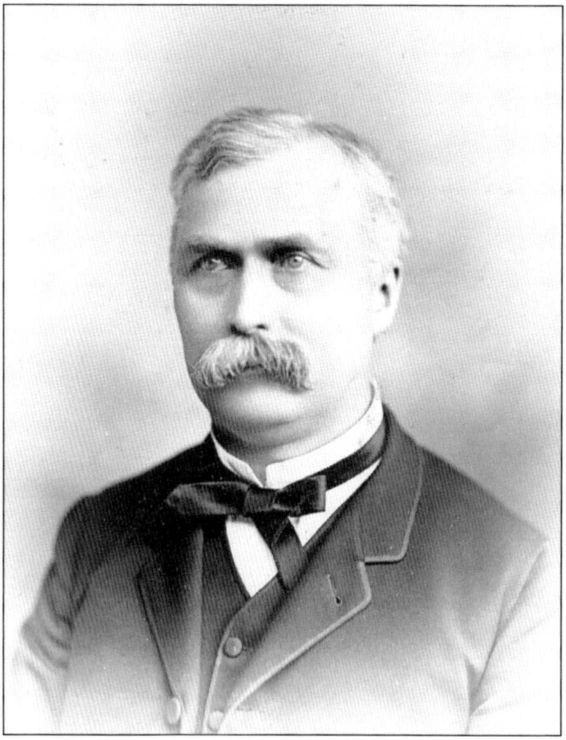

John T. Rines, 1834–1893, the oldest of the nine brothers and sisters, was from Athens, Maine, a small rural community north of Skowhegan. John and the Honorable J. P. Bass had worked together in a dry goods store in Lowell, Massachusetts, as young men and moved to Bangor in 1863 to seek employment. Eventually John formed the Rines Company and, with the help of Bass, erected a building on Main Street in 1869.

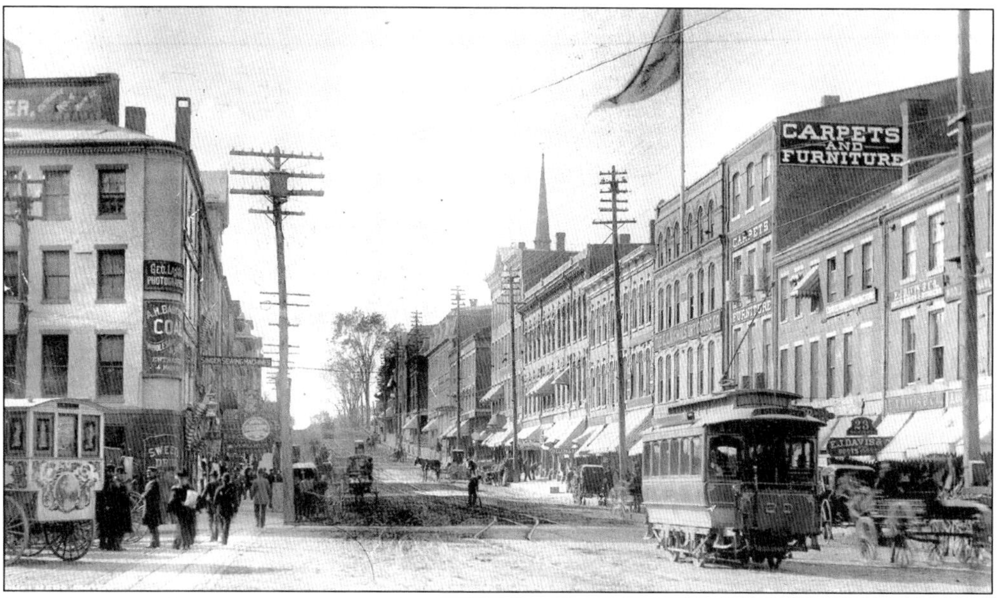

Main Street in Bangor, seen here at the beginning of the 20th century, was a city filled with hope and commercial promise, a far cry from the dwindling farming opportunities of rural Maine. When John T. Rines moved to Bangor in 1863, he saw a booming city teeming with land speculators, lumberjacks, businessmen, and most importantly, a burgeoning consumer population with expendable income. After partnering with E. C. Nichols, John opened his own dry goods store in 1869. It was located behind the second utility pole on the right. (Courtesy of the Maine Historic Preservation Commission.)

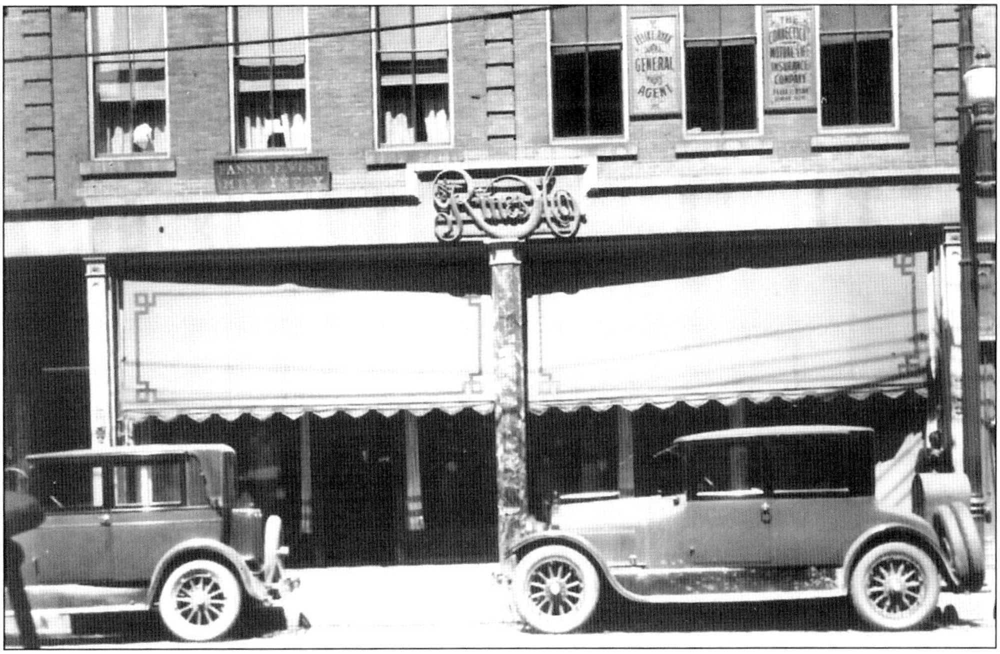

The Rines Block, erected by John Rines and J.P. Bass, was one of several dry goods stores along Main Street in Bangor, Maine. All four of John's brothers worked in this store in the 1870s and apprenticed at his side. John never lived in Portland, but all of his brothers moved there and took with them his business judgment and real-estate development expertise.

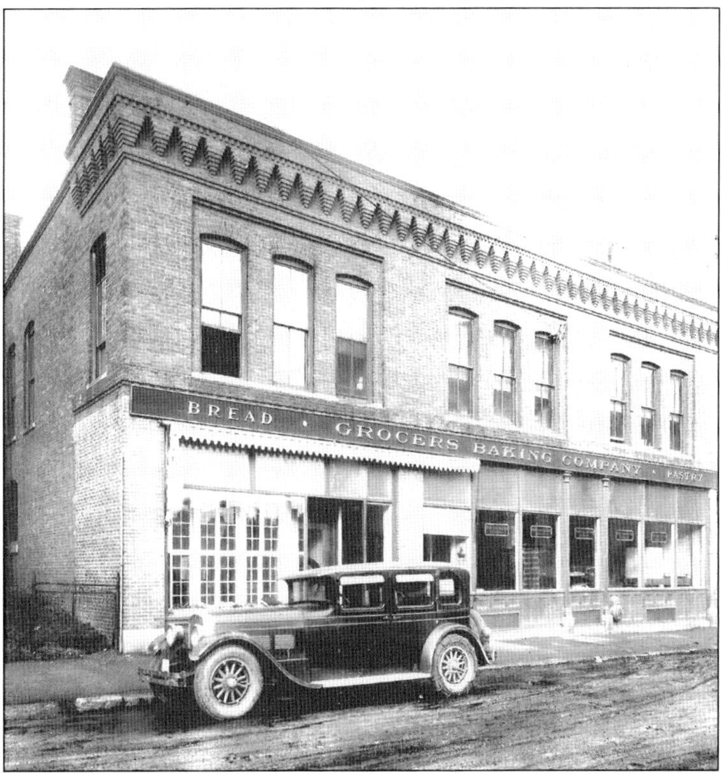

John T. Rines built the Rines Block in 1869 and this property on Columbia Street in Bangor just behind his building on Main Street. Rines "added much to the appearance and value of the real estate of the city . . . .Devoted to his business of which he was a thorough master, his business relations with all were of the most pleasant character and with none more so than with his employees, whom he treated with the utmost courtesy and unfailing consideration." (Obituary from July 28, 1893.)

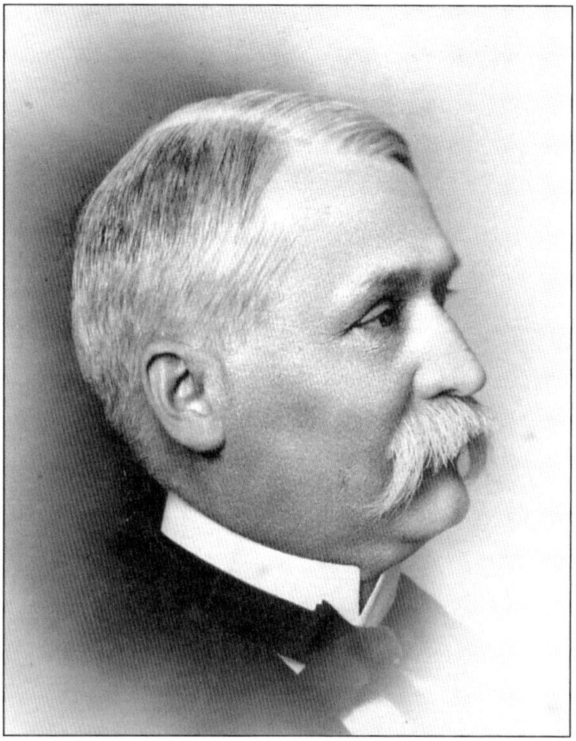

Albert S. Rines, 1848–1924, founded a small dry-goods store with his brother David at 261 Middle Street in Portland in 1874. Measuring 18 feet by 55 feet, the brothers' store had only two clerks.

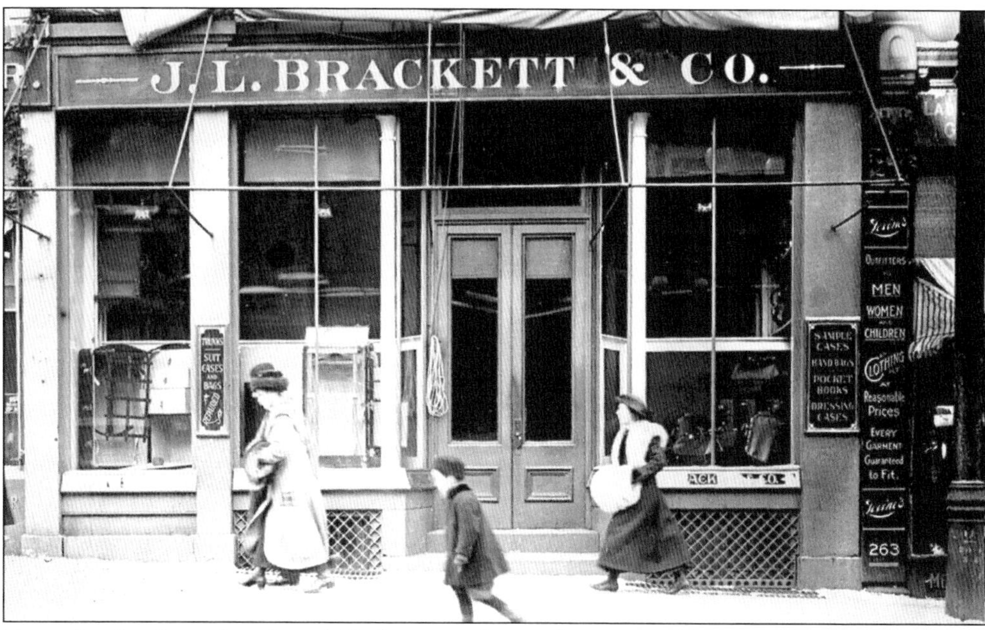

Two other brothers, Joseph and Hight, started a similar store a short time later at 265 Middle Street, seen here in 1900, just two doors away. In 1883, the four brothers formed the Rines Brothers Company and moved into the J. B. Brown block on Congress Street, a building built specifically for them. Relocating up Congress Street was a daring step for the brothers, for they were moving out of Portland's major retail district on Middle Street. (Collections of the Maine Historical Society.)

David T. Rines, 1845–1903, cofounded the original dry goods store at 261 Middle Street with Albert. When the brothers consolidated their operations with two other brothers to form the Rines Brothers Company, at 529 Congress Street, they took a risk. The store was a large, 40,000 square foot building. Fortunately, it was a successful endeavor and speedily took its place among the leading business concerns of the city. The Rines Brothers Company Store would establish a new location for the city's retail district.

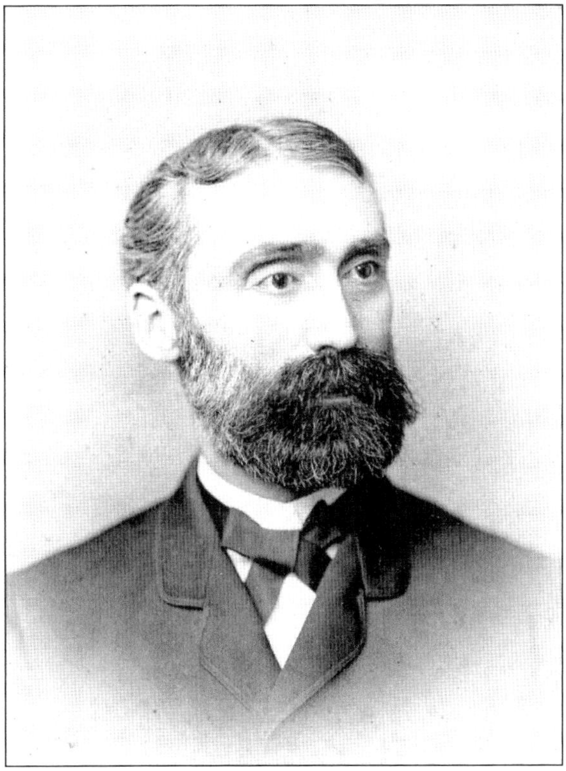

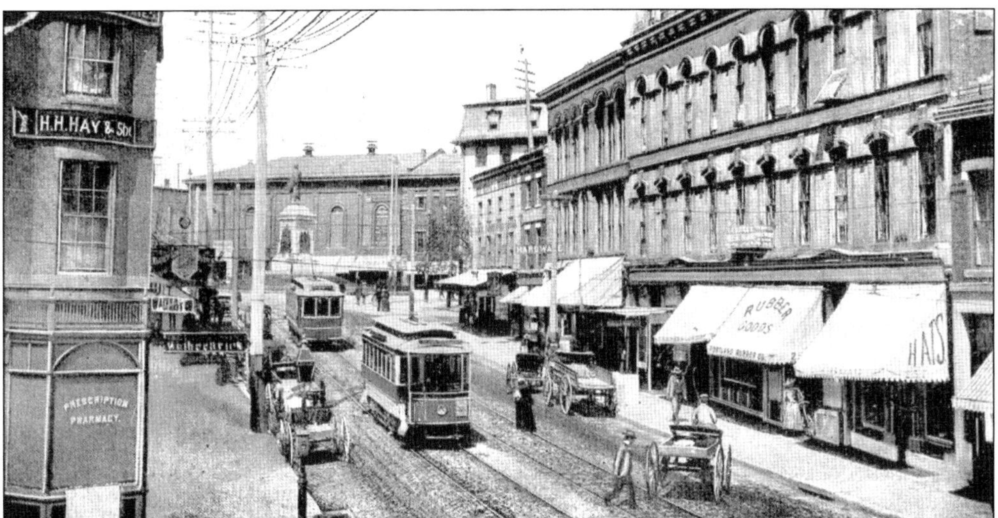

This view of Middle Street, with H. H. Hay and Sons on the left and the Liberty Statue of Monument Square in the distance, looked very similar to the street when the four Rines brothers operated two separate stores here in 1880. Their stores, 261 and 265 Middle Street, are on the right. (Courtesy of the Maine Historic Preservation Commission.)

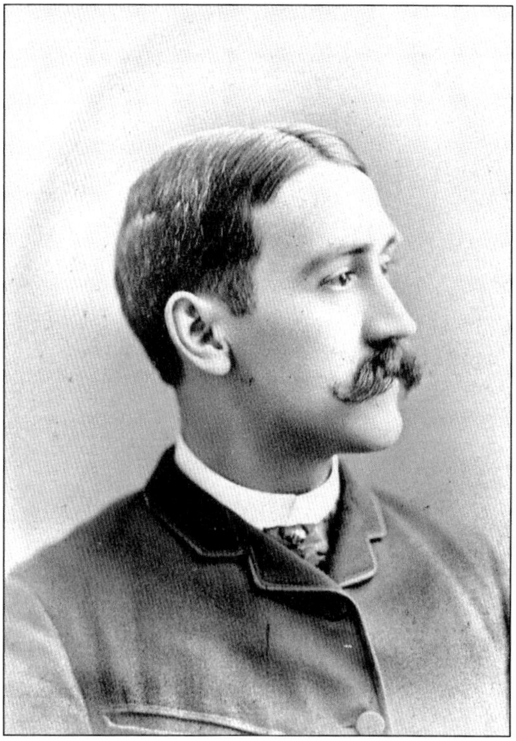

R. Hight Rines, 1853–1935, was a cofounder of the Rines Brothers Company Store along with his three older brothers. In 1893, he became the proprietor of the Columbia Hotel at 639 Congress Street, a property built and operated by his two brothers, Albert and David. A partner with his brothers in many real-estate holdings, he wrote the book *Panics, Facts to Keep in Mind Especially when General Business is Somewhat above Normal* in 1932.

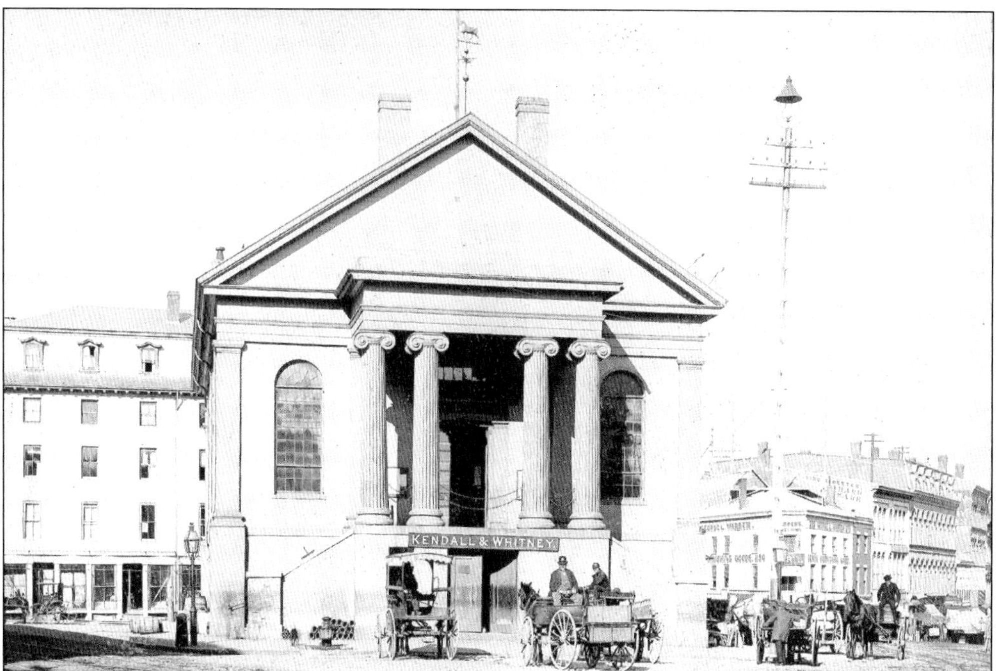

Old City Hall became the Kendall and Whitney store in late-19th-century Portland. This location is presently Monument Square. The original Rines brothers' stores on Middle Street, seen here in the background on the right, are presently the location of One City Center. (Courtesy of the Maine Historic Preservation Commission.)

Joseph H. Rines, 1841–1919, was 21 when he joined the Sixth Massachusetts Volunteers in 1862 to serve in the Union Army. After the war he started a career with Reed and Barton selling silverware, a job that took him around the world. He came to Portland to work with his three brothers in 1878. With a strong financial business sense, he became president of the Rines Brothers Company Store in 1900. He was the driving force behind the construction and operation of the Congress Square Hotel in 1896.

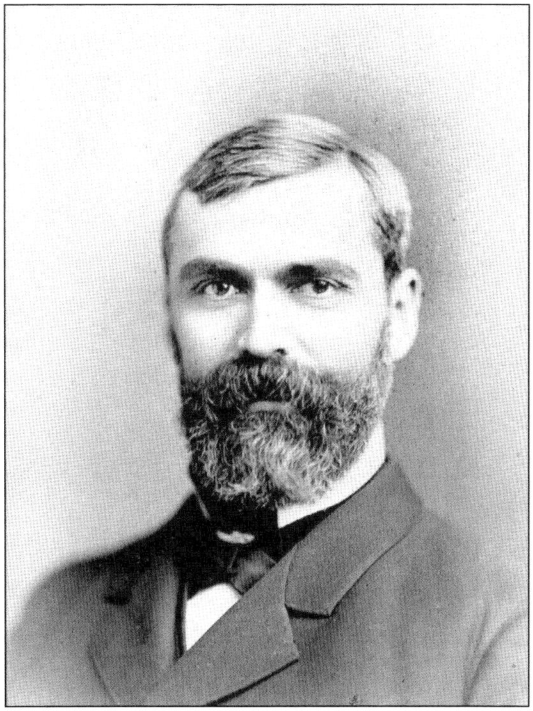

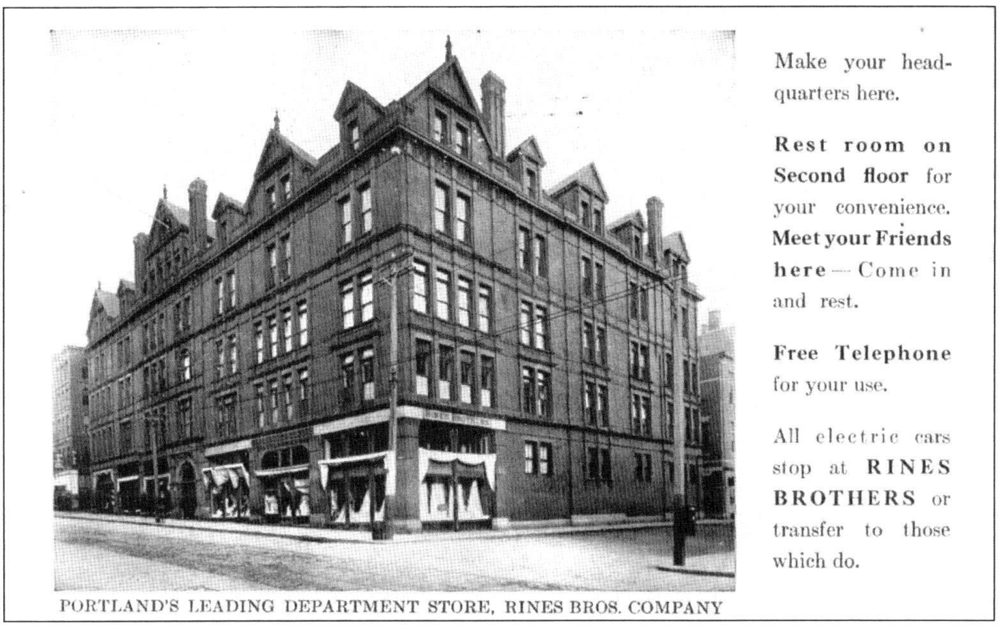

The Rines brothers moved into the relatively large five-story J. B. Brown Block on the corner of Casco and Congress streets in 1883. From employing only a few people on Middle Street, they eventually employed over 200 people in the J. B. Brown Block. The public was immediately taken by this large department store with its selection and variety of dresses, shoes, linens, gloves, and the latest ladies and men's fashions. The Rines Brothers Company Store would redefine Portland's retail center for the next century. (Courtesy of the Maine Historic Preservation Commission.)

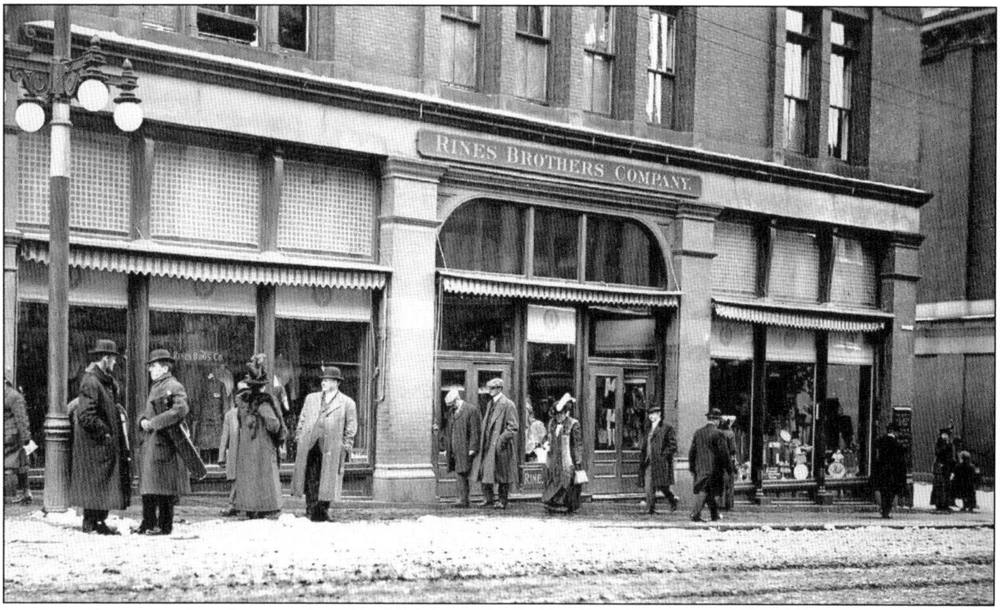

In this photograph taken in front of the Rines Brothers Company Store in 1912, everyone is wearing a hat. Fashions held a great deal of embedded power and clothing expressed much about the wearer. Whether small specialty shops or large department stores, retail stores lined the streets of Portland. (Collections of the Maine Historical Society.)

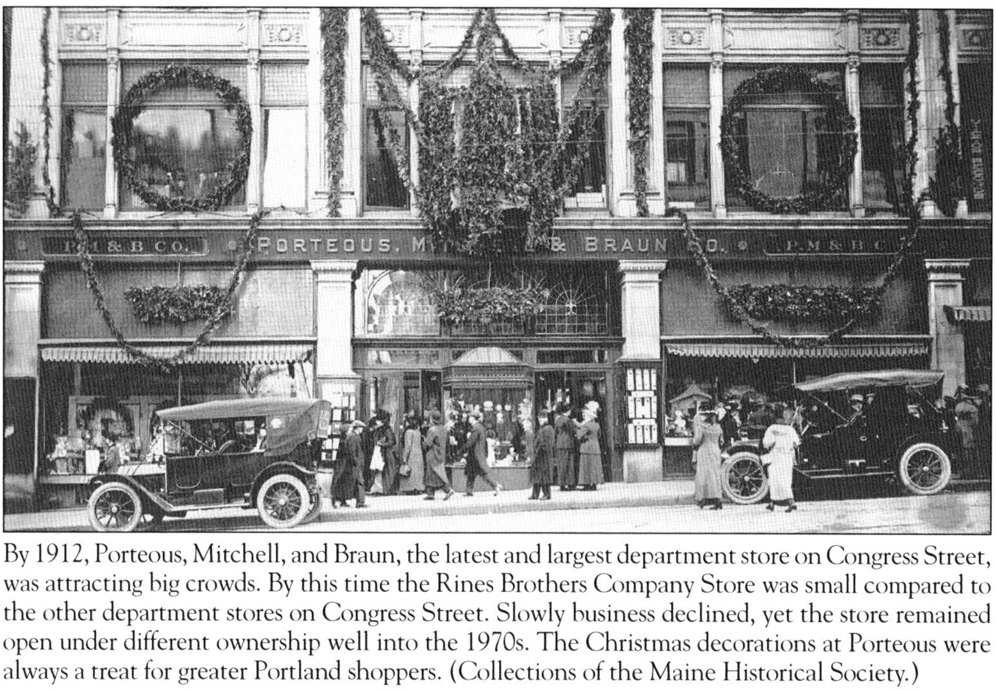

By 1912, Porteous, Mitchell, and Braun, the latest and largest department store on Congress Street, was attracting big crowds. By this time the Rines Brothers Company Store was small compared to the other department stores on Congress Street. Slowly business declined, yet the store remained open under different ownership well into the 1970s. The Christmas decorations at Porteous were always a treat for greater Portland shoppers. (Collections of the Maine Historical Society.)

This image depicts views down Congress Street from the Congress Square Hotel in Portland at the beginning of the 20th century. Libby's large department store is in the foreground and eventually the Porteous, Mitchell, and Braun department store would be built farther down the street. One can see by the trolley cars and traffic that Congress Street between Congress Square and Monument Square was becoming Portland's primary shopping area.

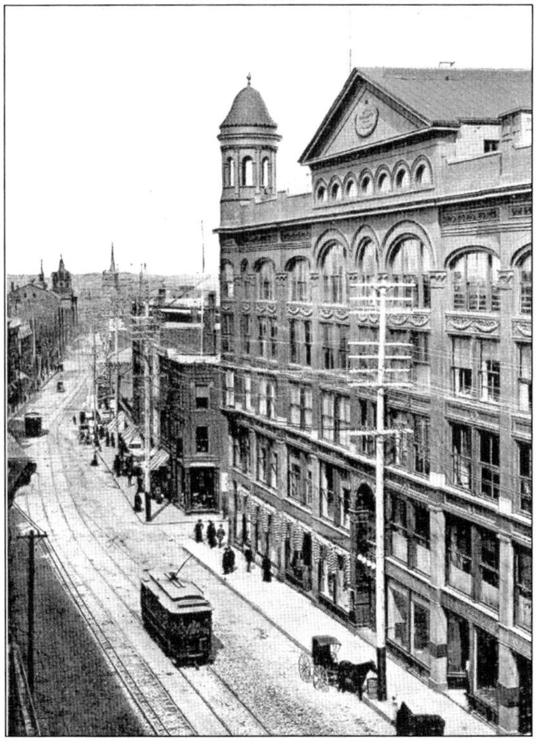

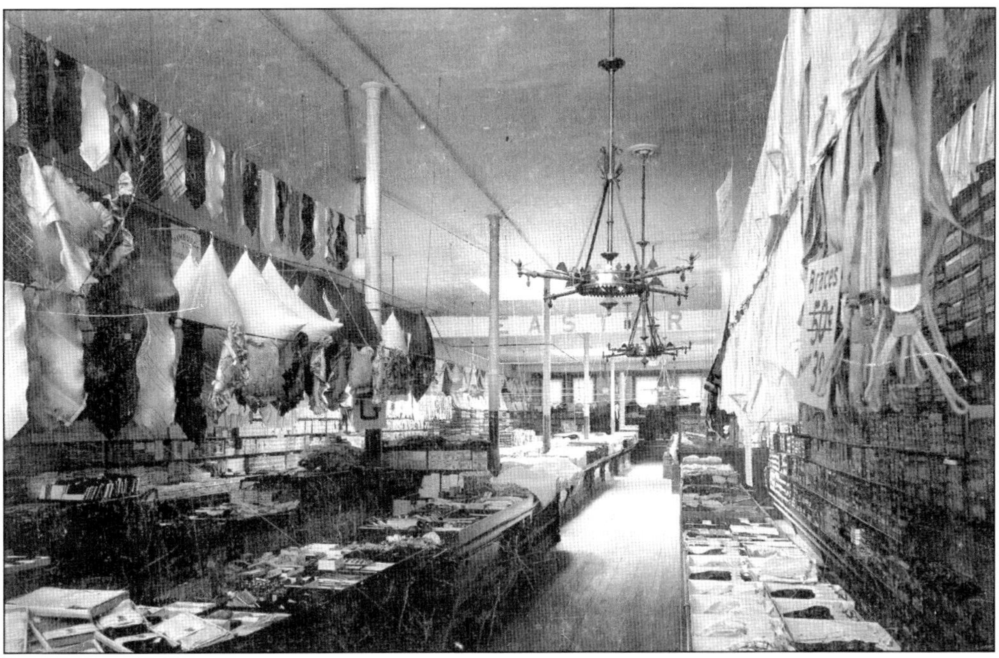

Quantity, accessibility, and price drew shoppers to the Congress Street department stores. Late-19th-century consumers with growing, expendable incomes found these stores luxurious and irresistible. This interior of the J. Libby department store shows the variety and quality that impressed late-19th-century Portland shoppers unaccustomed to such abundance. (Courtesy of the Maine Historic Preservation Commission.)

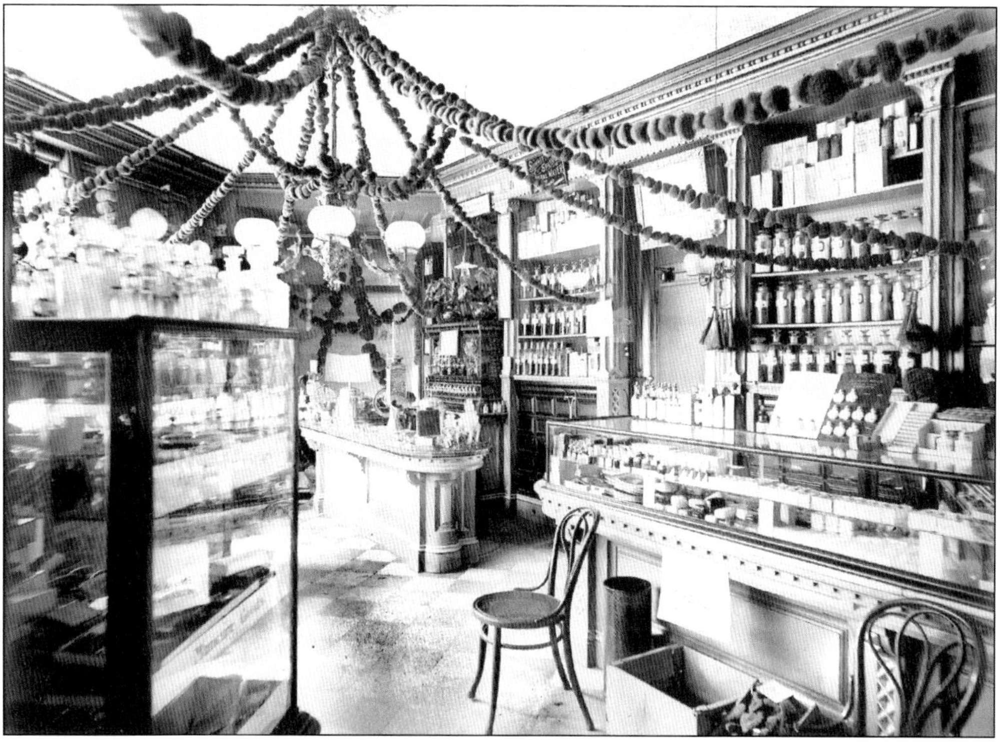

Luxurious displays, like this one in Hay's Drug store in Congress Square, were attractive to late-19th-century Portlanders. (Courtesy of the Maine Historic Preservation Commission.)

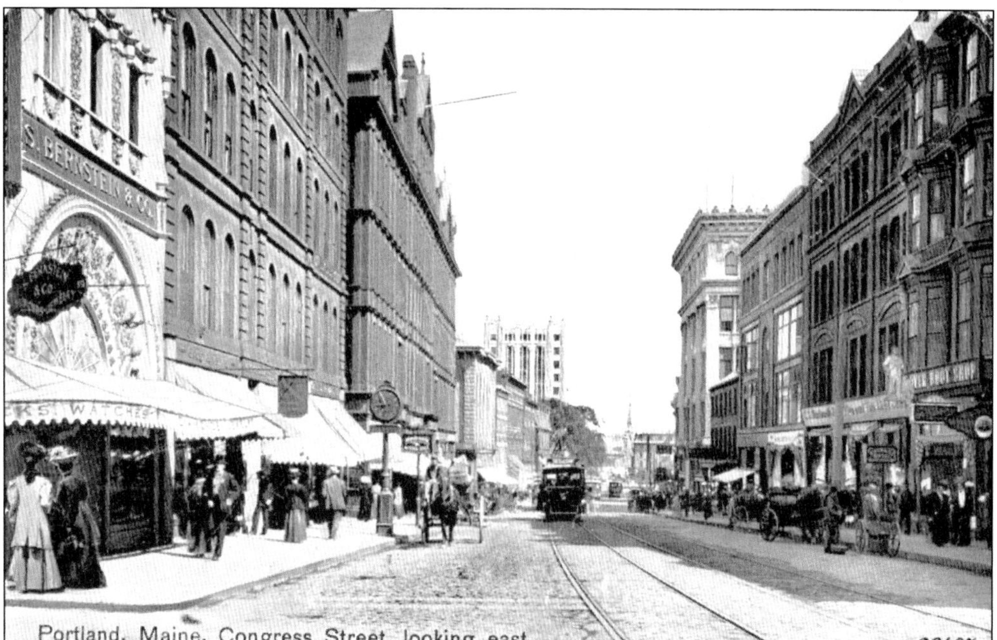

This is an early-20th-century view of Congress Street looking toward Monument Square with the Rines Brothers Company Store on the left. (Courtesy of the Maine Historic Preservation Commission.)

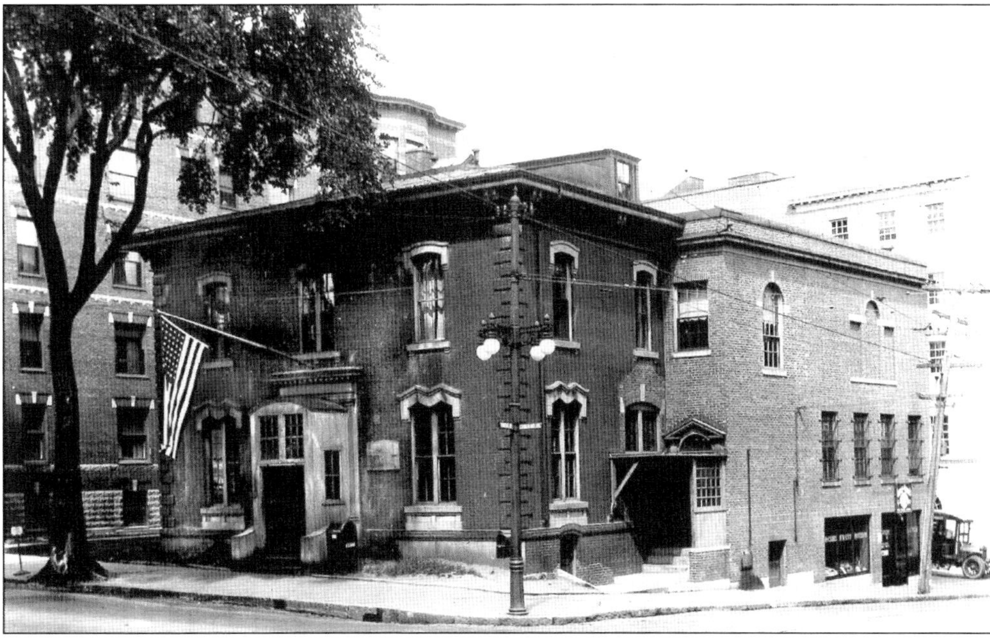

The Rines brothers began acquiring land and developing commercial buildings like this one in the late 19th century. Pictured here is the U.S. Substation at 415 Cumberland Avenue on the corner of Forest Avenue. This building has been home to many organizations including the Dorothy Mason School of Dance and Thomas Moser Furniture Gallery.

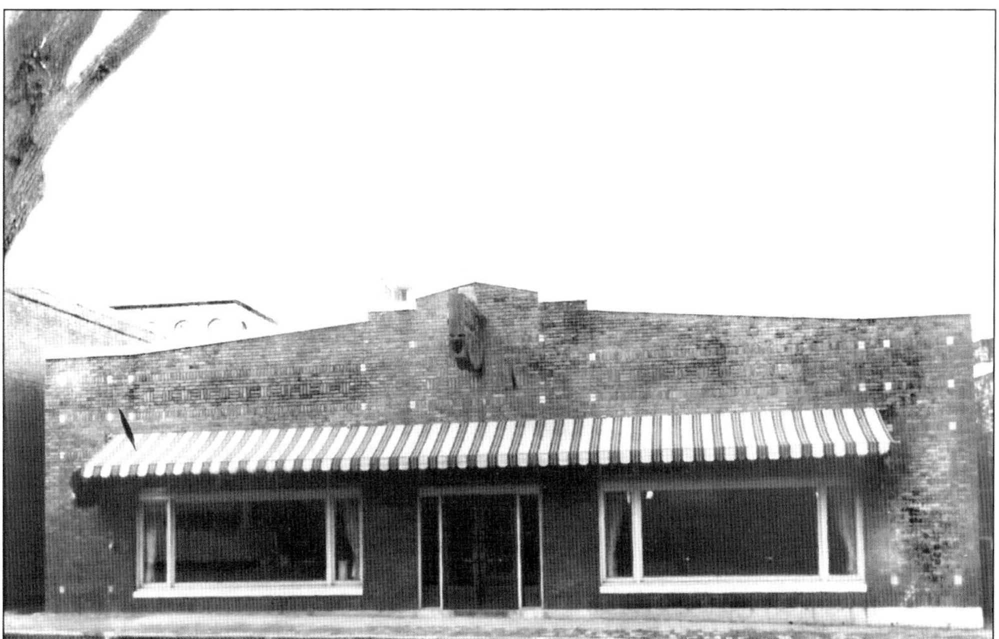

This restaurant at 92 Oak Street was a project of the Rines brothers. Years later this building would be the home to the Oak Street Theater.

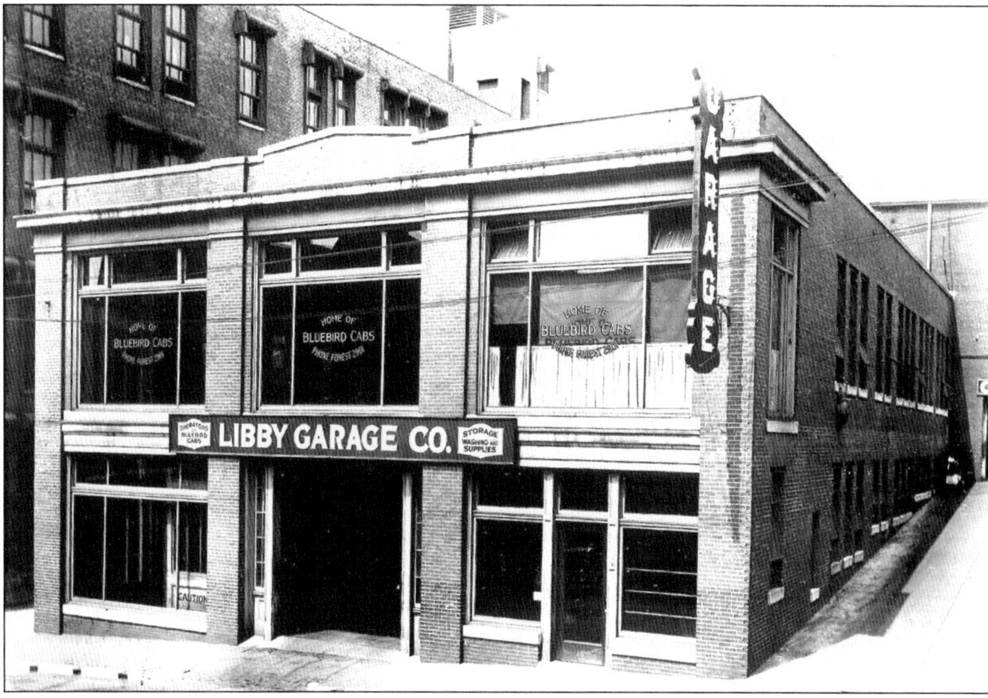

Transitioning from stabling horses to parking automobiles was a challenge for early-20th-century Portlanders. The Rines brothers realized that department store patrons and hotel guests needed parking for their cars. This garage on Forest Avenue was handy to their enterprises.

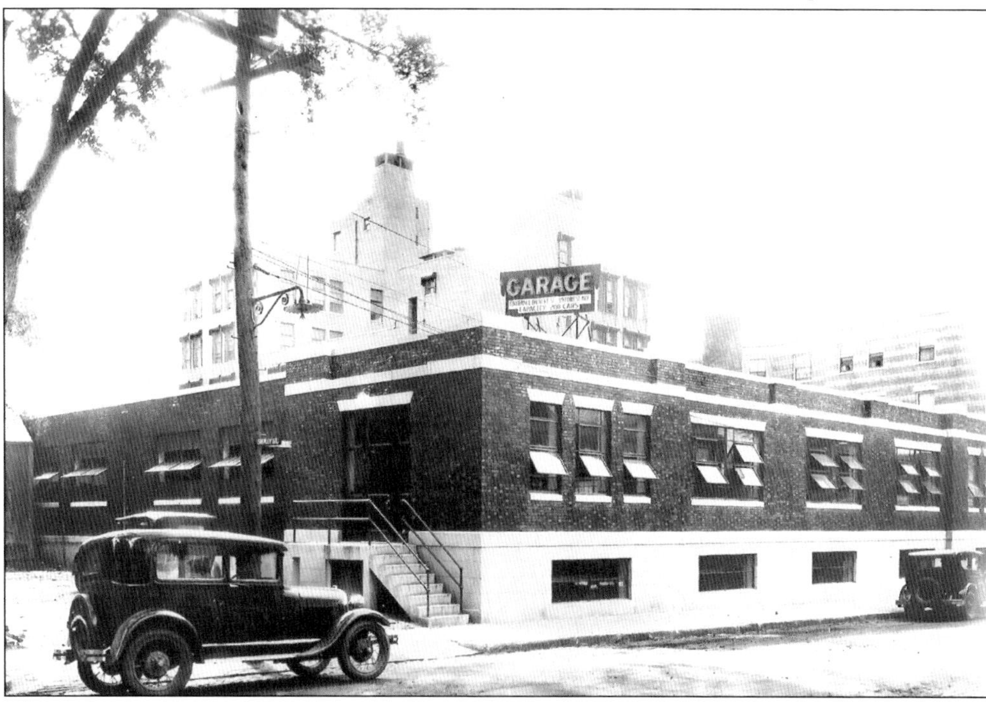

This is the rear view of the same garage opening out onto Oak Street just one half block from the Rines Brothers Company Store on Congress Street.

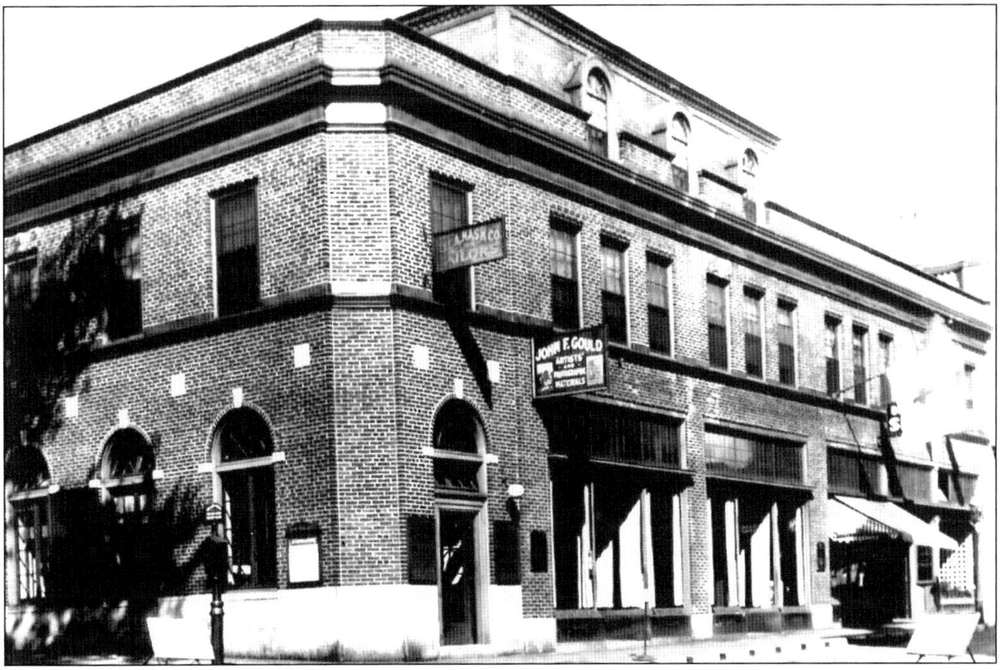

A look in the Cumberland County Registry of Deeds shows page after page of transactions by the Rines Real Estate Company and the four Rines brothers. By the beginning of the 20th century, they were among Portland's largest taxpayers. Here is a building built by the brothers on the corner of Brown and Free Streets, across from the present-day Cumberland County Civic Center.

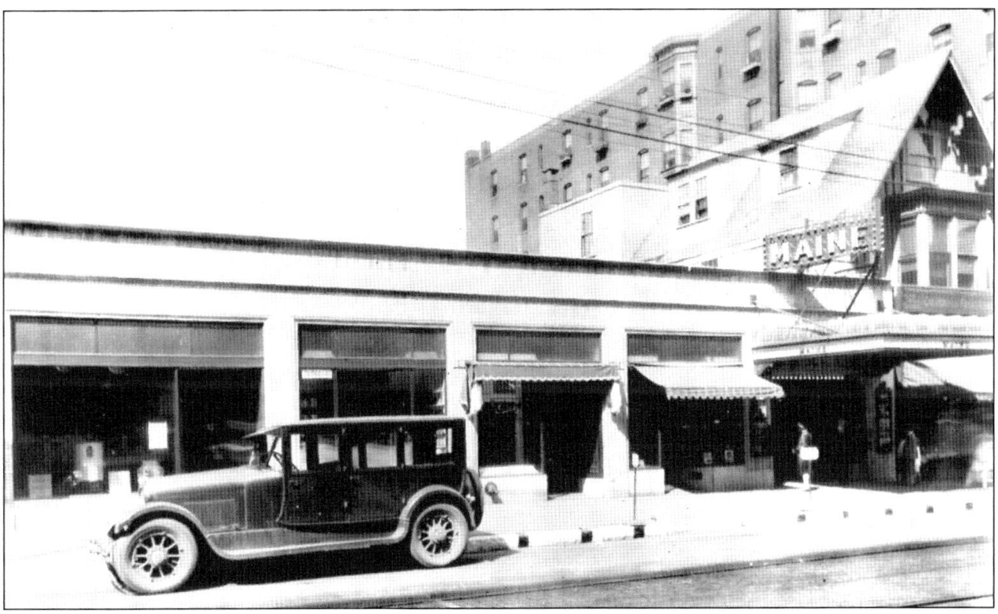

Whether developing restaurants, movie theaters, apartment houses, or bowling alleys, there were few popular businesses the brothers did not consider. Here is the Maine Theater at 637-641 Congress Street that they built. When the brothers realized that Portland lacked new, efficient and modern hotels, they entered that field, and built and operated some of Portland's finest.

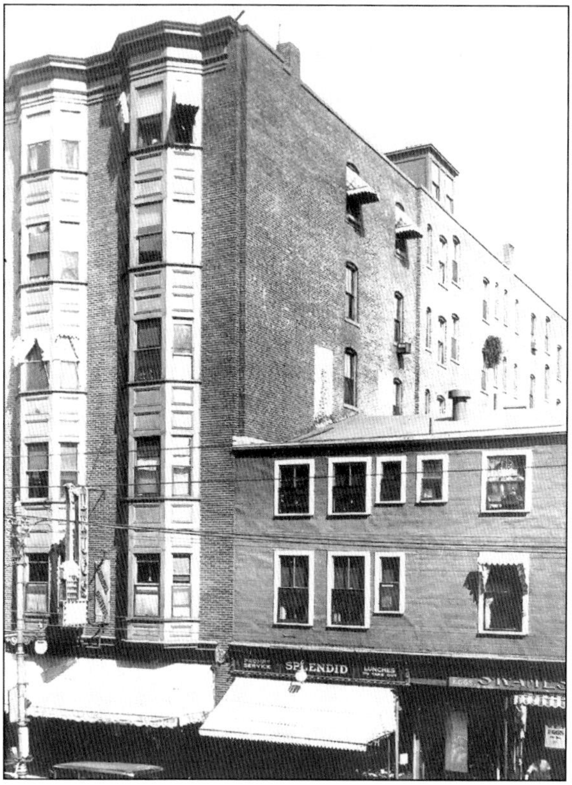

Often one brother would develop a property by himself such as the Burnham Arms apartments at 633 Congress Street built by Joseph Rines in 1903. Joseph eventually gave this building to his daughter-in-law Adeline Bond as a wedding present when she married Henry P. Rines in 1915.

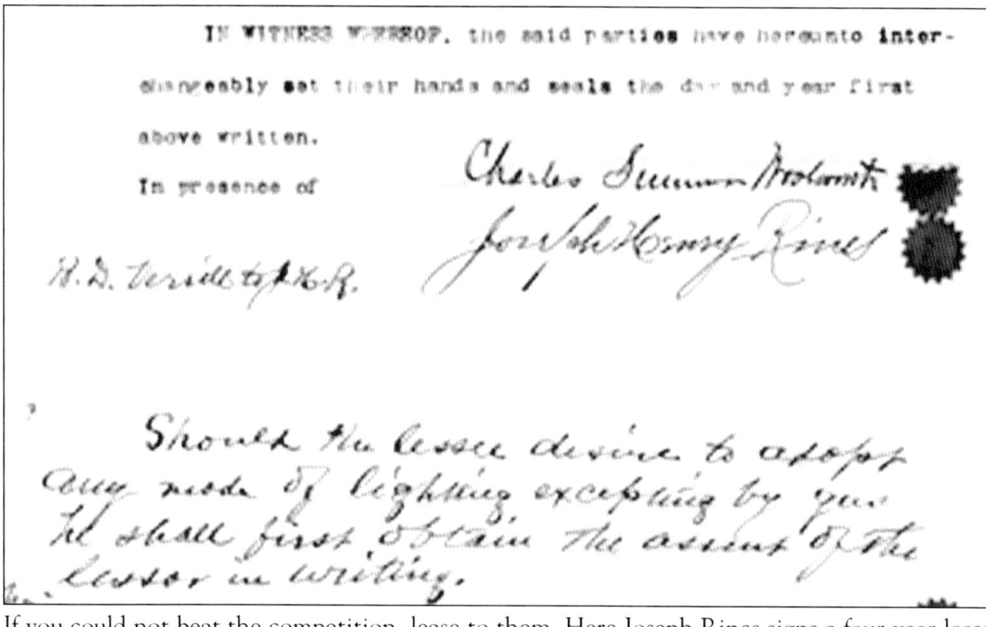

IN WITNESS WHEREOF, the said parties have hereunto interchangeably set their hands and seals the day and year first above written.

In presence of

Charles Sumner Woolworth

Joseph Henry Rines

H. D. Verrill to J.H.R.

Should the lessee desire to adopt any mode of lighting excepting by gas he shall first obtain the assent of the lessor in writing.

If you could not beat the competition, lease to them. Here Joseph Rines signs a four-year lease with Charles Summer Woolworth to rent one of Joseph's buildings to the five and dime store magnate's younger brother in 1895. Joseph bought and leased four buildings located directly across the street from the Rines Brothers Company Store in 1890. L. L. Bean presently occupies this same space in the former J. J. Newbury Building at 542 Congress Street.

Albert Rines, seen here at home in 1910, and his wife, Ada Ella, had no children. His home at 172 State Street below is presently the Conroy Tully Funeral Home. It was filled with fine antiques of considerable value. (Courtesy of Paul Tully.)

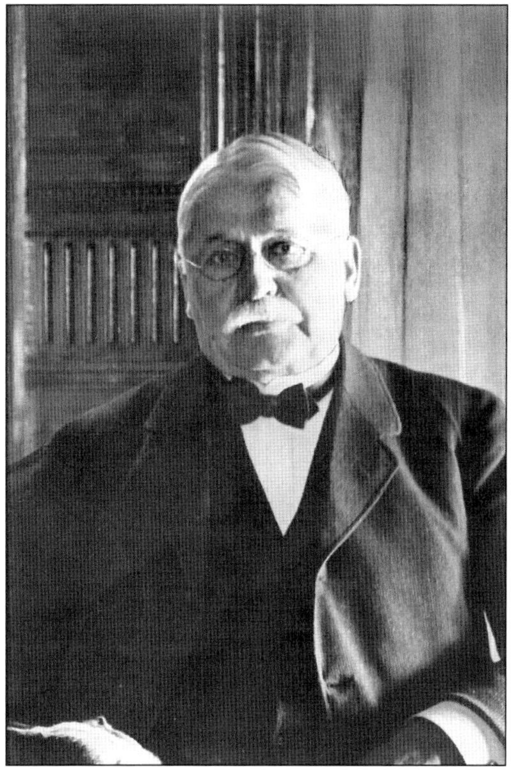

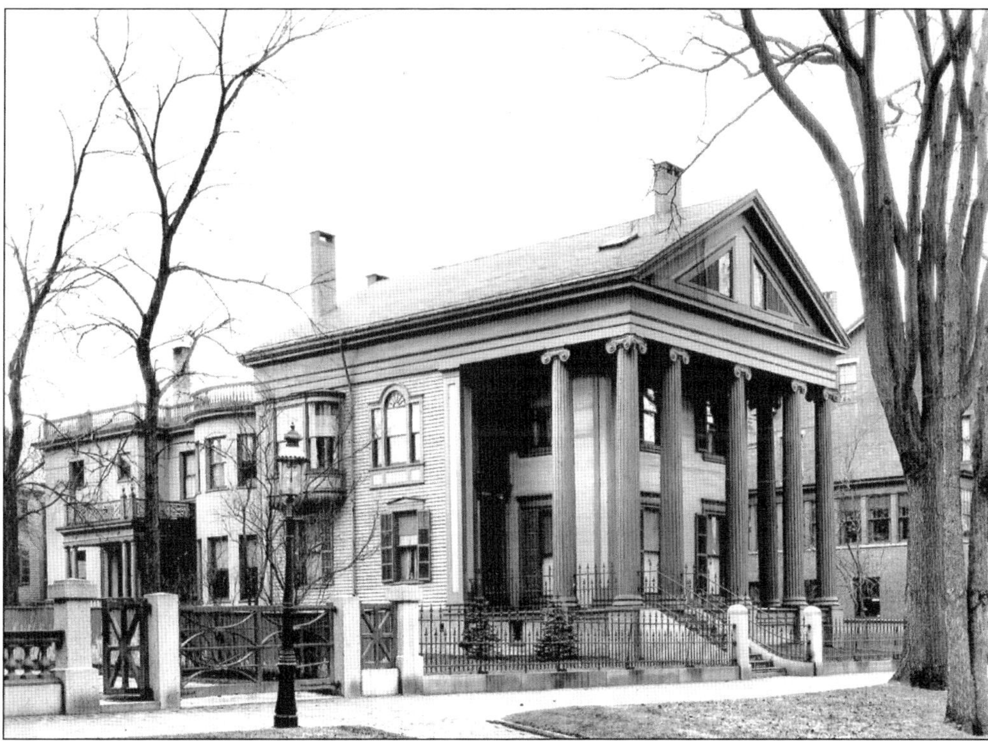

The Albert Rines home is pictured here in 1910. (Courtesy of Paul Tully.)

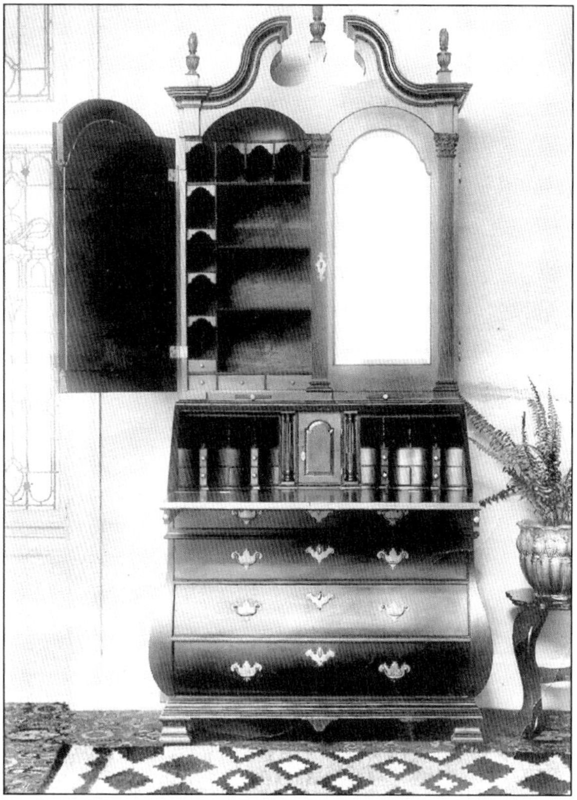

Albert's passion was collecting antiques. His chauffeur, a luxury in 1915 Portland, would drive him through the country. If Albert saw a house that appeared as though it might contain precious old furniture, he would stop and inquire if the homeowner had any old chairs, desks, or bureaus they might wish to sell him. Nine times out of ten, they did not.

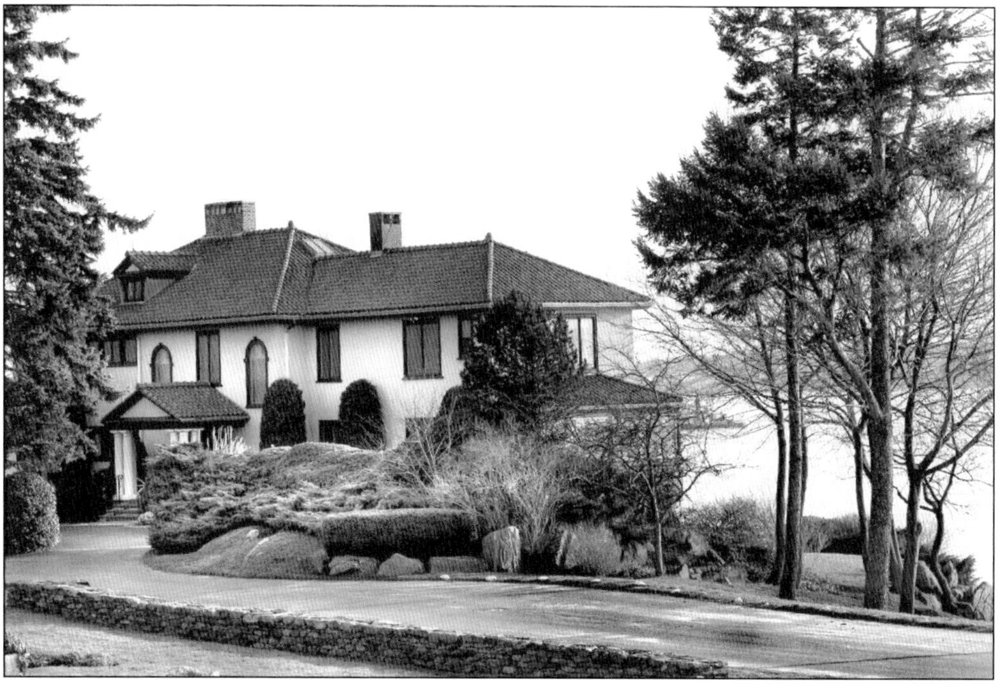

Albert Rines built a summer home in Ottawa Park on the shore in Cape Elizabeth, which still stands today. A few years after his death in 1924, his houses and furnishings were separated and sold.

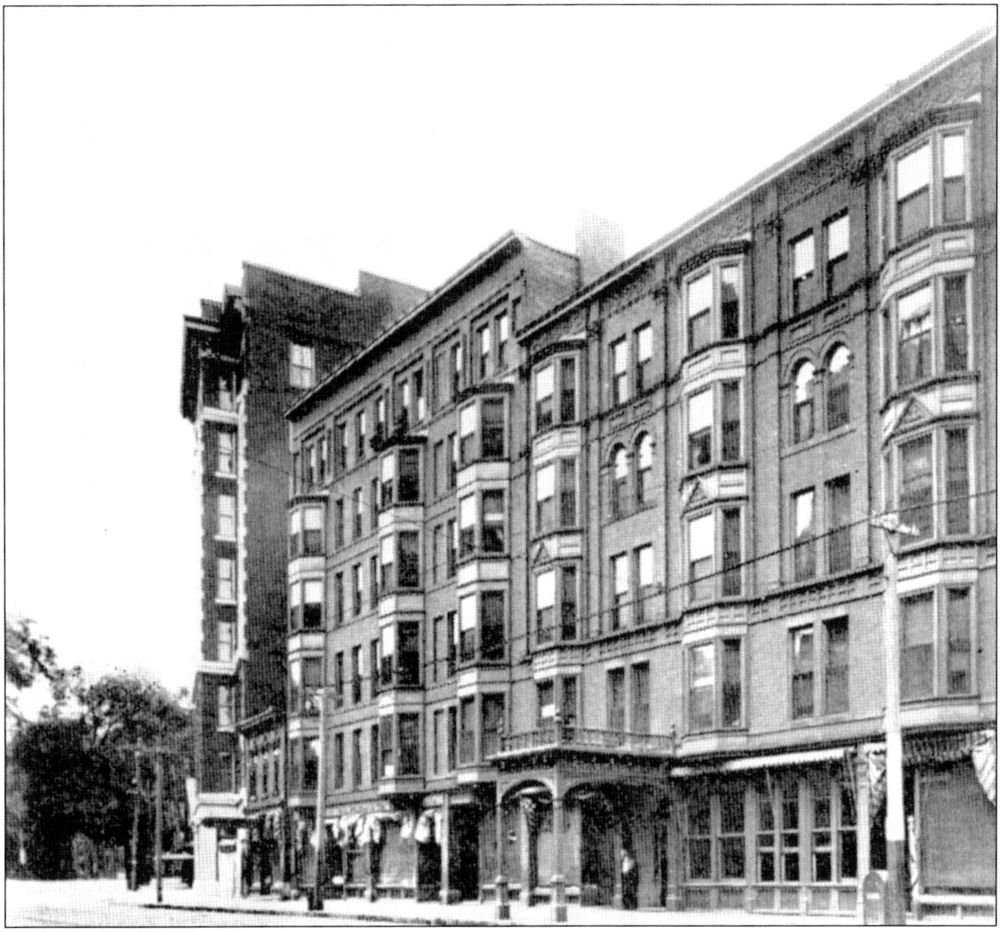

Pictured here is the Columbia Hotel at 645 Congress Street, a property of the Rines Real Estate Company. Built in 1894 and named after the Columbia Exposition of 1893 in Chicago, it was one of Portland's largest. David T. and Albert S. Rines were the owners and R. Hight Rines was the manager. (Courtesy of the Maine Historic Preservation Commission.)

The Hotel

THE HOTEL solid and safe in construction, amply supplied with fire escapes, is planned upon generous lines to insure large cool and airy chambers. It attracts the visitor by its homelike appearance and pleasant surroundings.

Albert and David Rines were co-owners of the Columbia Hotel when this booklet was published in the early 1900s. (Courtesy of the Maine Historic Preservation Commission.)

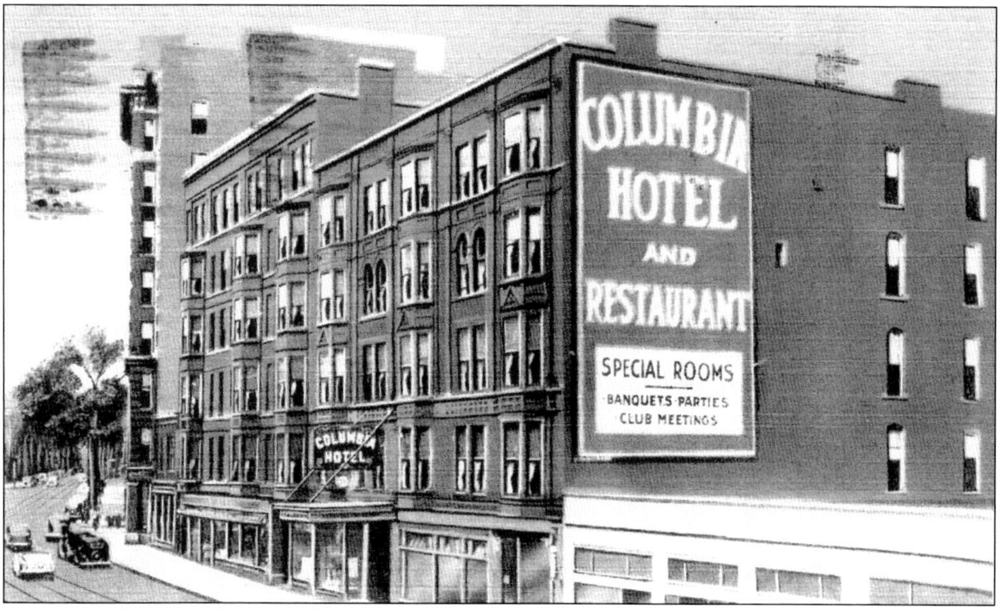

The Columbia Hotel operated on the American Plan with rates starting from $2.50.

The Hotel

THE HOTEL is complete in its own Steam and Electric plants.

The Steam Heating is so arranged as to furnish comfortable heat in late Spring and early Fall as well as in Winter.

The Electrical plant is modern and up to date for the proper lighting of the house and the running of the safe and noiseless elevator.

The management and owners have endeavored to raise the standard of the Hotel to the standard of a First Class Home, and are not sparing of Expense to gain the desired end.

The hotel is operated on the American plan. Rates from $2.50 to $5.00 per day. Special weekly rates. Inquiries may be directed to

COLUMBIA HOTEL, Portland, Maine,

Walter L. Palmer, Manager.

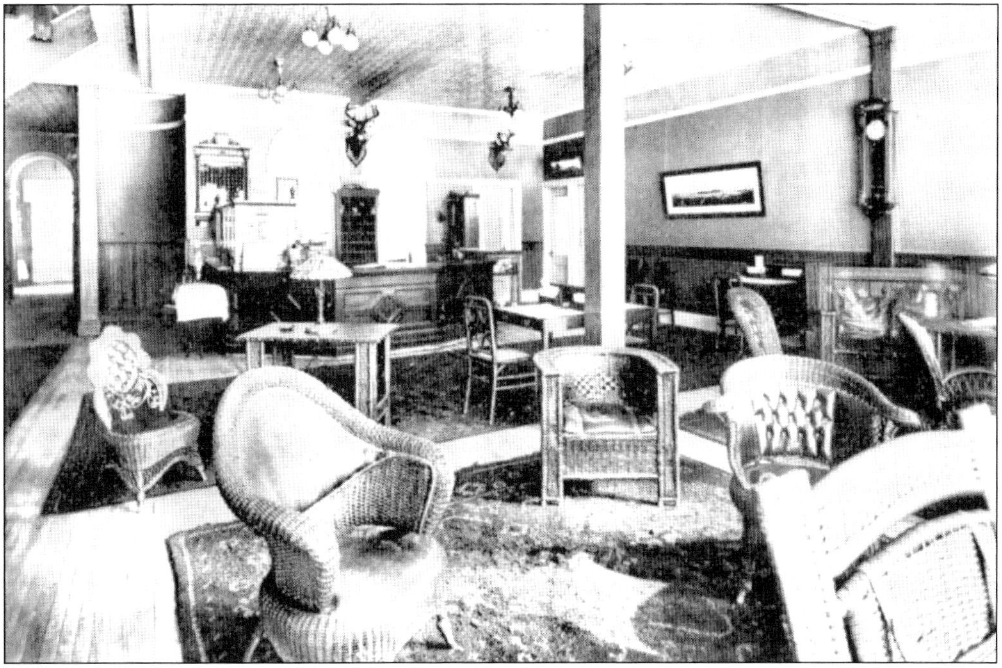

The office and the adjoining lounge in Columbia Hotel were advertised as "most attractive."

The Office

IS pleasantly situated on the street floor and is most attractive.

The lounging room adjoining is commodious and restful.

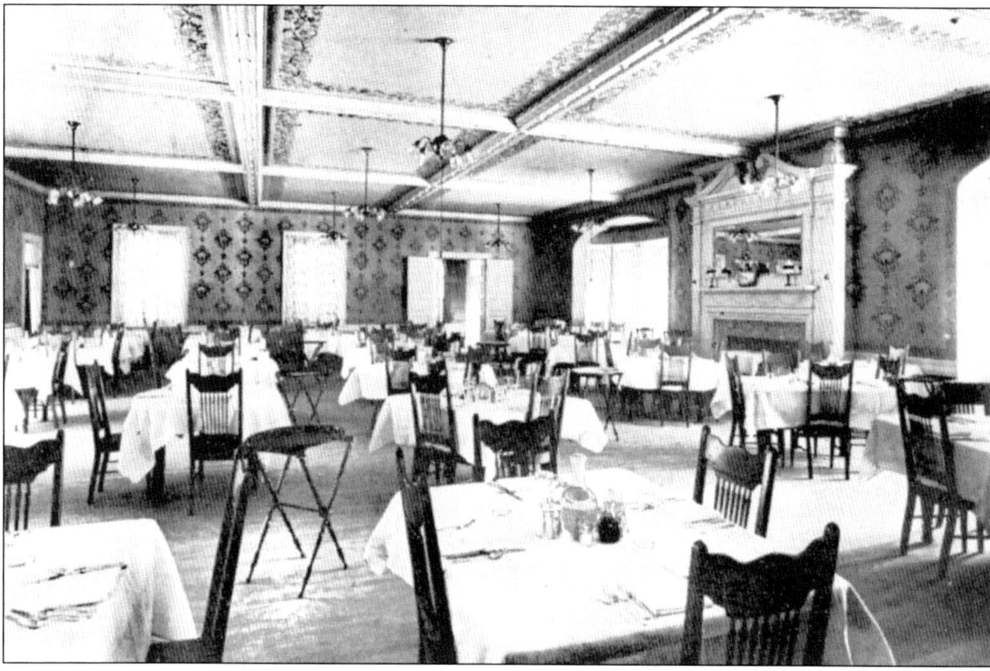

The Columbia Hotel offered a large dining room.

The Dining Room.

A Large, Cool, and Pleasing Dining Room with a well trained corps of waitresses to insure correct service.

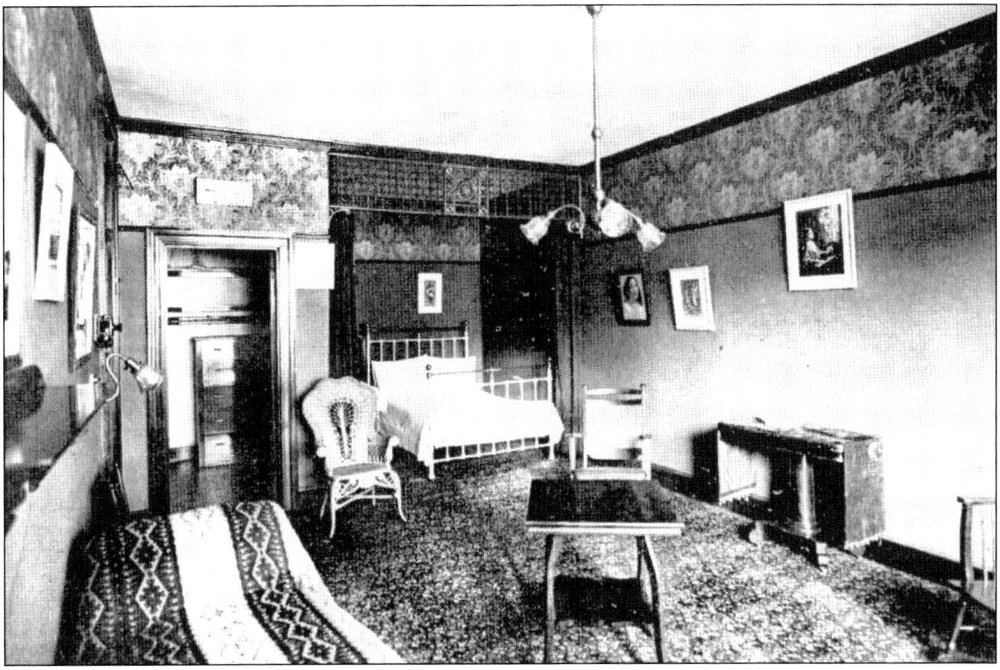

The rooms at the Columbia Hotel had single rooms, double rooms, and suites.

The Rooms.

ROOMS are single and double or en suite with parlor, bedroom and bath. The situation of the house makes every room cheerful and pleasant.

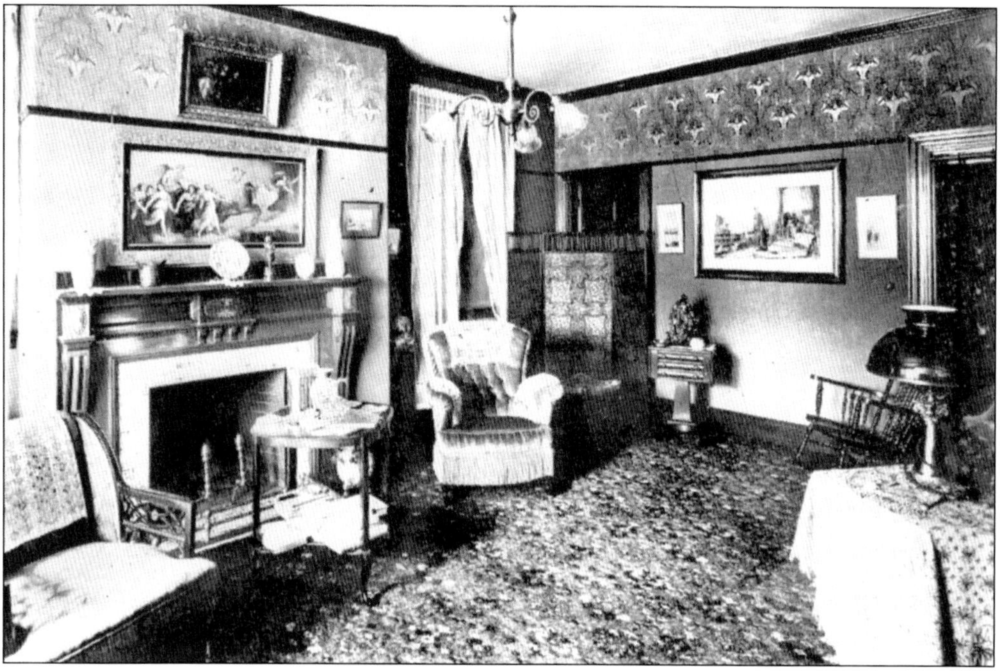

Suites at the Columbia Hotel included a parlor, bedroom, and bath.

The Suites

CONSISTING of Parlor, Bedroom and Bath are homelike and attractive in their decorations and furnishings. Private telephone in every room, connecting with all parts of the hotel and outside world.

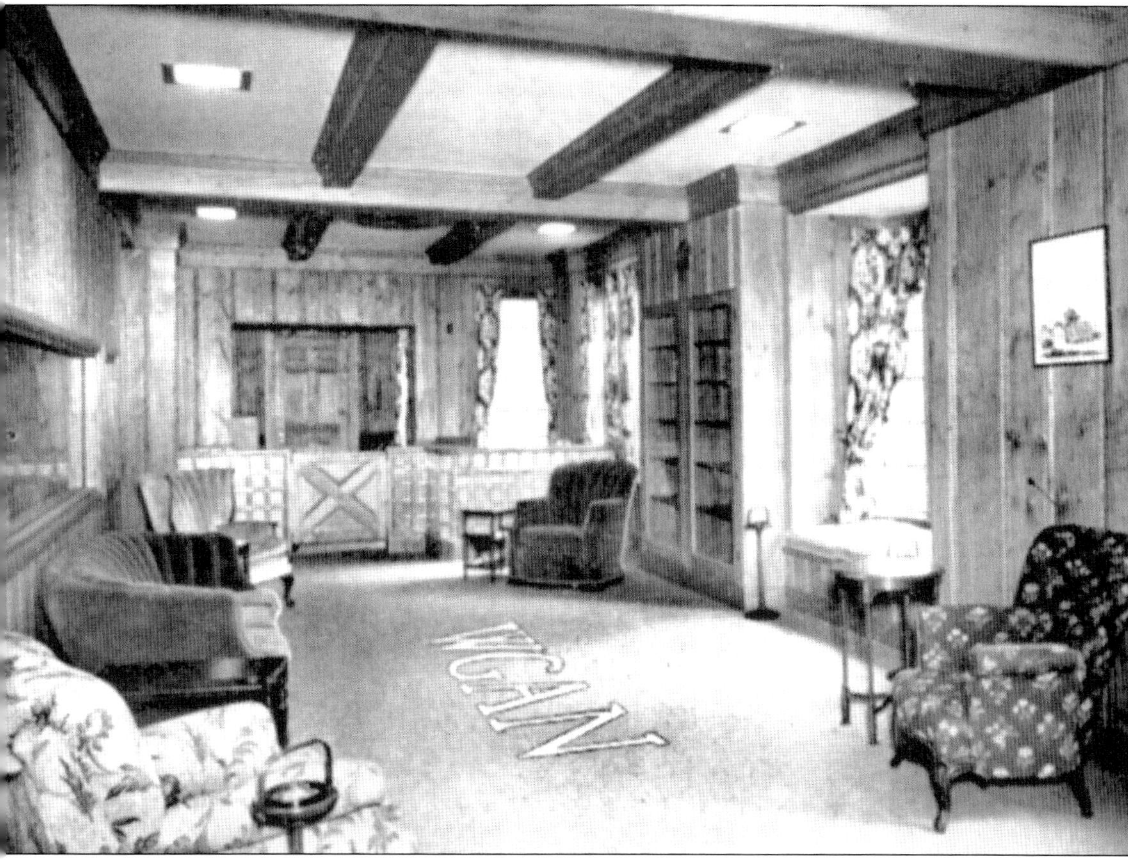

Ironically, WGAN Radio, while not owned or operated by Rines family members, maintained its studios in the Columbia Hotel in the 1930s and 1940s. This must have created some consternation among family members at the WCSH Radio studios, located just down the street on the top floor of the Congress Square Hotel. The Columbia Hotel management's cousin, Henry Rines, owned both the Congress Square Hotel and WCSH Radio at that time.

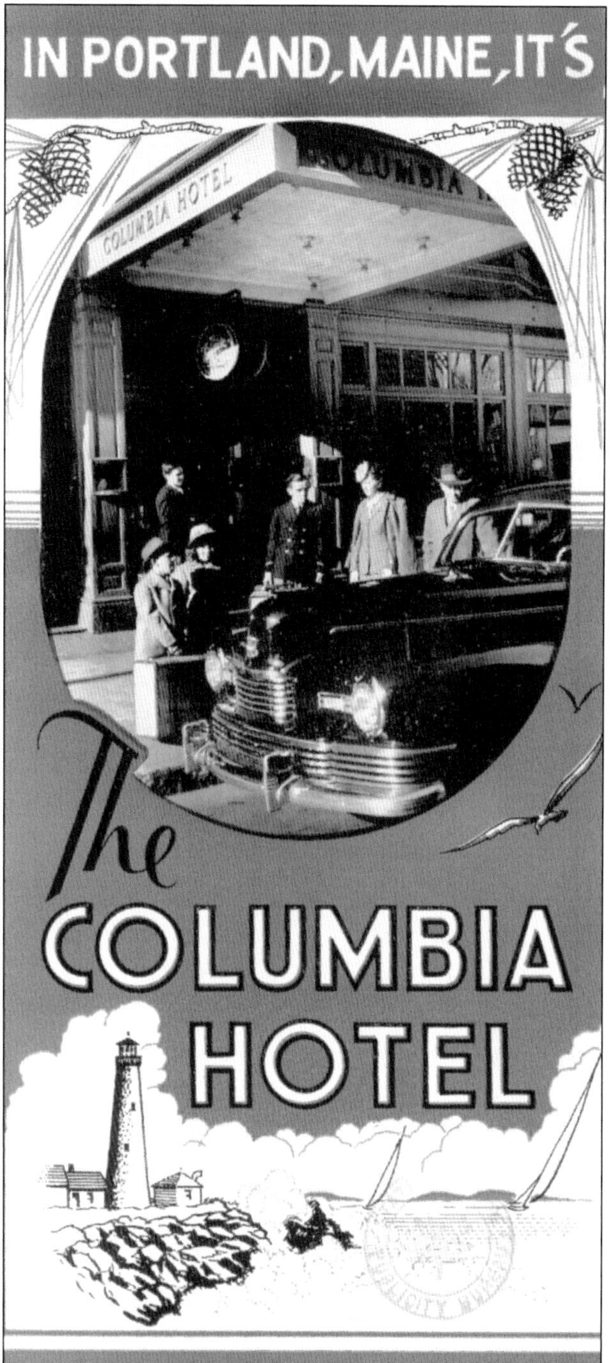

The ownership of the Columbia Hotel fell to the heirs of Albert and David Rines' sisters, Ann-Sarah and Hannah. The heirs ran the hotel until 1952. Since then, the hotel has had several owners including the Best Western Hotel and the Executive Inn. Today the hotel has been greatly modernized and serves as a dormitory for students of the University of Southern Maine and the Maine College of Art. (Courtesy of the Maine Historic Preservation Commission.)

Two

Joseph Henry Rines Led Two Lives

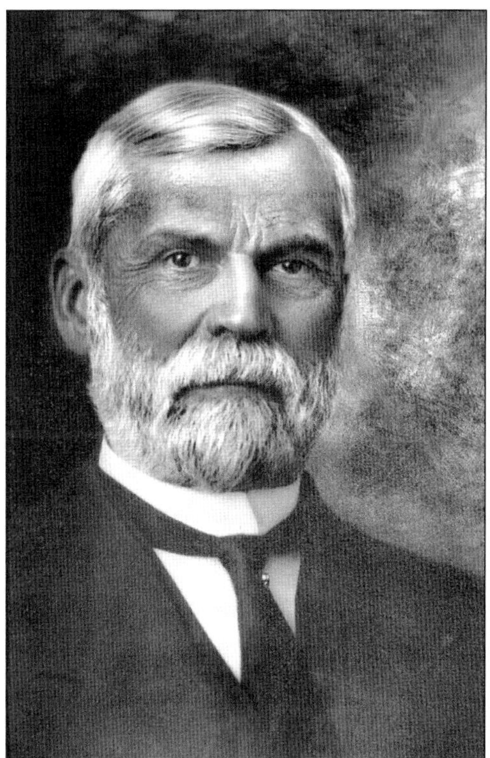

Having traveled the world for Reed and Barton silversmiths of Taunton, Massachusetts, Joseph Henry Rines had stayed in some of America and Europe's finest hotels. Soon after opening the Rines Brothers Company Store on Congress Street in 1883, Joseph realized that Portland lacked a modern hotel. When Joseph died in 1919, he was considered one of the foremost hoteliers in the country, having built and operated the Congress Square Hotel, which was considered one of the grandest in New England.

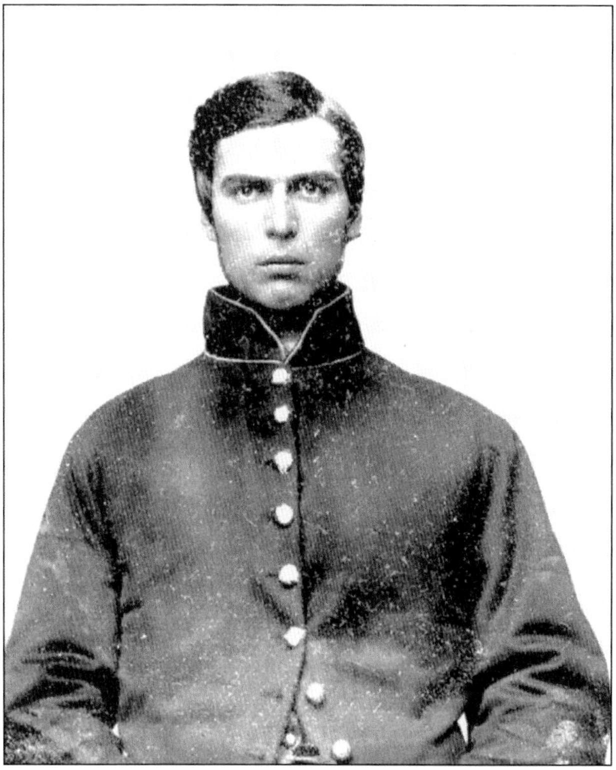

Joseph Rines joined the Sixth Massachusetts Volunteers in September 1862. (Courtesy of Walnut Crest Farm.)

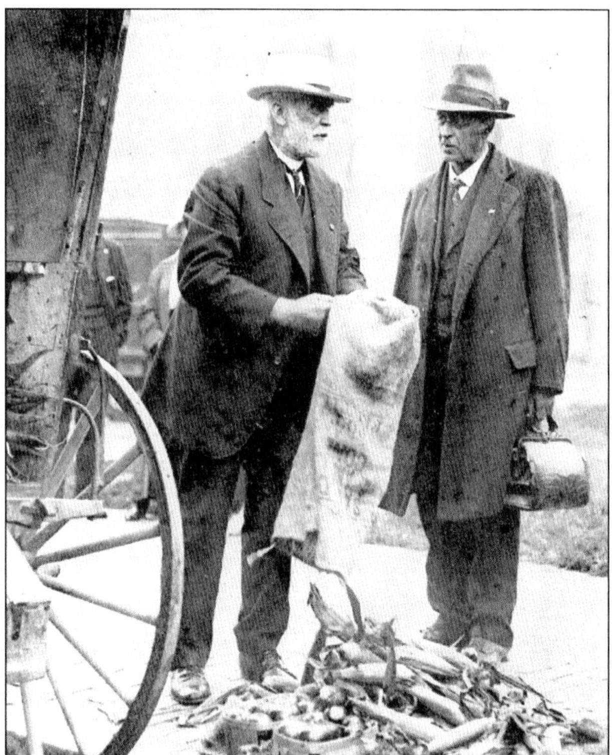

Joseph Rines's business career did not satisfy all his yearnings. He wanted to return to farming, a skill he learned as a young boy in Athens, Maine. He made the best of all his passions. He was one of the founders of the Portland Farmers Club (seen here at left on opening day, August 25, 1917). He was very public-spirited and used his real-estate acumen to help the city obtain land for school playgrounds.

"In his long and useful life from a boy on a Maine farm, as a soldier in the Civil War, traveling salesman, merchant, hotel proprietor, and farmer, [Joseph] Rines advanced in acquiring valuable experience, achieved more than ordinary property and demonstrated the highest traits of the sterling Yankee character." (Obituary from *Portland Press Herald*, June 25, 1919.)

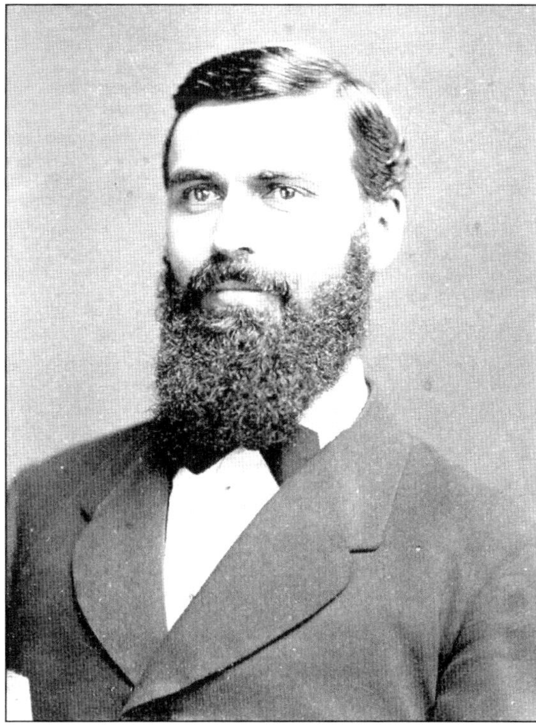

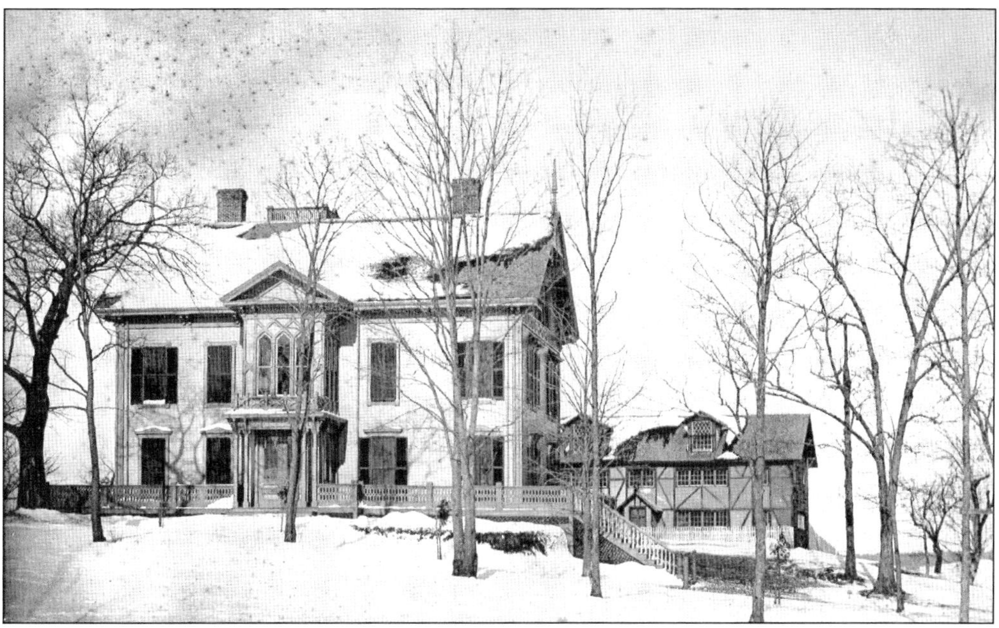

Joseph Rines purchased the former James Phinney Baxter mansion and property in Gorham in 1894. "Walnut Crest" would fulfill one of Joseph's other passions, farming. Joseph enjoyed raising cattle and sheep. Walnut Crest supplied most of the dairy products for the Columbia and Congress Square Hotels and later the Eastland Hotel and Danish Village. Joseph's grandson Bernard Rines and his sons Dale, Mathew, and Stephen run the farm today. (Courtesy of Walnut Crest Farm.)

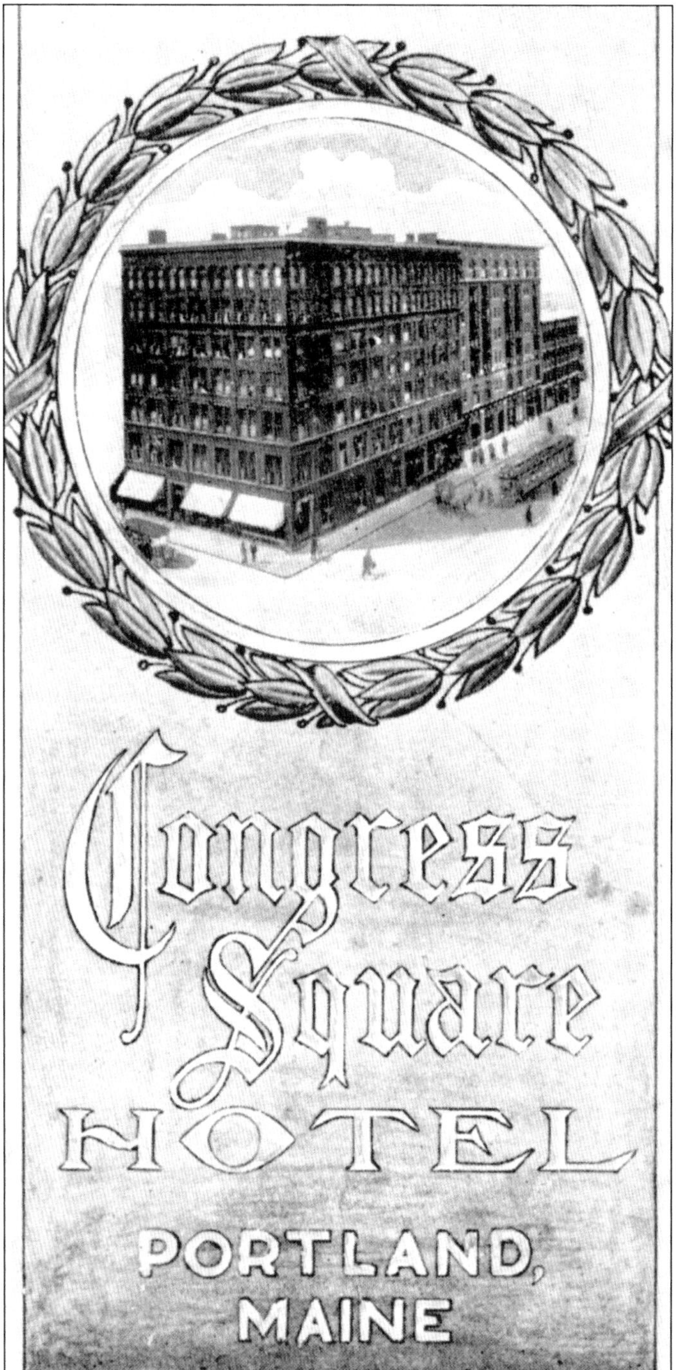

Joseph Rines built the Congress Square Hotel with the financial help of his brothers, two of whom, Albert and David, had just finished the completion of the Columbia Hotel two blocks away. The Congress Square Hotel was Joseph's brainchild and he wanted it to bring to Portland the elegance of the finest luxury hotels he had frequented while selling silverware across the United States and Europe.

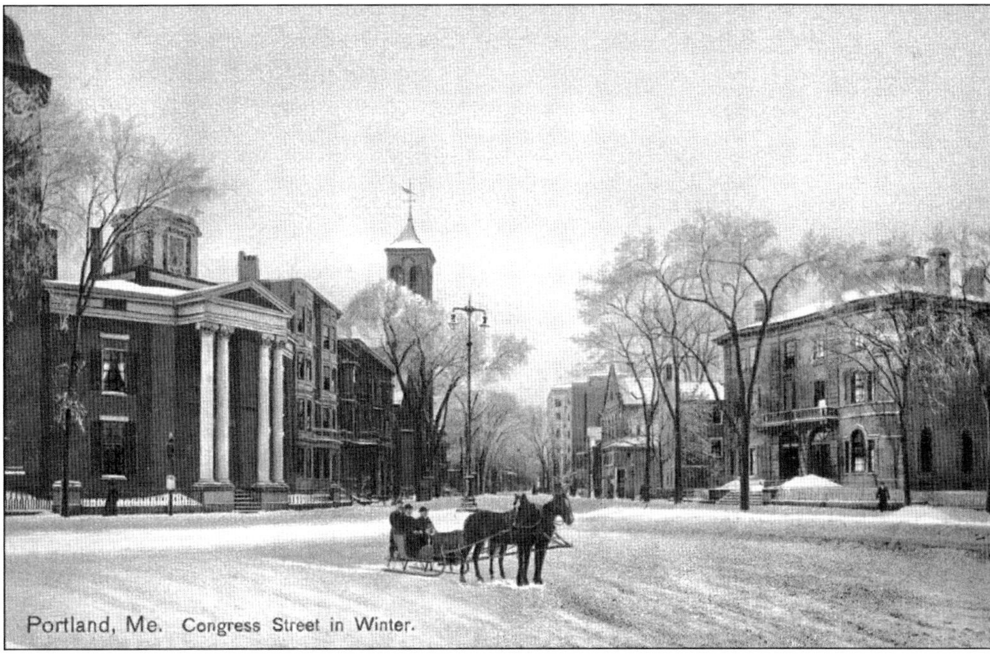

One of Maine's busiest intersections today, Portland's Congress Square is shown here in the early 1900s. The church on the left is presently the location of the WCSH6 Television studios, owned by the Rines family until 1998. The former Baxter Library building is seen in the distance on the right. (Collections of the Maine Historical Society.)

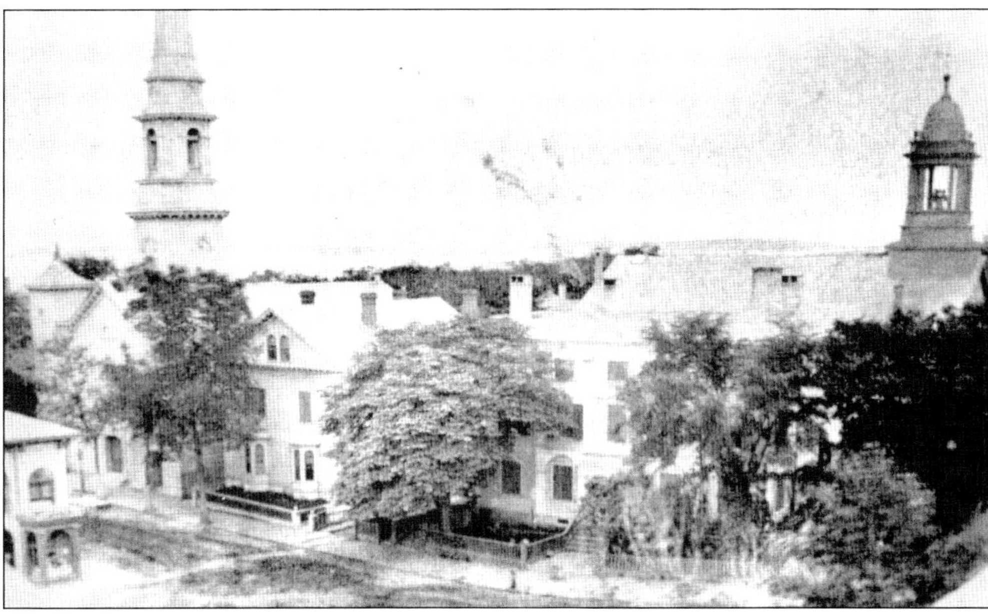

This is one of Portland's oldest photographs of Congress Square, taken in the 1860s. The only recognizable feature is the Hay Drug Store building on the left. The church above it is presently the Children's Museum of Maine while the house and church on the right are located where the Portland Museum of Art is today. (Collections of the Maine Historical Society.)

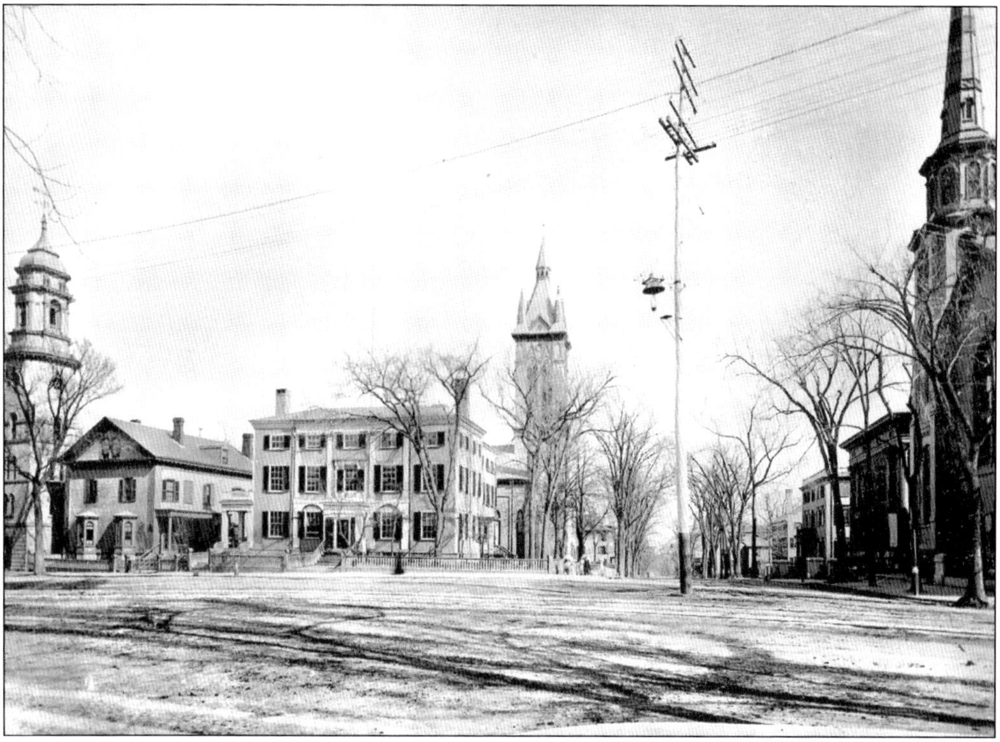

Dirt roads and newly installed electricity can be seen in Congress Square in the late 1880s. The mansion in the center, located in Congress Square, is presently the location of the Portland Museum of Art. The church on the left would eventually become the chamber of commerce's headquarters in 1920, and the Children's Museum of Maine in 1990.

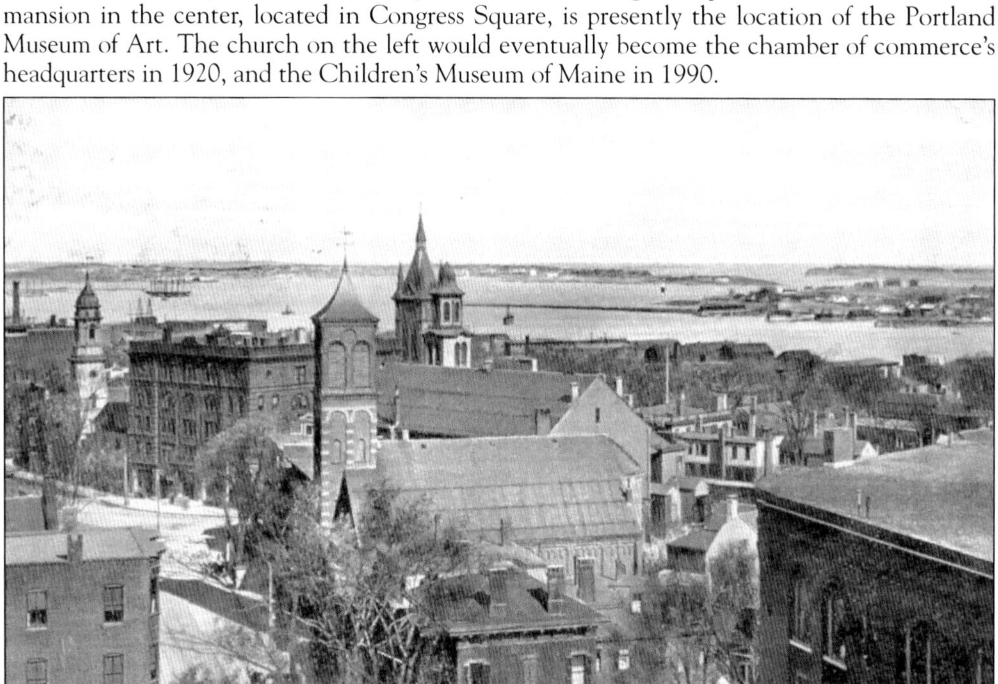

Congress Square in 1910 contained several churches and many personal residences. Casco Bay and the islands can be seen in the distance.

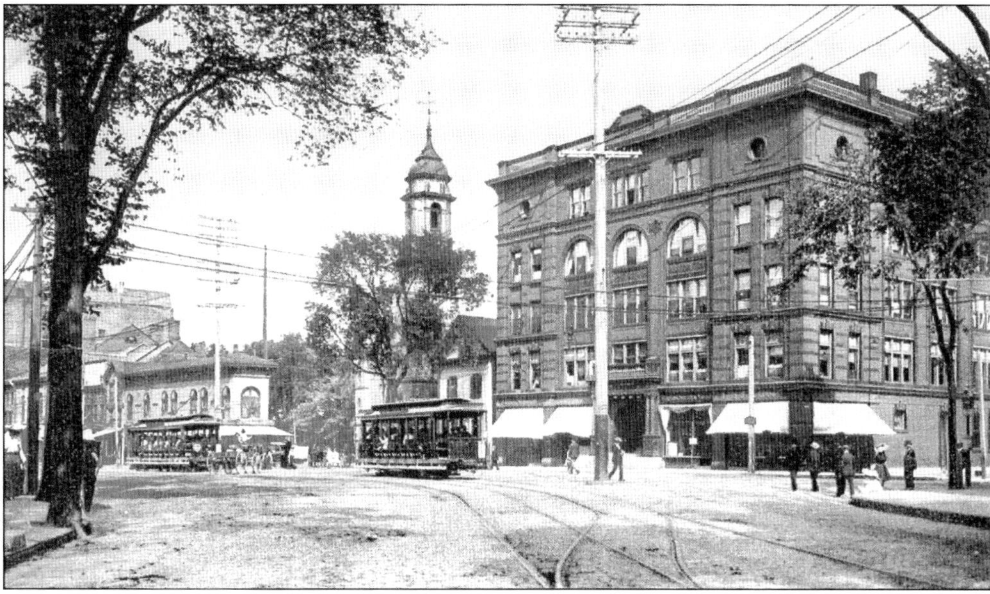

Congress Square began to change into a commercial district with drug stores, hotels, trolley cars, and electricity, as seen here in 1910.

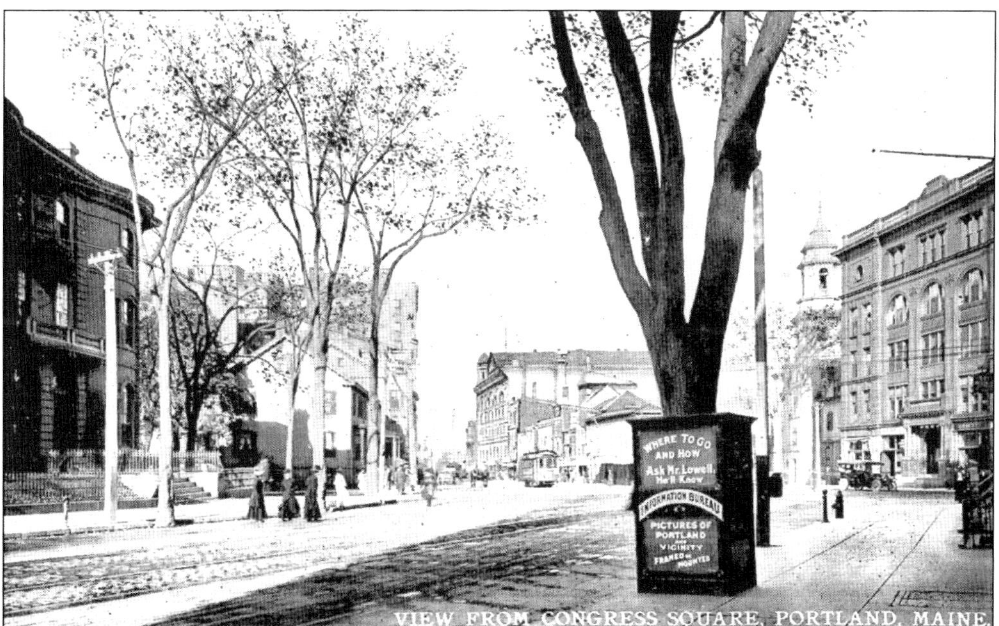

Congress Square, as seen here in 1911, started to take on the look of a big city.

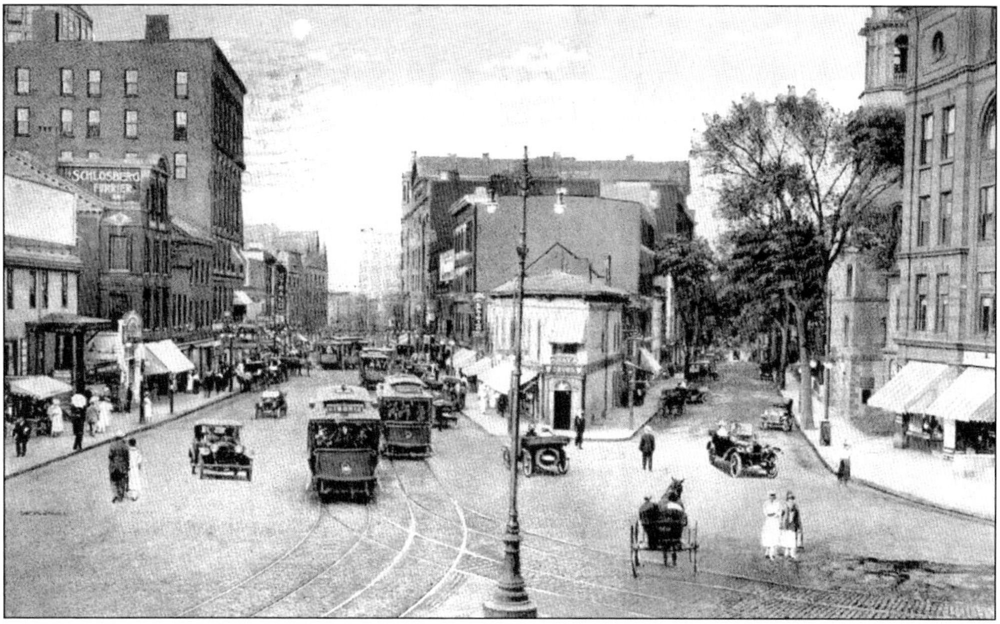

By 1920, the automobile was becoming more predominant than the horse. Congress Square was also becoming a major crossroads for commerce and traffic.

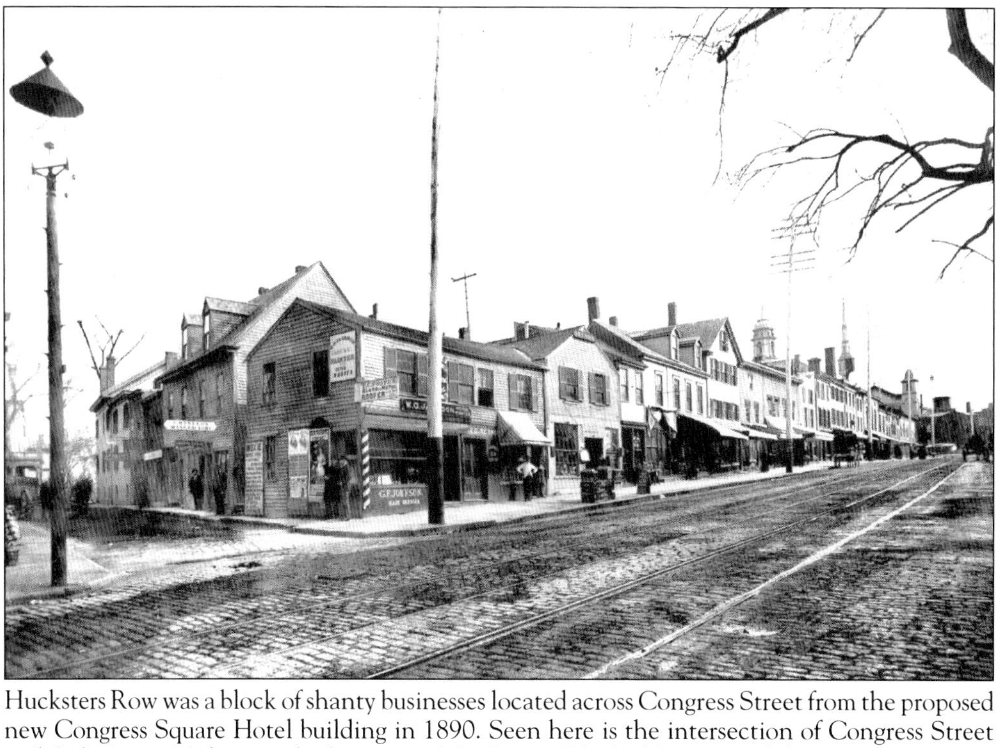
Hucksters Row was a block of shanty businesses located across Congress Street from the proposed new Congress Square Hotel building in 1890. Seen here is the intersection of Congress Street and Oak Street. Today it is the location of the Baxter Block. (Courtesy of the Maine Historical Preservation Commission.)

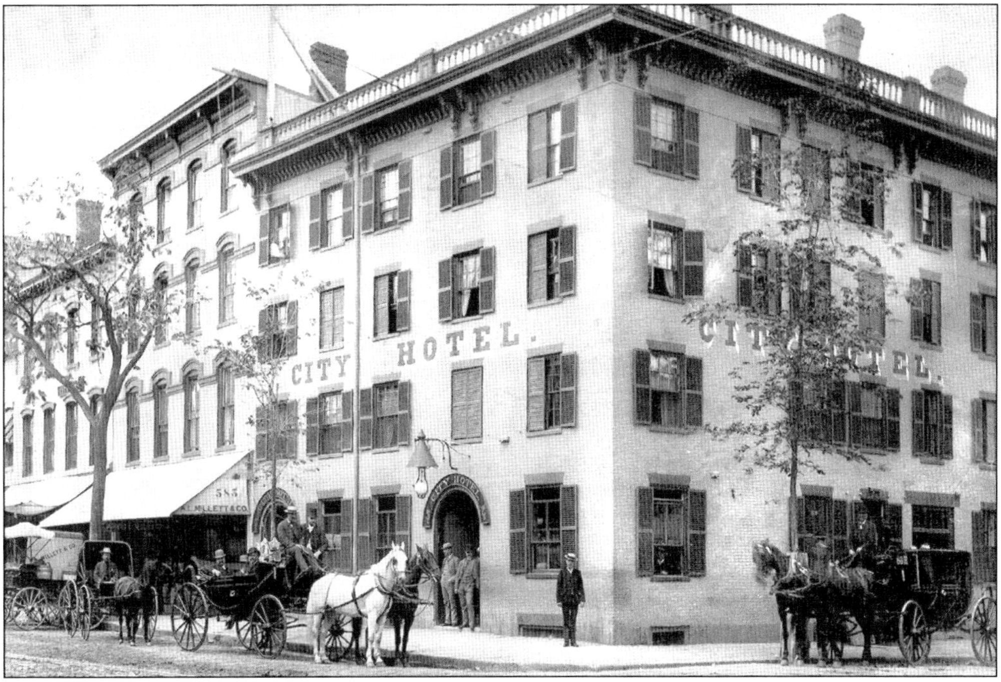

The City Hotel stood on the corner of Congress Street and Forest Avenue (then Green Street). It was torn down to make room for the Congress Square Hotel in 1894. (Collections of the Maine Historical Society.)

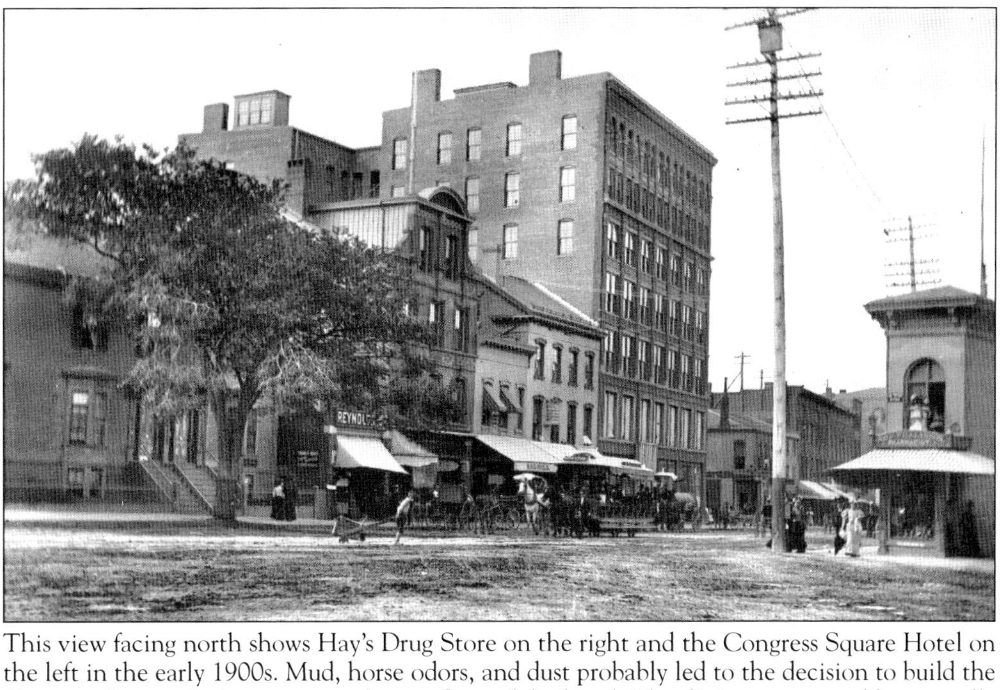

This view facing north shows Hay's Drug Store on the right and the Congress Square Hotel on the left in the early 1900s. Mud, horse odors, and dust probably led to the decision to build the Congress Square dining room on the top floor of the hotel. The dining room would eventually become the studios of WCSH Radio and Television between 1925 and 1976. (Courtesy of the Maine Historic Preservation Commission.)

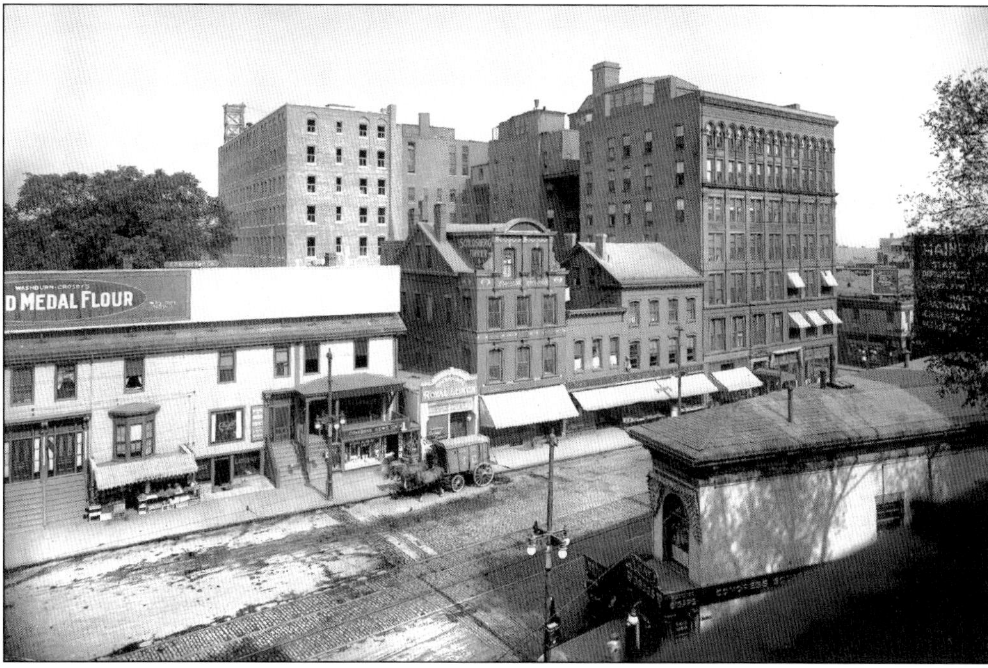

This image is a view of Congress Square around 1910 looking toward the new Congress Square Hotel. Congress Square Park is located here today on the left, and behind it the Eastland Hotel, built in 1927. (Collections of the Maine Historical Society.)

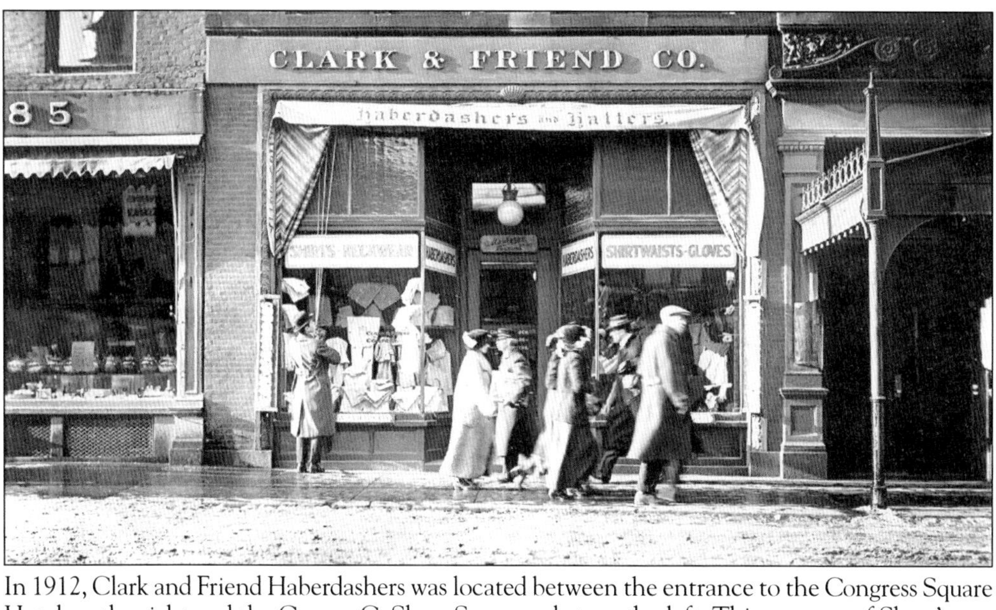

In 1912, Clark and Friend Haberdashers was located between the entrance to the Congress Square Hotel on the right and the George C. Shaw Supermarket on the left. This was one of Shaw's two original stores first located here in Portland. (Collections of the Maine Historical Society.)

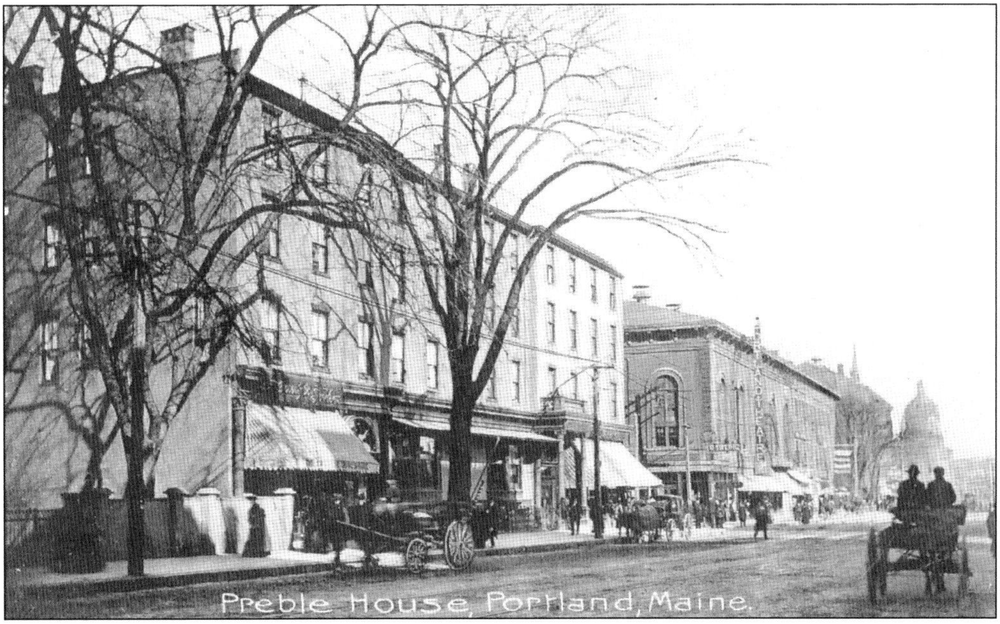

There were many hotels in Portland that catered to the increasing visitor population. By the beginning of the 20th century, 2,000 businessmen, railroad and steamboat passengers, and tourists a day were seeking nighttime accommodations in Portland. The Preble House, seen here located next to the Longfellow House, was considered attractive lodging.

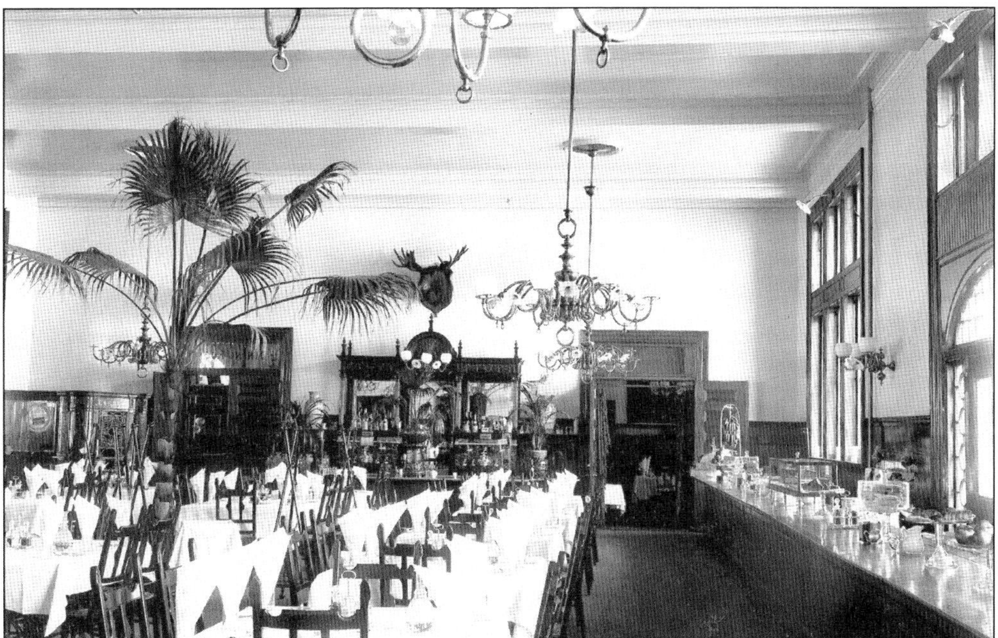

Fine dining was not unusual during the beginning of the 20th century in Portland. Even the public dining room at Union Station, Portland's major railroad station, shown here, was elaborate. Note the fine linen table clothes and crystal glassware. (Courtesy of the Maine Historic Preservation Commission.)

Congress Square Hotel

American Plan

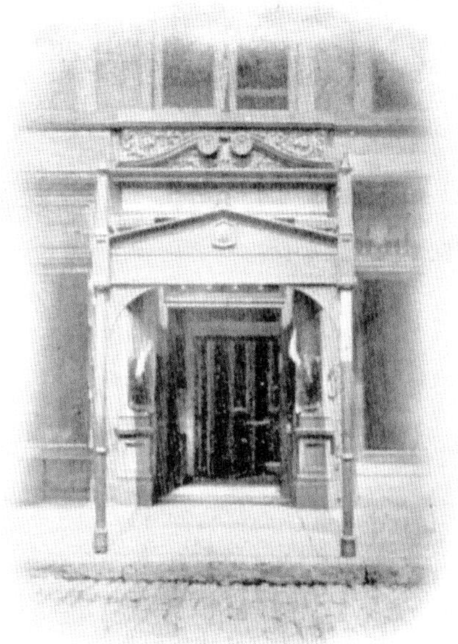

Congress Street and Forest Avenue

Ten minutes from Union Station

Portland, Maine

Most nights some 2,000 people on average needed hotel accommodations in the commercially booming city of Portland. The railroad and shipping lines brought businessmen and tourists from all over the east coast and Canada. People moved easily from New York, Boston, and Montreal, and Portland was the closest port for export to Europe when the St. Lawrence Seaway was frozen solid in the winter. (Courtesy of the Maine Historic Preservation Commission.)

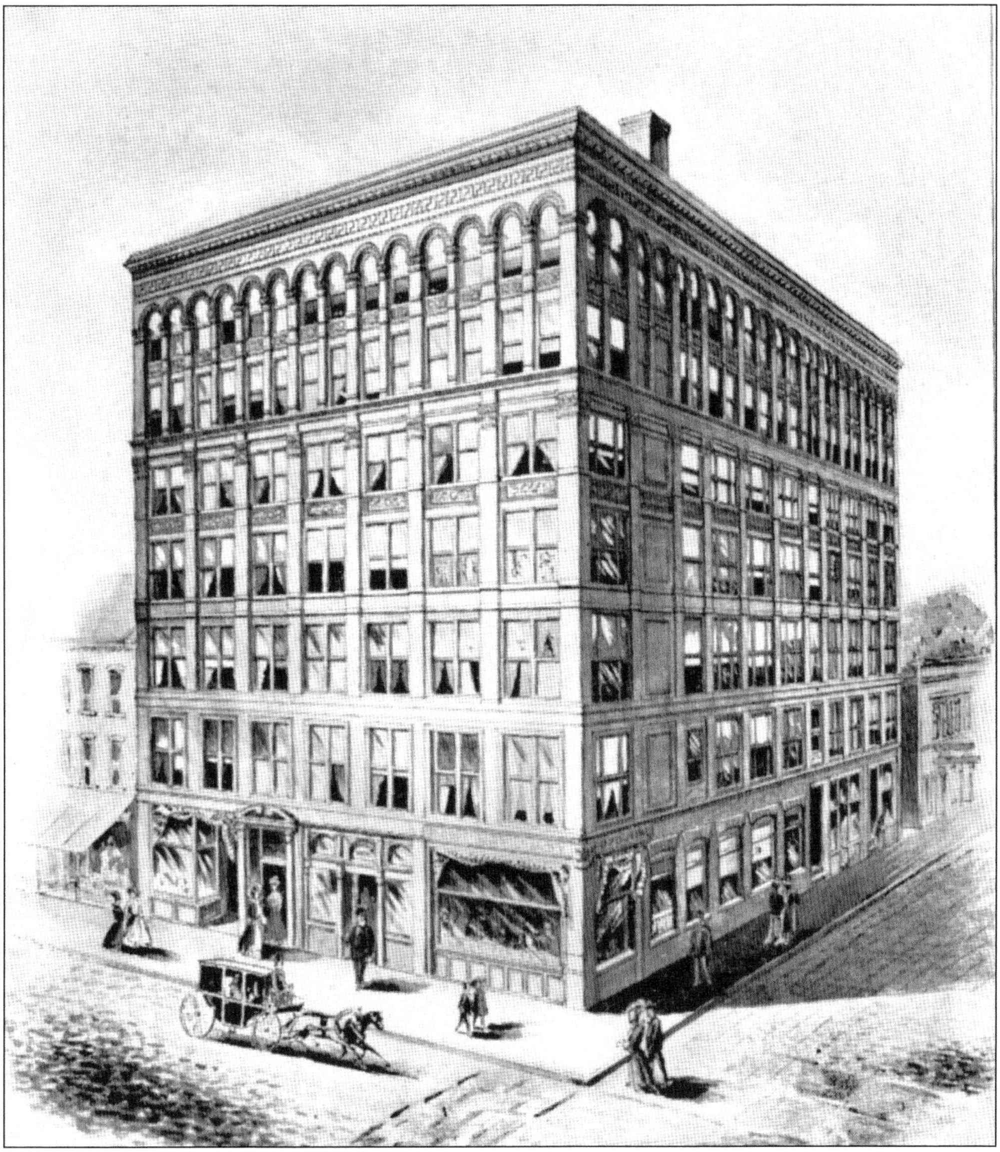
This illustration shows the Congress Square Hotel when it opened in 1896. (Courtesy of the Maine Historic Preservation Commission.)

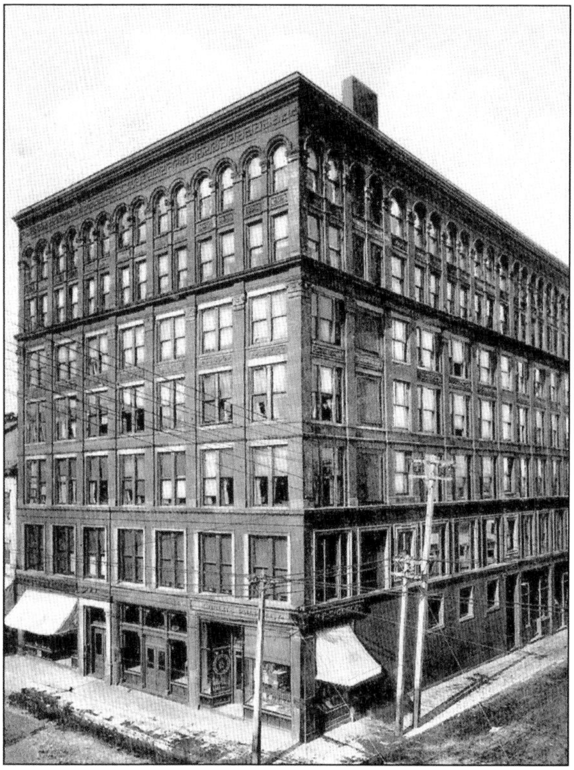

Responding to the increasing occupancy, the Congress Square Hotel was added onto several times. The original hotel was built in 1896 and additions were added over the next dozen years. To the left is the original building in 1896 and below as it appeared in 1910 with additions. A portion of the top floor where the dining facilities were located would become the studios of WCSH Radio in 1925 and WCSH Television in 1953.

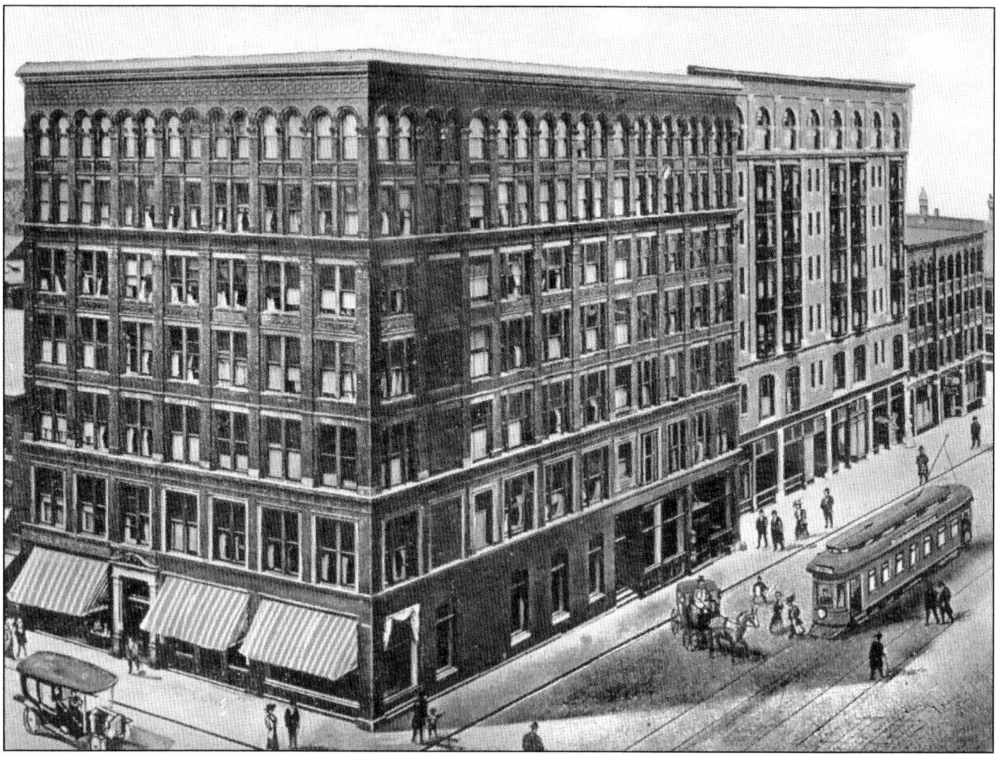

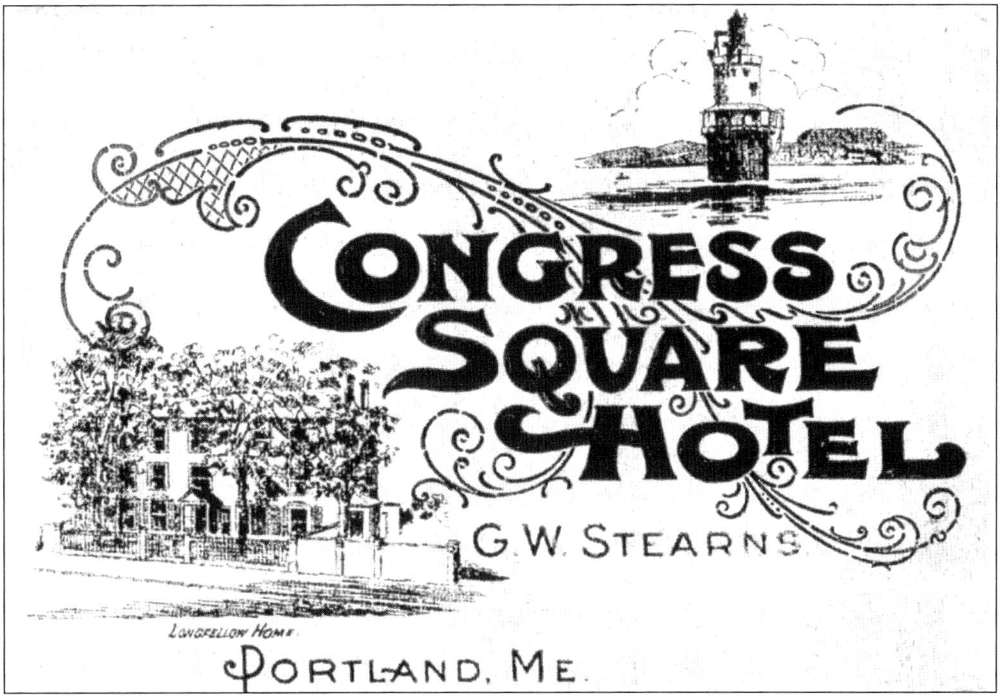

G. W. Stearns was the proprietor for the Rines brothers when the Congress Square Hotel opened in 1896. (Courtesy of the Maine Historic Preservation Commission.)

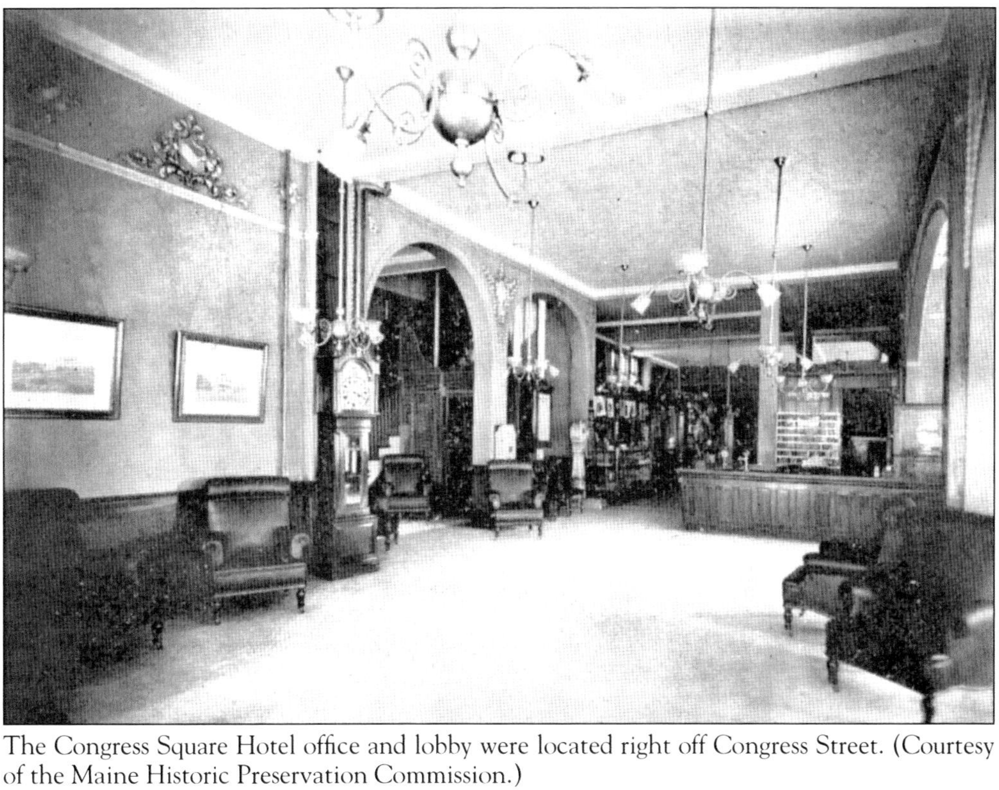

The Congress Square Hotel office and lobby were located right off Congress Street. (Courtesy of the Maine Historic Preservation Commission.)

THE CONGRESS SQUARE HOTEL

How to reach the Congress Square Hotel from railroad stations and steamers.

Taxicab service and a most efficient trolley car service from every train and steamer.

All trolley lines pass the Congress Square Hotel.

TARIFF

American Plan only.

Rates from $3.50 without bath; from $4.00 with bath, according to location.

Weekly rates on application.

This is the rate plan for the Congress Square Hotel in the early 1900s.

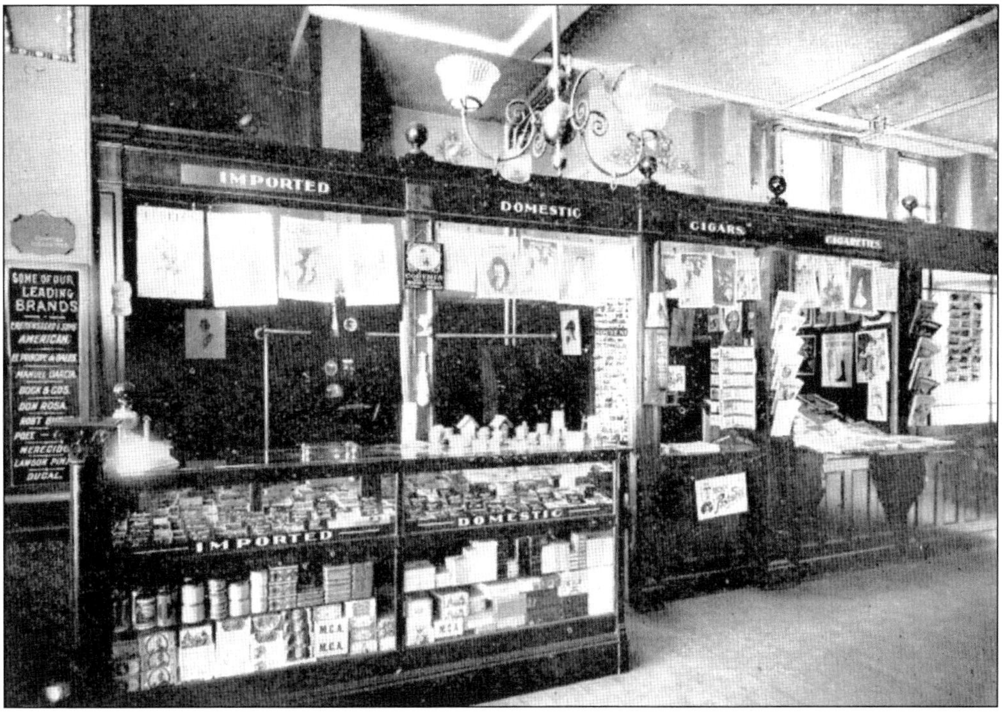

The public could come to the Congress Square Hotel to acquire the latest news in print. Later they would tune to WCSH, located in the same building, to receive their news on radio and television.

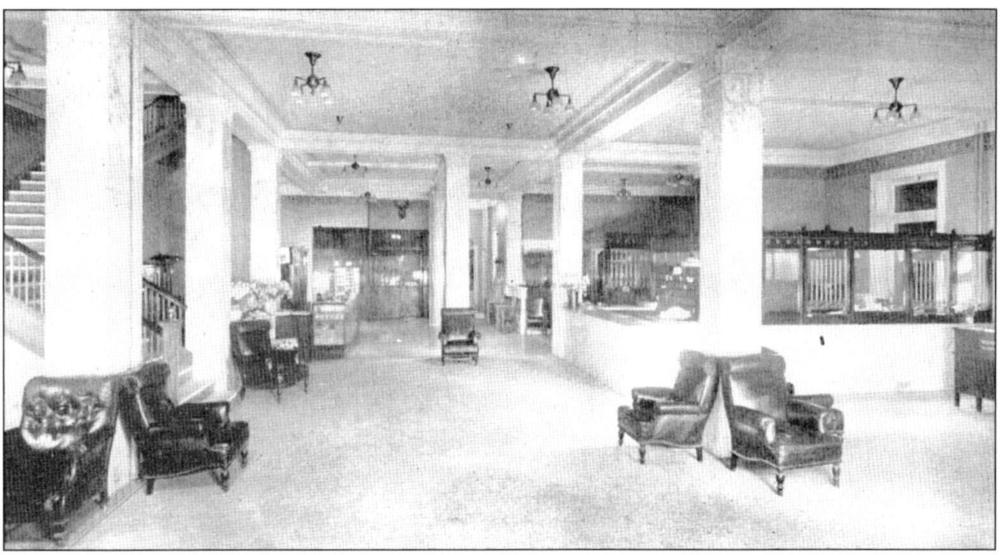

The Congress Square Hotel, approached from Congress Street, had one of the city's first elevators. Some of the fine woodwork in the lobby can still be seen today at Congress Square Associates.

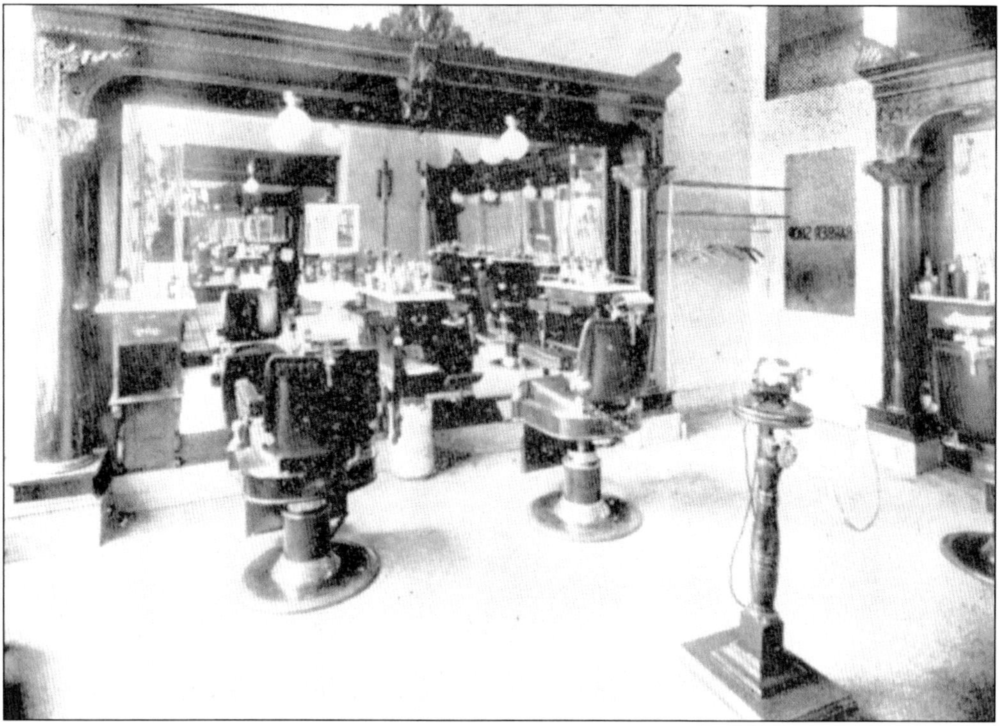

The Congress Square Hotel barbershop was as popular as it was modern.

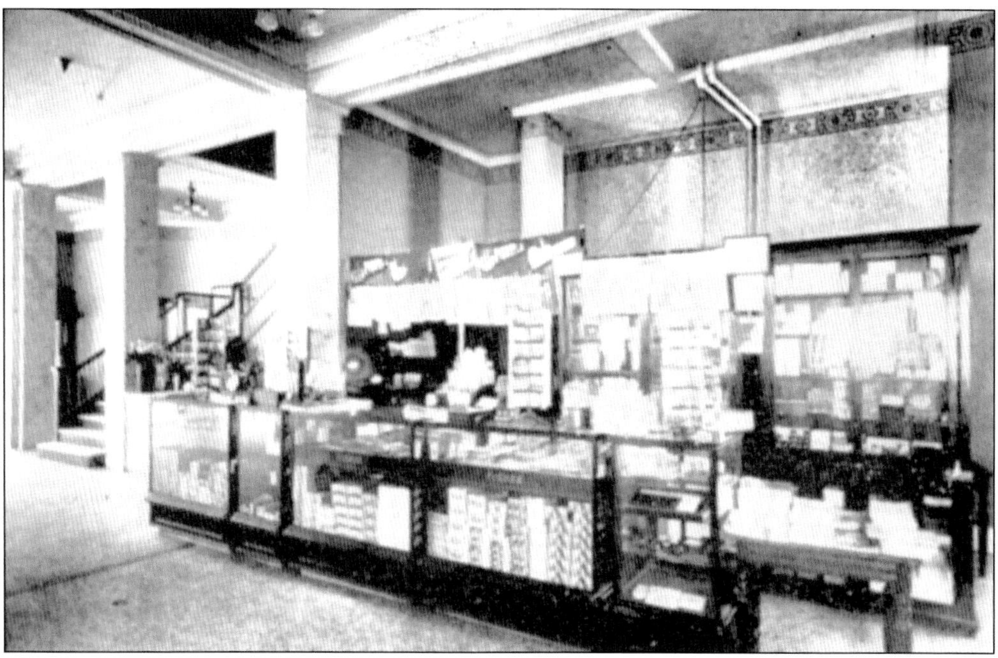

The Congress Square Hotel sundries store was located in the lobby.

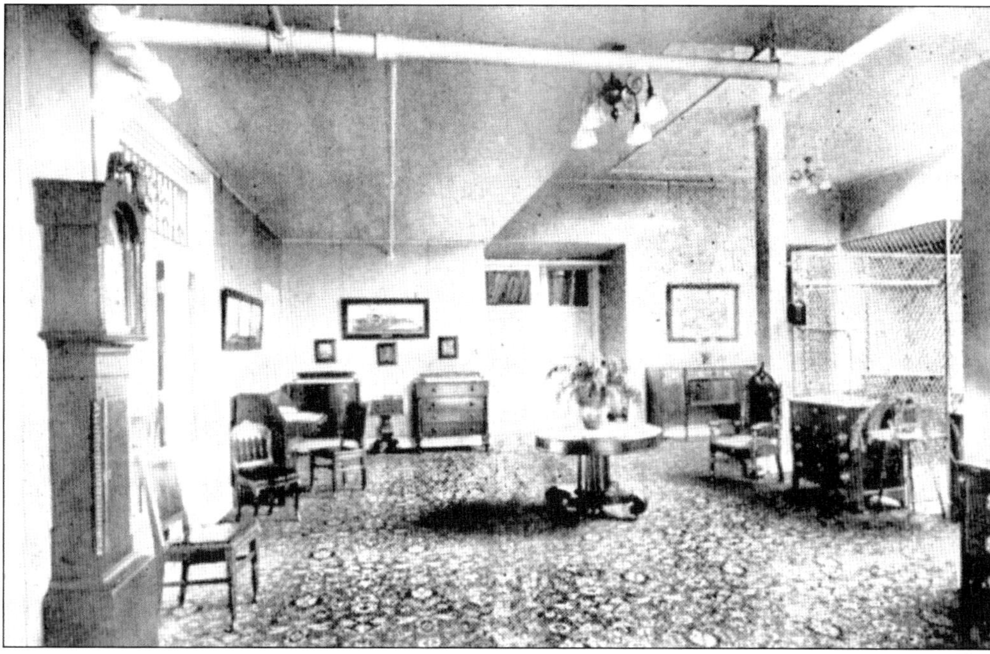

The Congress Square Hotel haberdashery was laid out with fine furnishings.

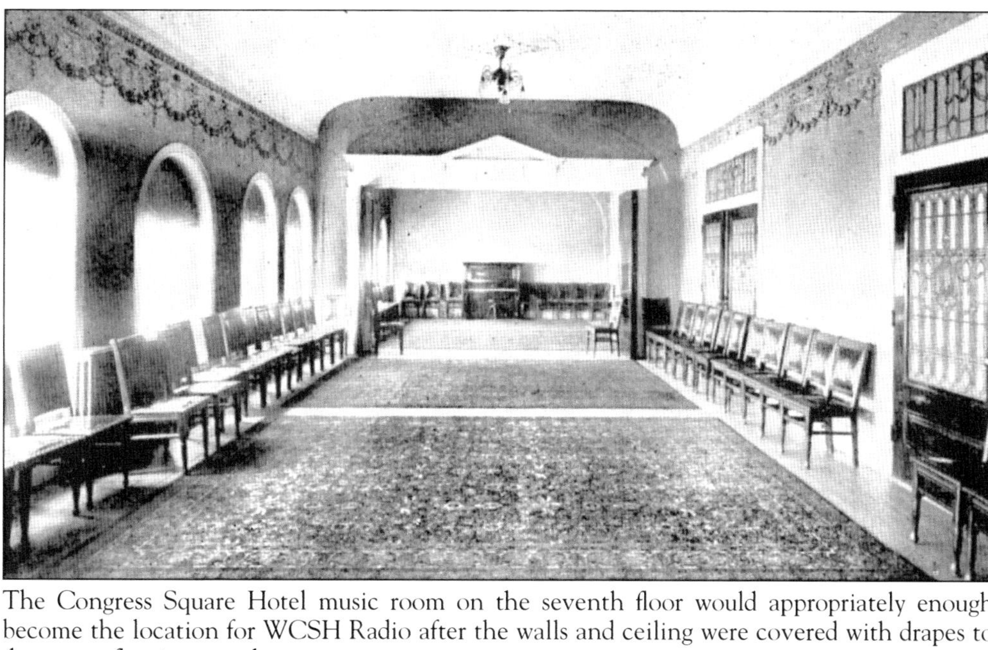

The Congress Square Hotel music room on the seventh floor would appropriately enough become the location for WCSH Radio after the walls and ceiling were covered with drapes to dampen reflective sounds.

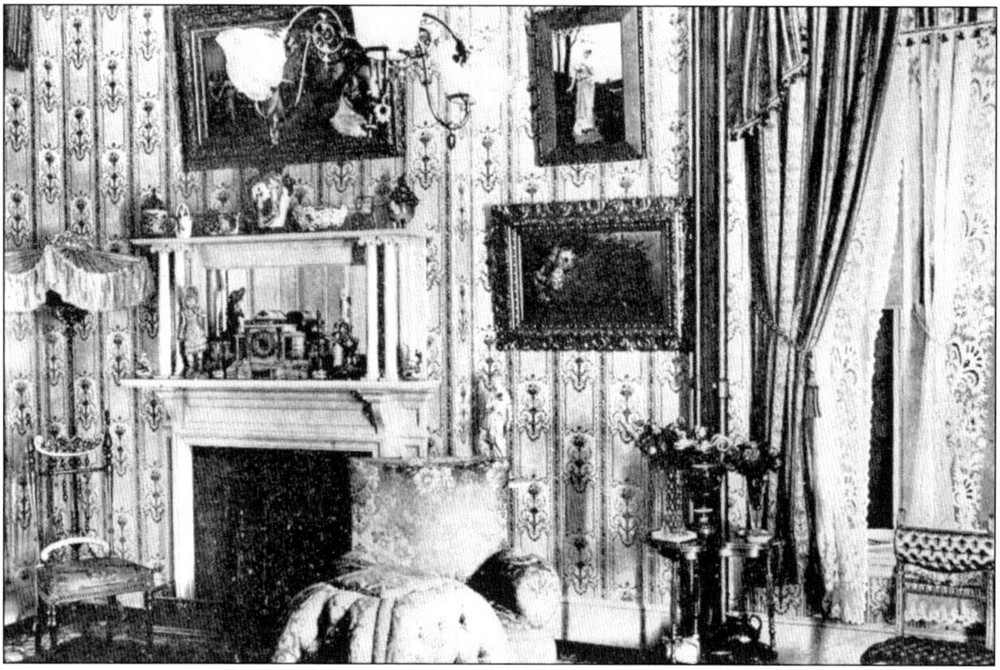

While a company president may have stayed in this suite, Joseph Rines remembered his stays in hotels as a salesman, living on a limited budget. The hotel purposefully offered a more modest Pullman Suite, small rooms that were much more affordable for the tradesman and salesman working on slim means.

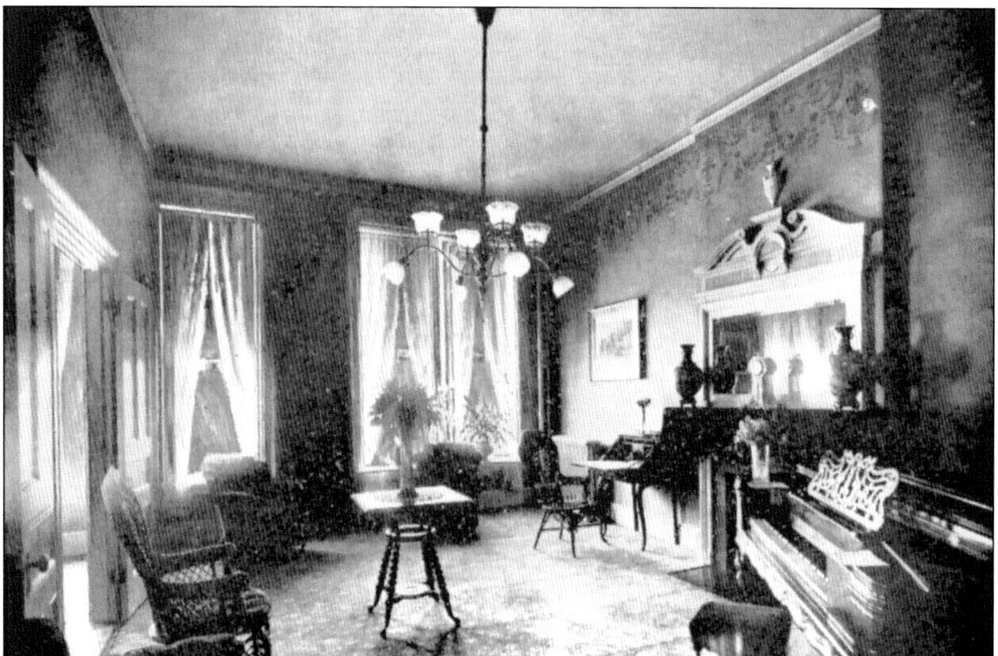

The ornate detail and lavish surroundings of the Congress Square Hotel parlor impressed travelers.

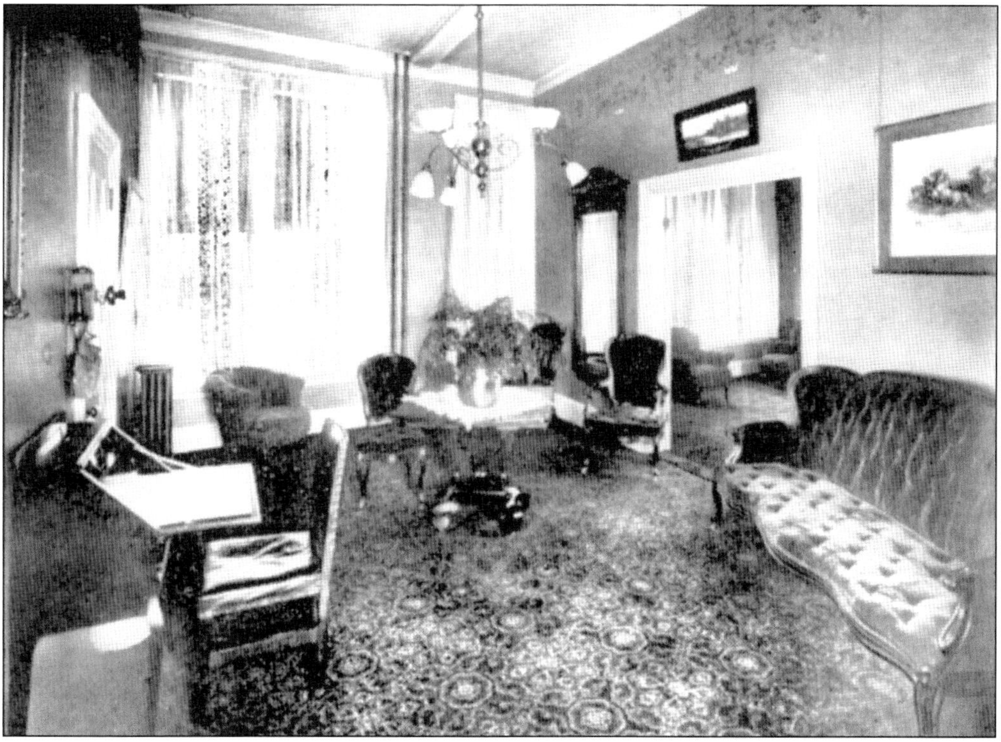

The American Room is shown here with its fine furnishings.

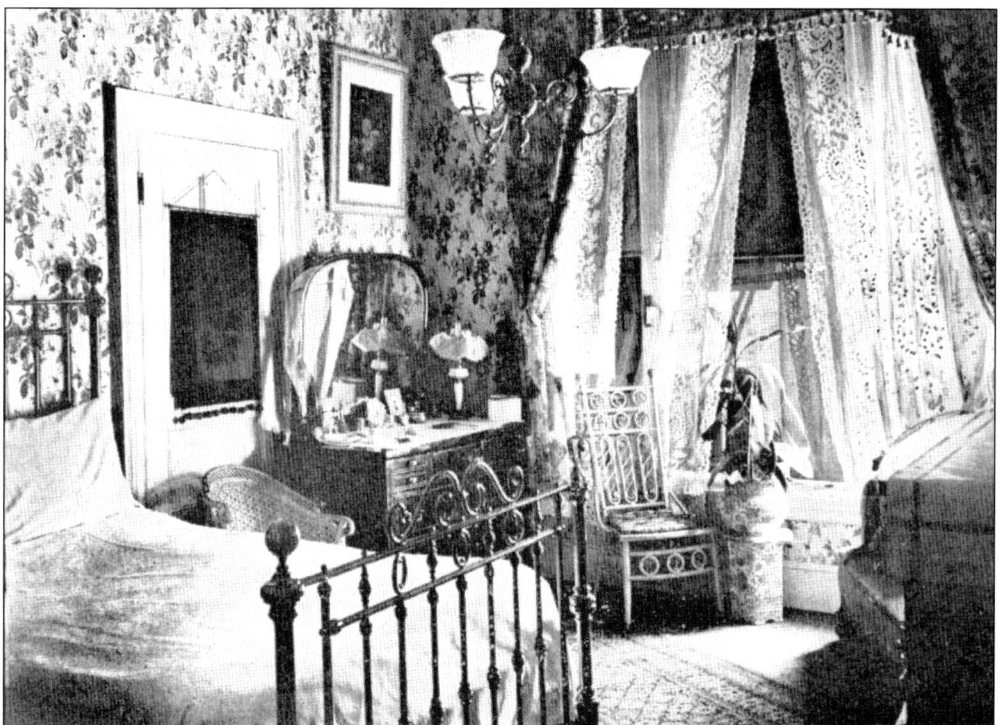

Seen here in this 1910 photo is the Congress Square Hotel Sleeping Chamber.

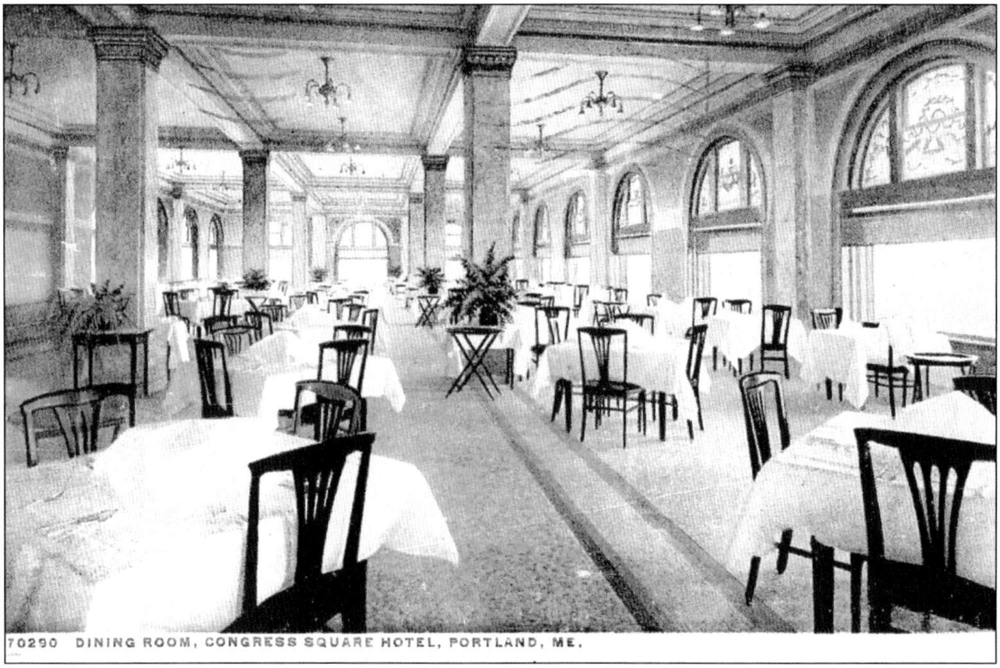

The Congress Square Hotel's seventh floor main dining room offered a spectacular view of the White Mountains in one direction and Casco Bay in the other. It was a favorite haunt of 1930s best-selling author Kenneth Roberts. He maintained that his favorite pea soup was served here.

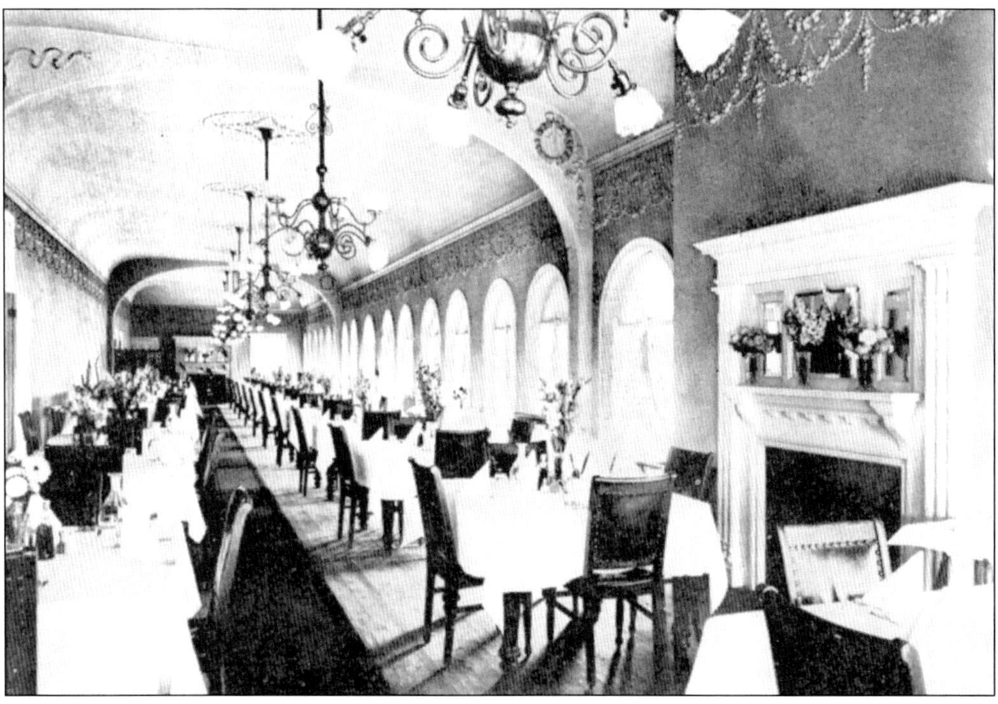

Congress Square Hotel's seventh floor dining room extension was taken over by WCSH Radio in 1925.

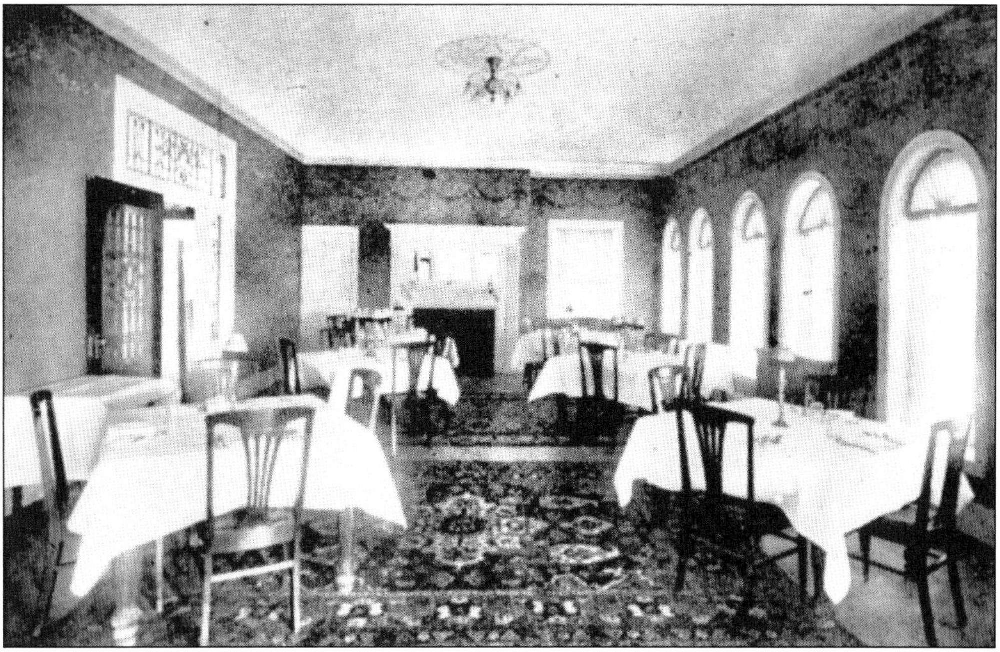

The Congress Square Hotel private banquet room facility was one of Portland's most luxurious.

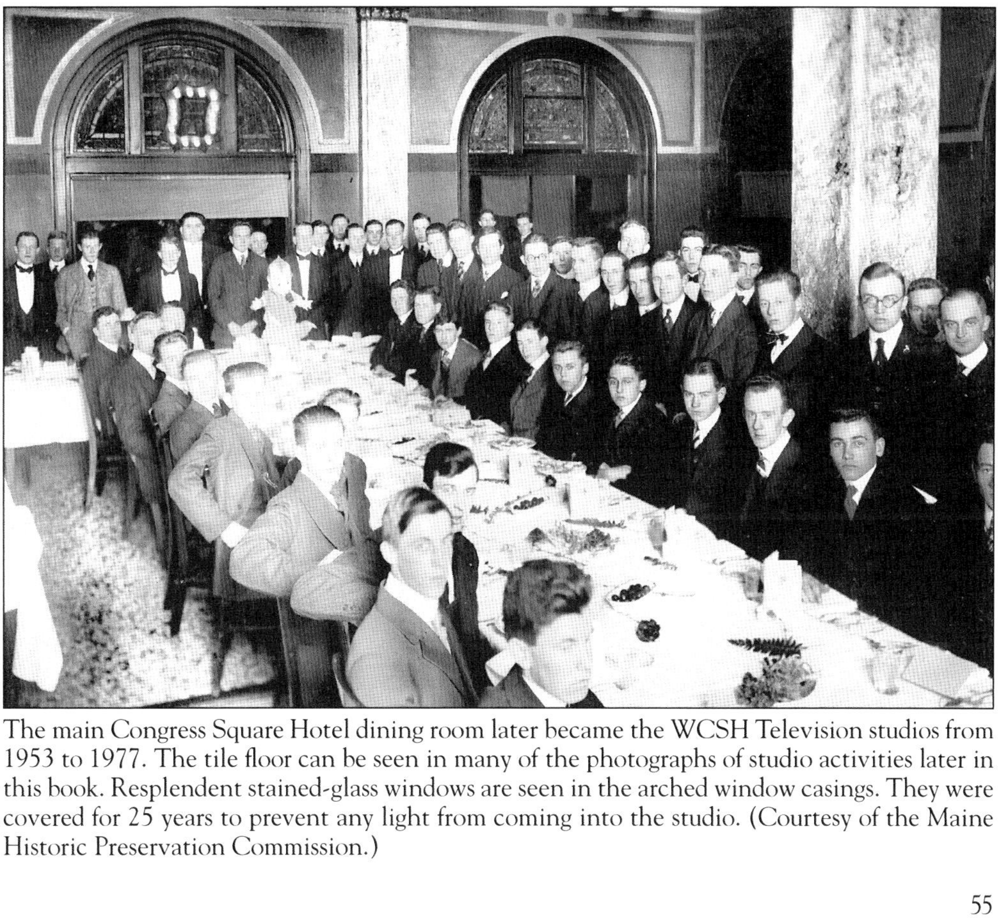

The main Congress Square Hotel dining room later became the WCSH Television studios from 1953 to 1977. The tile floor can be seen in many of the photographs of studio activities later in this book. Resplendent stained-glass windows are seen in the arched window casings. They were covered for 25 years to prevent any light from coming into the studio. (Courtesy of the Maine Historic Preservation Commission.)

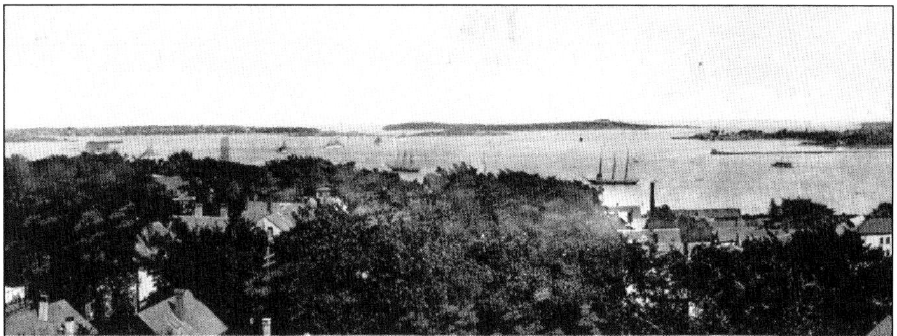

VIEW OF PORTLAND HARBOR FROM THE CONGRESS SQUARE DINING ROOM.

Dinner

CONSOMME PRINTANIERE

CLAM CHOWDER

OLIVES CUCUMBERS CELERY

BOILED HADDOCK, CAPER SAUCE
POMMES HOLLANDAISE

EASTERN BLUEFISH A LA ANDALOUSE
LATTICE POTATOES

BOILED CORNED BEEF AND CABBAGE

FRIED SWEETBREADS, PUREE OF TOMATO
SAUTE OF CHICKEN LIVERS WITH MUSHROOMS
CREAMED LOBSTER EN PETITE BOUCHEE
FRUIT FRITTERS, GLACE AU COGNAC

ROAST SIRLOIN OF BEEF AU JUS
MASHED POTATOES SPINACH

SADDLE OF MUTTON, APPLE JELLY
BOILED POTATOES SQUASH

YOUNG TURKEY, CRANBERRY SAUCE
WAX BEANS PICKLED BEETS TOMATOES

WALDORF SALAD DRESSED LETTUCE

APPLE PIE CUSTARD PIE MINCE PIE

BAKED INDIAN PUDDING, HARD SAUCE
VANILLA ICE CREAM, ASSORTED CAKE
PEACH SHORTCAKE, WHIPPED CREAM
ORANGE MARMALADE
PRESERVES

NUTS SALTED PEANUTS RAISINS
SALTINES, SODA AND BENT'S WATER CRACKERS
NEUFCHATEL, EDAM, AMERICAN AND ROQUEFORT CHEESE
DATES FIGS
FRUIT
COFFEE

HOURS FOR MEALS:

BREAKFAST, 6 TO 9.30 A. M.
DINNER, 12.00 TO 2.15 P. M.
SUPPER, 6 TO 8.30 P. M.

SUNDAY:
BREAKFAST, 8 TO 10 A. M.
DINNER, 1 TO 2.30 P. M.
SUPPER, 6 TO 8 P. M.

G. W. STEARNS, Mgr.

JANUARY 12, 1909

(Clips for mailing may be procured at the office) OVER

This is the Congress Square Hotel dinner menu for January 12, 1909. (Courtesy of the Maine Historic Preservation Commission.)

Special dinners, reasonably priced, were always available at the Congress Square Hotel.

Special Dinner

$1.50 per Person

Served from 6 to 8

White Bean Soup aux Croutons
or
Consomme Vermicelli

Olives *Dill Pickle*

Broiled Mackerel, Maitre d'Hotel

CHOICE OF

Broiled Lamb Chops, with Bacon

Fricassee of Chicken, w.th Noodles

Mashed or Boiled Potatoes *Lima Beans*

Cucumber Salad

Pineapple Meringue Pie or Banana Shortcake
or
Ice Cream

Cake

Tea *Coffee* *Milk*

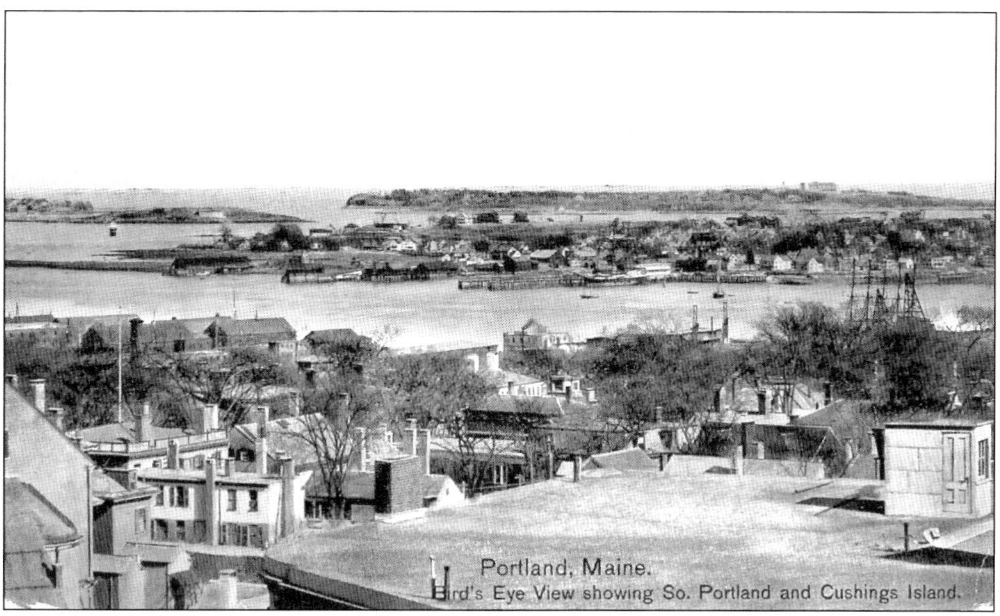

A view of the Fore River could be seen from the Congress Square Hotel dining room.

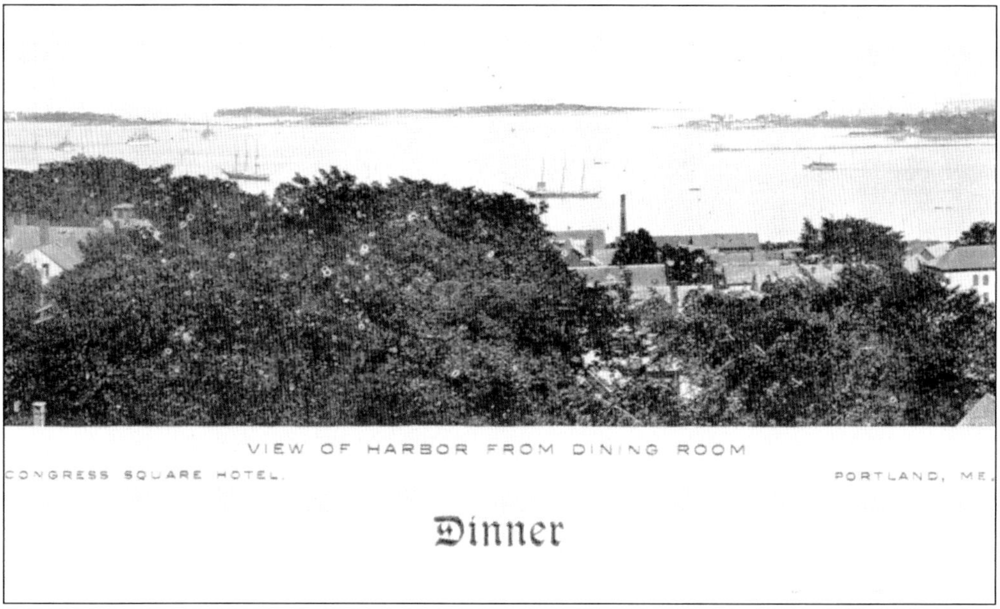

Diners at the Congress Square Hotel were treated to views of Casco Bay and the White Mountains.

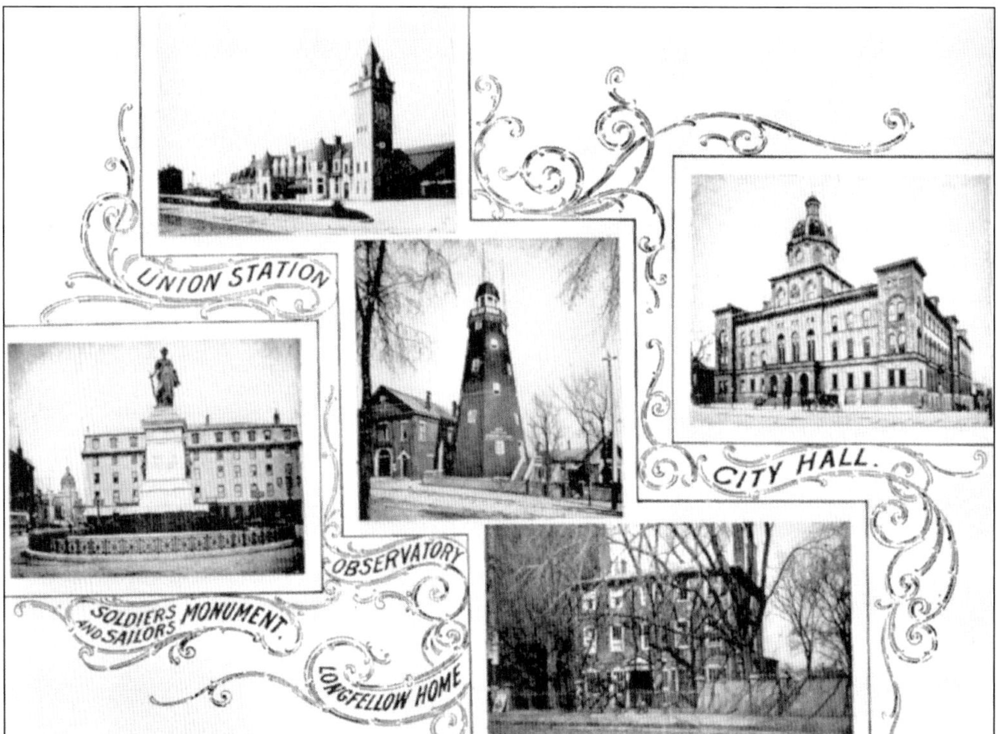

Early-20th-century postcards of Portland landmarks were labeled on the opposite side with a Congress Square Hotel letterhead and were freely available to patrons.

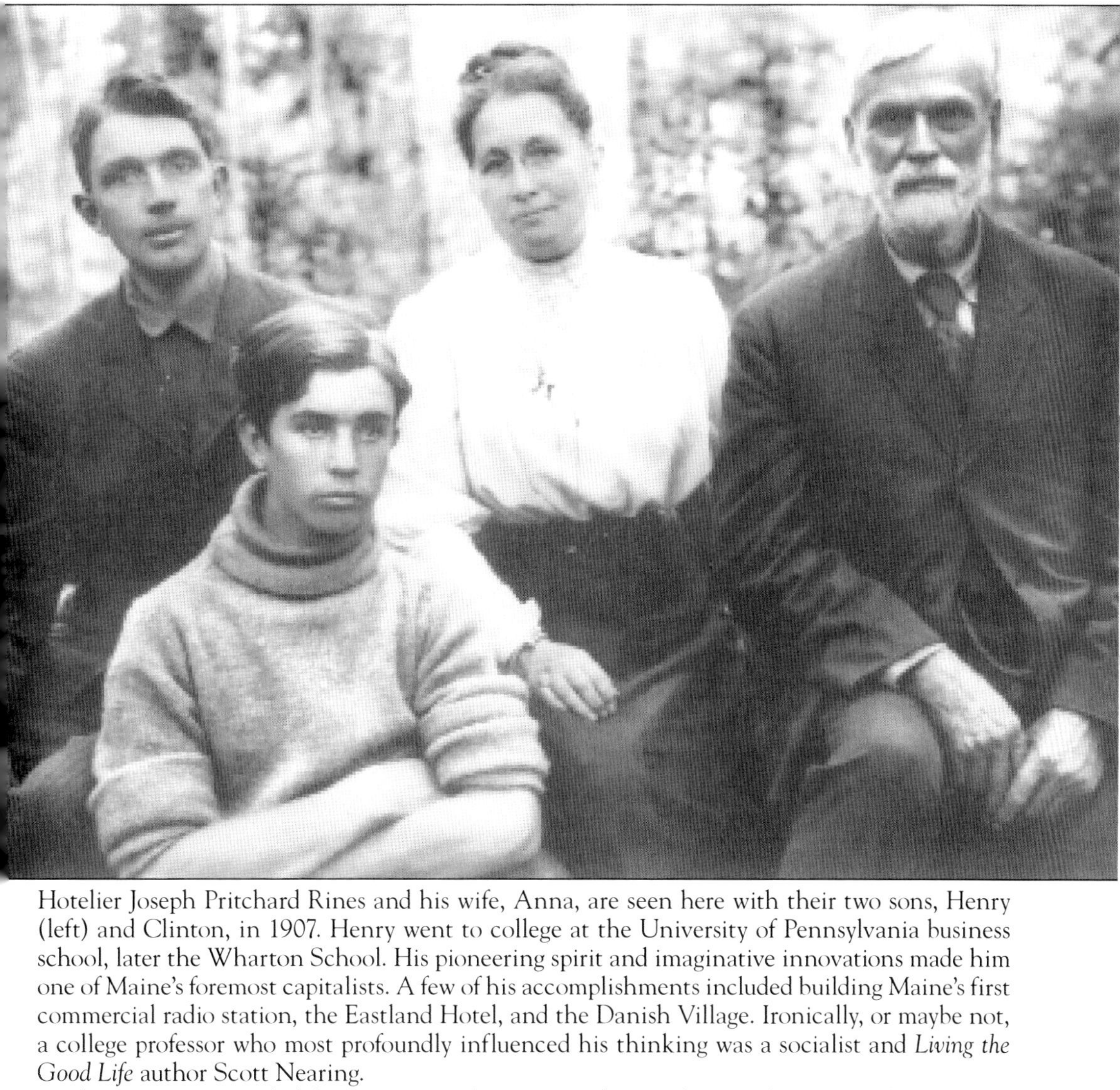

Hotelier Joseph Pritchard Rines and his wife, Anna, are seen here with their two sons, Henry (left) and Clinton, in 1907. Henry went to college at the University of Pennsylvania business school, later the Wharton School. His pioneering spirit and imaginative innovations made him one of Maine's foremost capitalists. A few of his accomplishments included building Maine's first commercial radio station, the Eastland Hotel, and the Danish Village. Ironically, or maybe not, a college professor who most profoundly influenced his thinking was a socialist and *Living the Good Life* author Scott Nearing.

Clinton Rines attended the University of New Hampshire and ran Walnut Crest, the farm that Joseph had purchased in Gorham, Maine. The farm supplied meat, vegetables, and dairy products to the Columbia, the Congress Square Hotel, the Eastland Hotel, and the Danish Village.

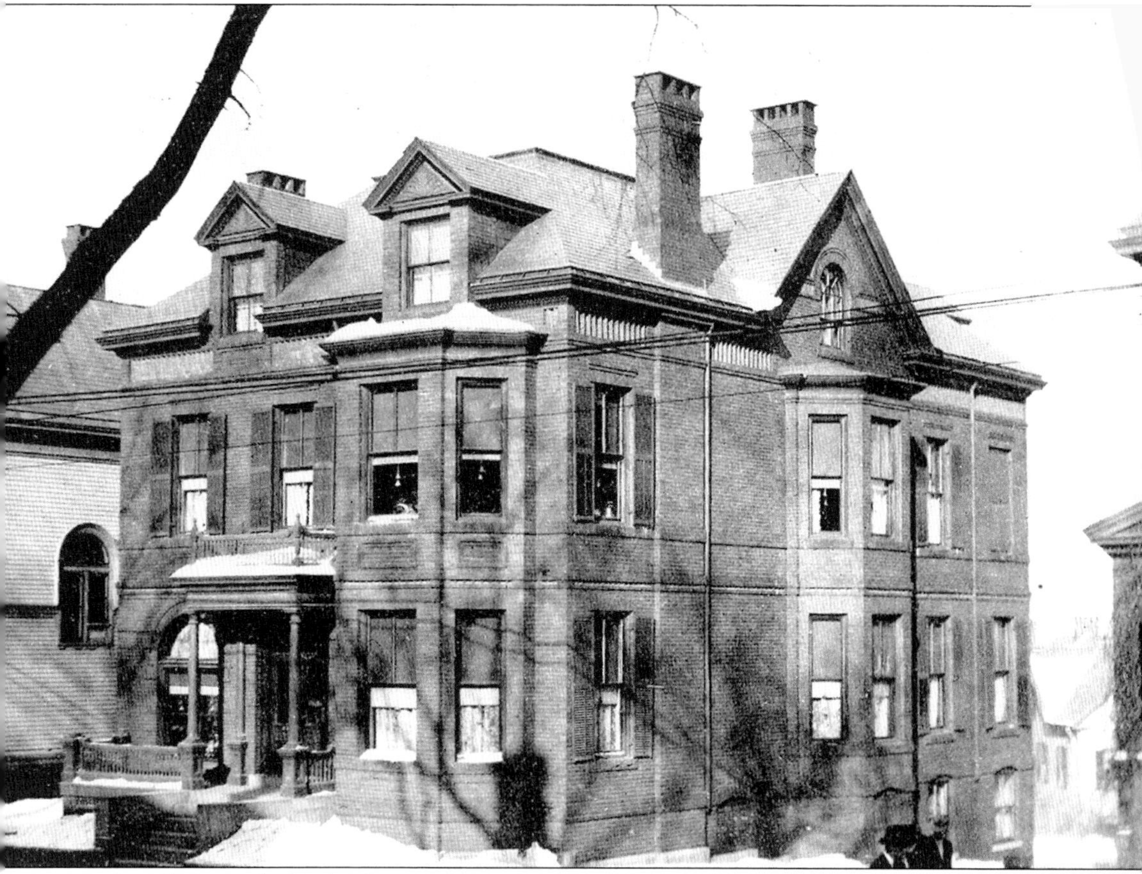

Joseph Rines built this home at 769 Congress Street in 1894. It was designed by Frederick Thompson and Francis Fassett. After Rines died in 1919, his son Henry lived in the home for a short period while his new home was being built in Cape Elizabeth. Both of Henry's children, Mary and William were born in this house. Eventually this building became the Roma Cafe and was run for many years by the Marino family as a quality Italian restaurant. The Roma is operated today by Peter Landrigan and is noted for its fine cuisine and sophisticated atmosphere.

Three

Henry Pritchard Rines, an Enlightened Entrepreneur

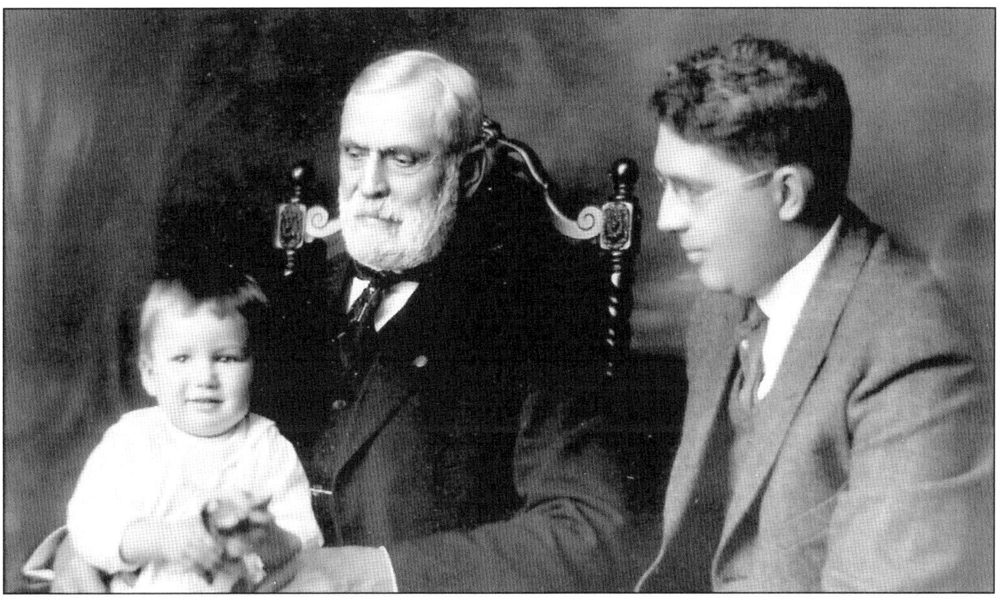

Henry Pritchard Rines, right, and his father Joseph Rines, admire Henry's infant son, William, in 1918. Necessity begets ingenuity as Henry Rines sought a vehicle to promote his expansive new investment, the luxurious Eastland Hotel. The inspiration walked through the door when William Foss was seeking a backer to help build a radio station in Portland. The state of Maine would never be the same, as Henry would build a string of radio stations from Bangor all the way to New Hampshire introducing NBC to northern New England.

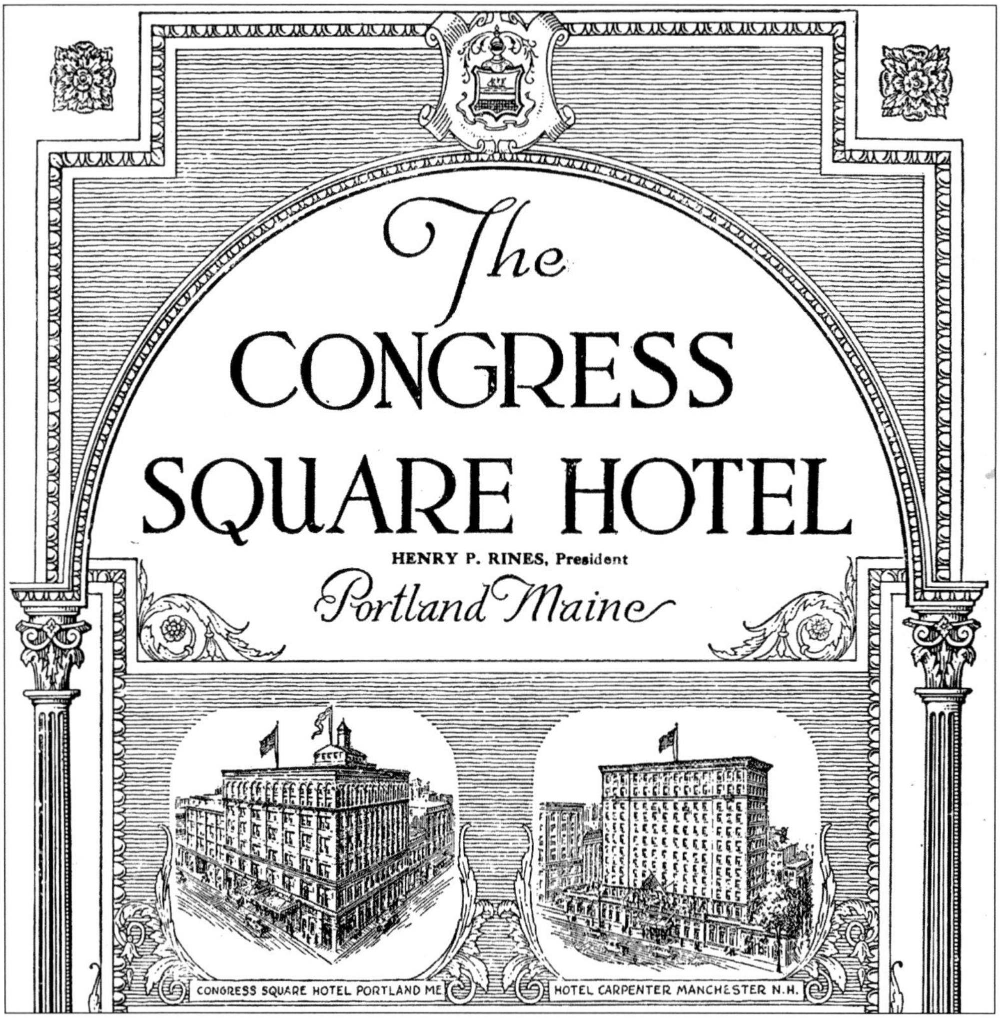

The Congress Square Hotel had many tasty items on the menu in 1920, including fried lobster for $1.75. (Courtesy of the Maine Historic Preservation Commission.)

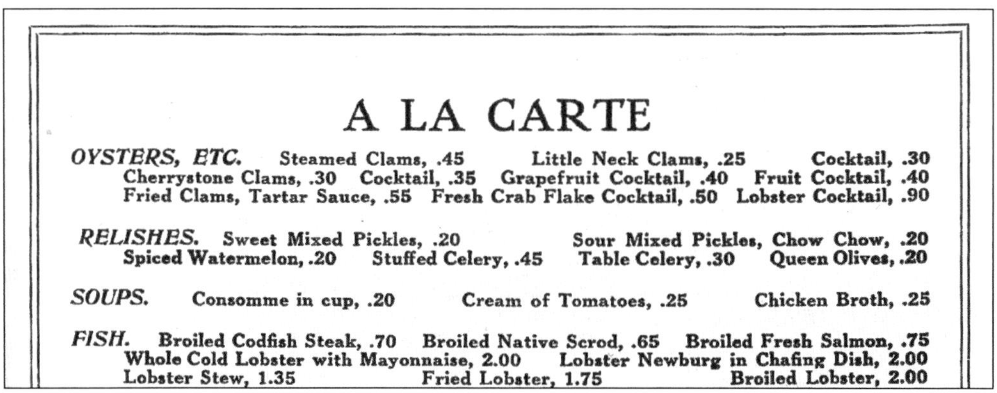

A LA CARTE

OYSTERS, ETC. **Steamed Clams, .45 Little Neck Clams, .25 Cocktail, .30 Cherrystone Clams, .30 Cocktail, .35 Grapefruit Cocktail, .40 Fruit Cocktail, .40 Fried Clams, Tartar Sauce, .55 Fresh Crab Flake Cocktail, .50 Lobster Cocktail, .90**

RELISHES. **Sweet Mixed Pickles, .20 Sour Mixed Pickles, Chow Chow, .20 Spiced Watermelon, .20 Stuffed Celery, .45 Table Celery, .30 Queen Olives, .20**

SOUPS. **Consomme in cup, .20 Cream of Tomatoes, .25 Chicken Broth, .25**

FISH. **Broiled Codfish Steak, .70 Broiled Native Scrod, .65 Broiled Fresh Salmon, .75 Whole Cold Lobster with Mayonnaise, 2.00 Lobster Newburg in Chafing Dish, 2.00 Lobster Stew, 1.35 Fried Lobster, 1.75 Broiled Lobster, 2.00**

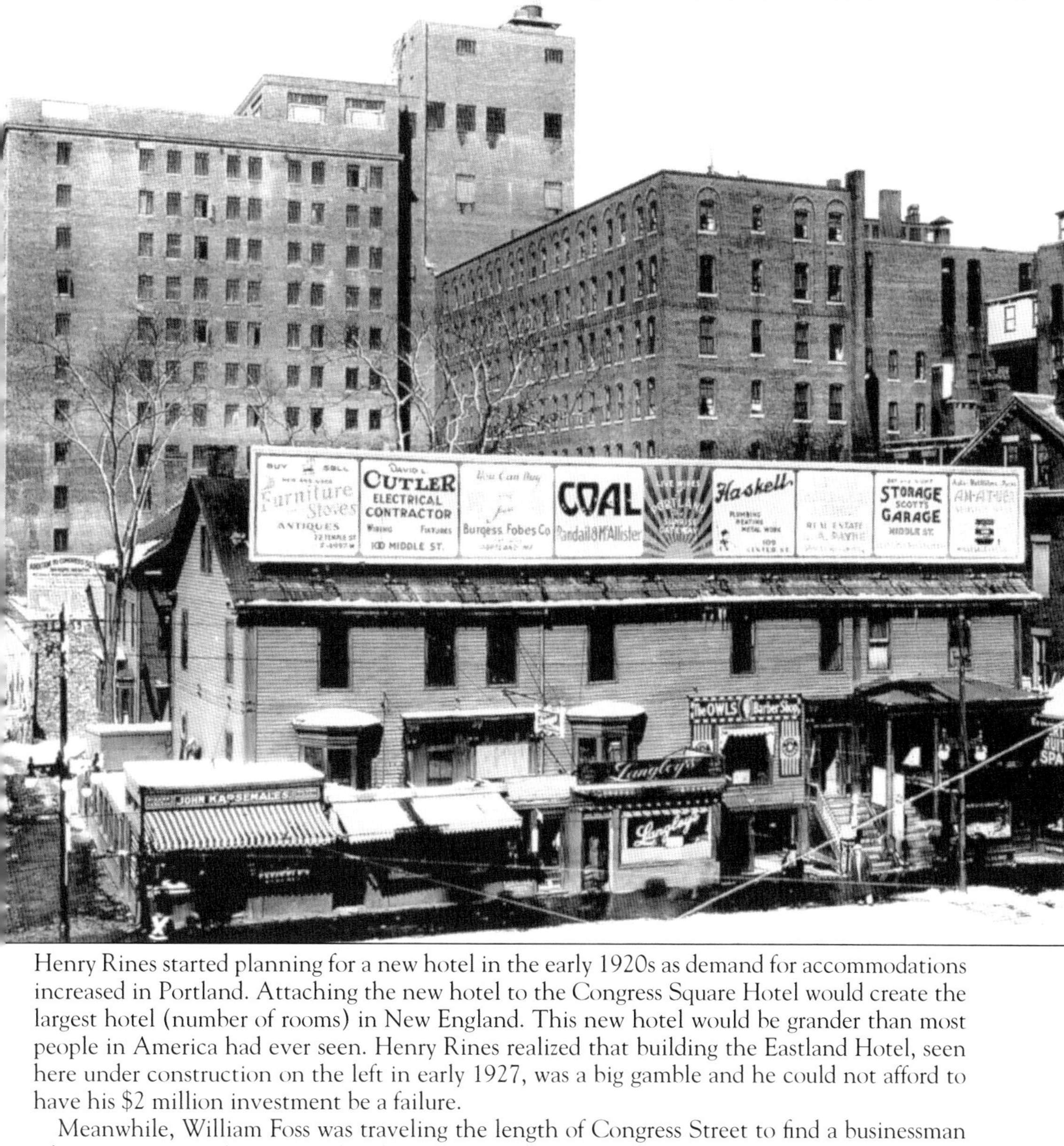

Henry Rines started planning for a new hotel in the early 1920s as demand for accommodations increased in Portland. Attaching the new hotel to the Congress Square Hotel would create the largest hotel (number of rooms) in New England. This new hotel would be grander than most people in America had ever seen. Henry Rines realized that building the Eastland Hotel, seen here under construction on the left in early 1927, was a big gamble and he could not afford to have his $2 million investment be a failure.

Meanwhile, William Foss was traveling the length of Congress Street to find a businessman adventurous enough to consider the new and still-evolving technology called radio. Every businessman that Foss approached felt that the industry was too infantile and speculative, except for one man. Henry Rines embraced new and innovative ideas and certainly the design of his new hotel showed that. He realized right away that radio and the opening of his new business would create a perfect fit. (Collections of the Maine Historical Society.)

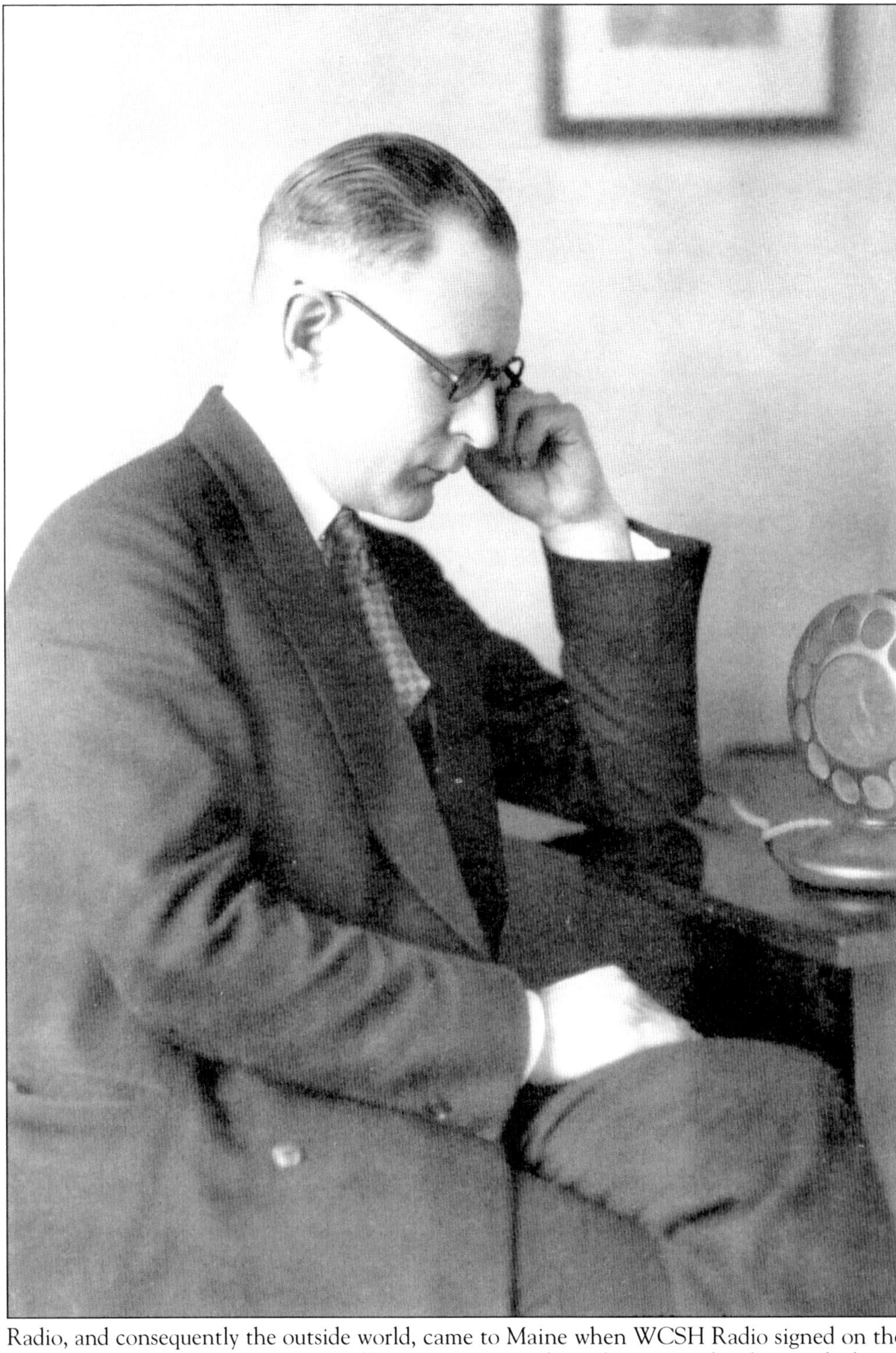

Radio, and consequently the outside world, came to Maine when WCSH Radio signed on the air in 1925. Here station manager William Foss contemplates this new technology and what it might mean to the world.

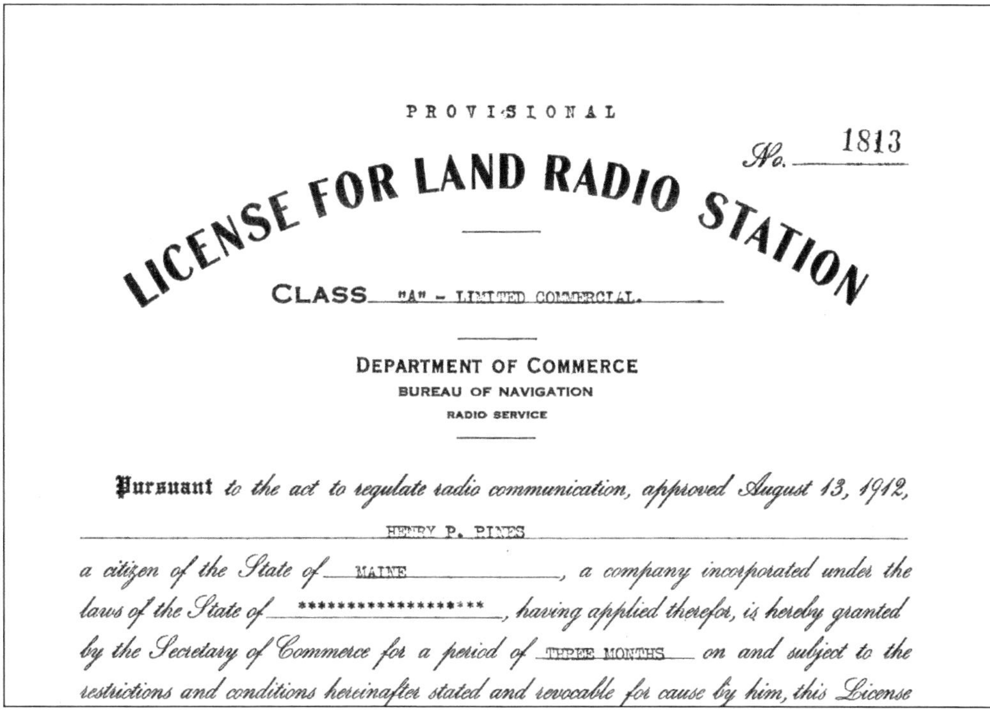

PROVISIONAL

No. 1813

LICENSE FOR LAND RADIO STATION

CLASS "A" - LIMITED COMMERCIAL.

DEPARTMENT OF COMMERCE
BUREAU OF NAVIGATION
RADIO SERVICE

Pursuant *to the act to regulate radio communication, approved August 13, 1912,* HENRY P. RINES *a citizen of the State of* MAINE*, a company incorporated under the laws of the State of* *********************, having applied therefor, is hereby granted by the Secretary of Commerce for a period of* THREE MONTHS *on and subject to the restrictions and conditions hereinafter stated and revocable for cause by him, this License*

Maine's first commercial radio station license for a land radio station was issued to Henry Rines on June 14, 1925.

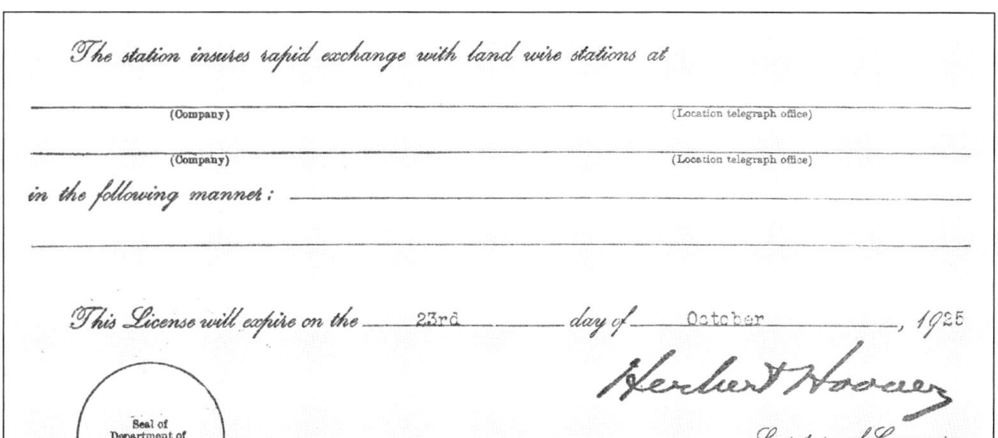

The station insures rapid exchange with land wire stations at

(Company) (Location telegraph office)

(Company) (Location telegraph office)

in the following manner:

This License will expire on the 23rd *day of* October*, 1925*

Herbert Hoover

Secretary of Commerce.

Seal of Department of Commerce

Secretary of Commerce Herbert Hoover signed WCSH Radio's first license to broadcast and the radio station made its inaugural broadcast transmission on July 13, 1925.

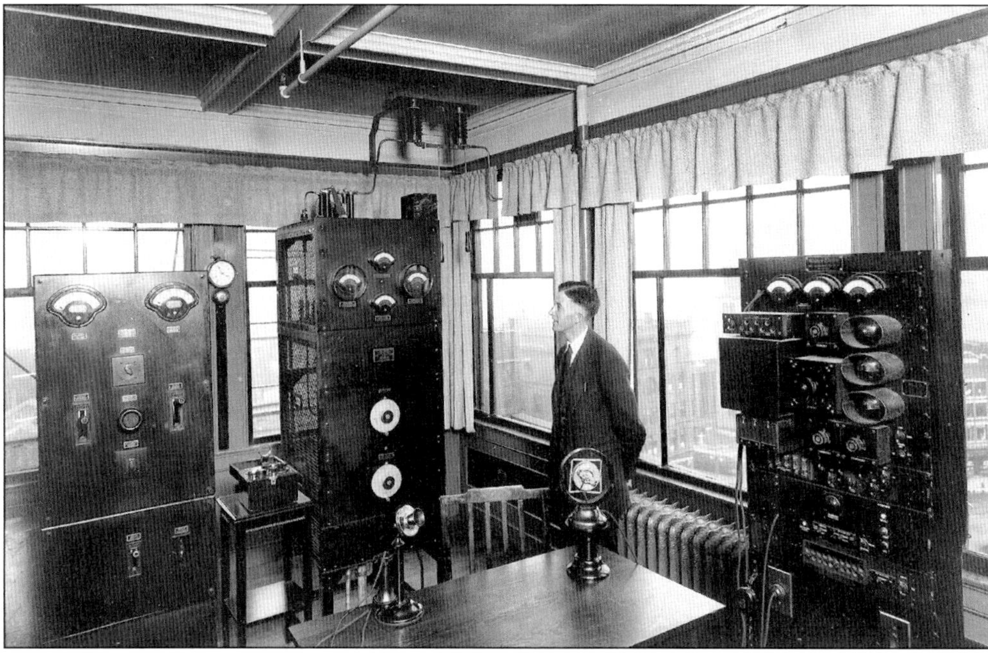

Henry Rines applied for and received permission to broadcast from atop the family hotel, thus the call letters, WCSH, for Congress Square Hotel. Here WCSH Radio's first chief engineer, Jimmy Nicholson, looks over the transmission equipment. Congress Square can be seen through the windows behind.

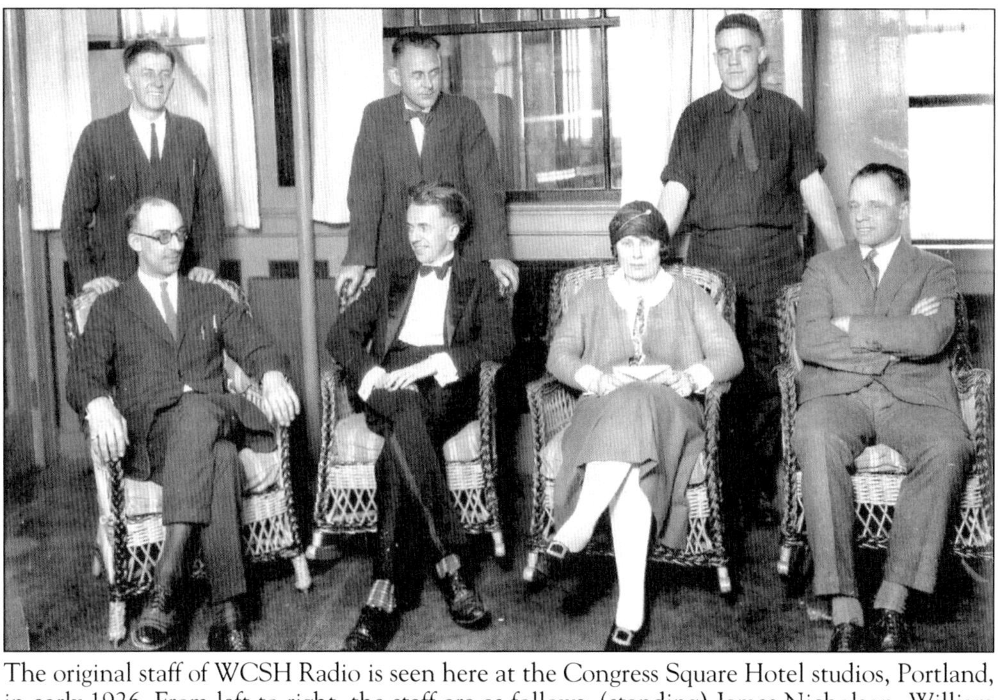

The original staff of WCSH Radio is seen here at the Congress Square Hotel studios, Portland, in early 1926. From left to right, the staff are as follows: (standing) James Nicholson, William Foss (Station Manager), and John Fraser; (seated) Linwood Pitman, J. Daniel MacDonald, Gwendolyn C. Marshall, and Archie Legreau.

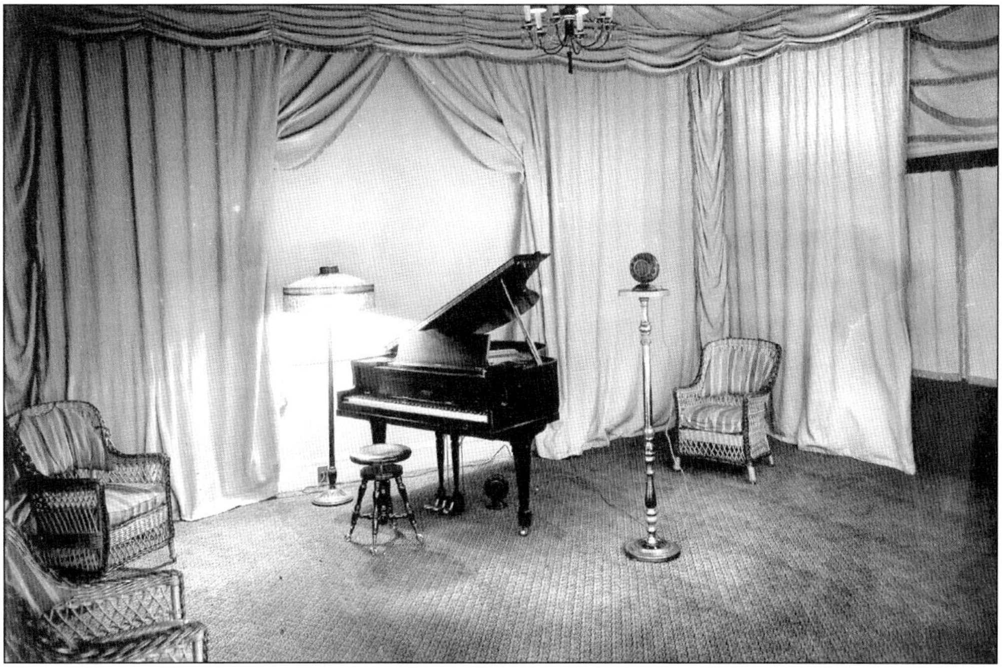

WCSH Radio's first studio barely looked like the radio studios of today. Draped in monks cloth to dampen sound, the studio was sweltering when Gov. Ralph O. Brewster and Henry P. Rines gave the inaugural speech on WCSH Radio. The speech was at 7:30 p.m. on July 13, 1925.

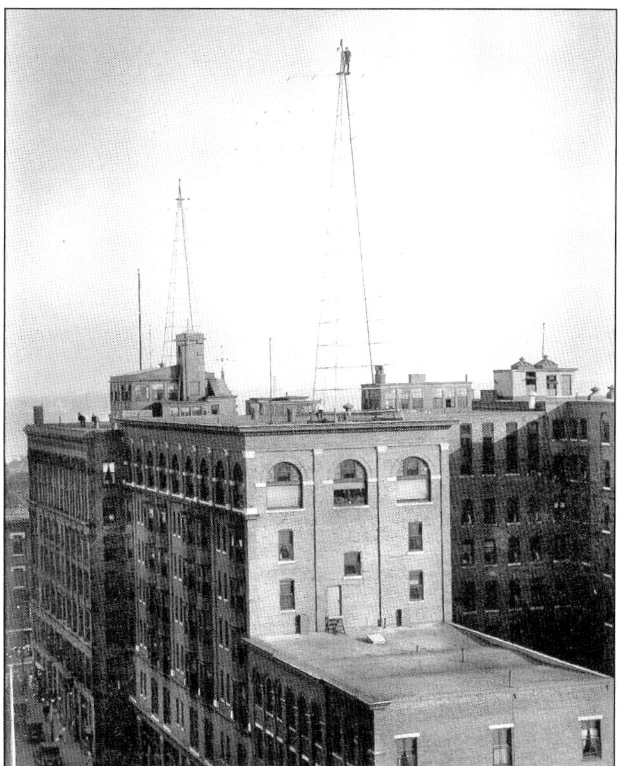

From 1925 through 1930, the WCSH Radio transmission antenna and tower were located on the top of the Congress Square Hotel. Jimmy Nicholson, the radio engineer on top of the tower, probably had a good, if unsettling, view of greater Portland.

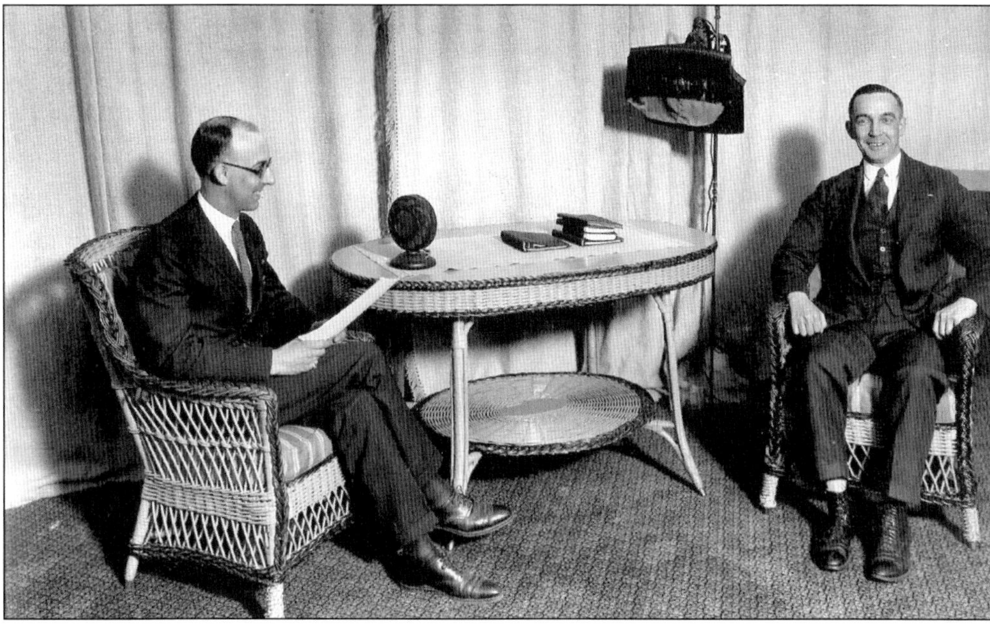

Radio comedian Eddie Cantor was the first of many nationally recognized talents to visit the WCSH Radio studios in the 1920s. Cantor (right) is seen with program director Linwood Pitman in 1926. Internationally renowned personalities like Charles Lindbergh, Amelia Earhart, Admiral Byrd, and orchestra leaders Tommy Dorsey and Rudy Vallee made appearances in the Portland studio.

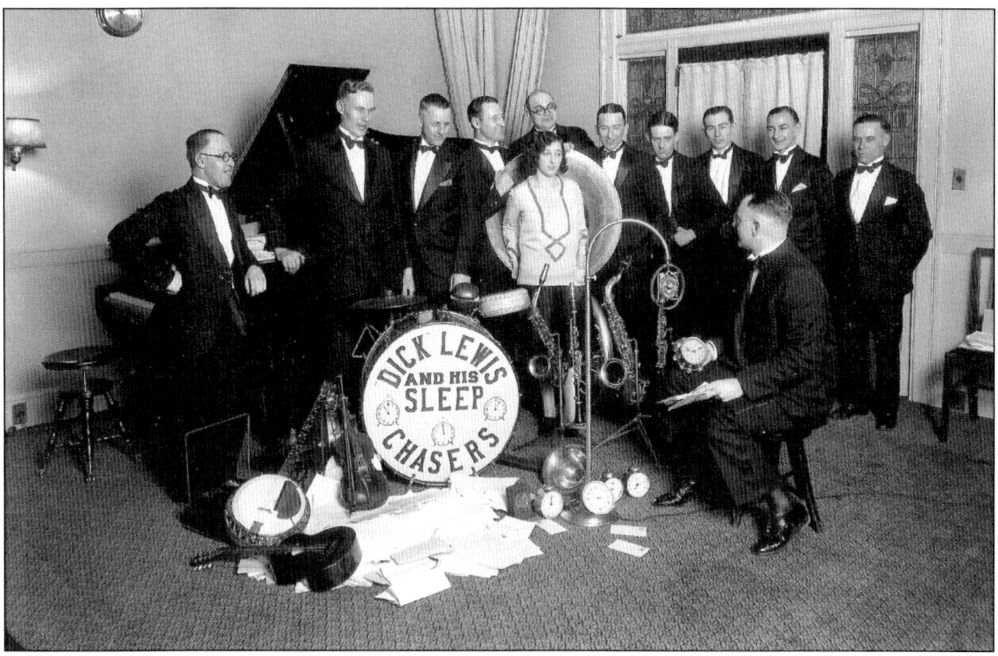

Early radio had no recording devices until the mid-1950s. Much of the programming was live. A popular band in the 1920s and 1930s was Dick Lewis and his Sleep Chasers. Dick Lewis (at the piano) chats with WCSH Radio station manager Bill Foss (holding the clock). The woman is Lucille Potter (Lavin) whose daughter Linda starred in the network television series *Alice*.

The National Broadcasting Corporation (NBC) radio network was incorporated in the fall of 1926 and WCSH Radio was one of the 26 flagship radio stations to join. Here Fibber McGee and Molly, a very popular early radio program, broadcast live from the NBC studios in New York City. By the 1990s, WCSH Radio and Television would be the oldest NBC affiliate in the country still operating under the original ownership.

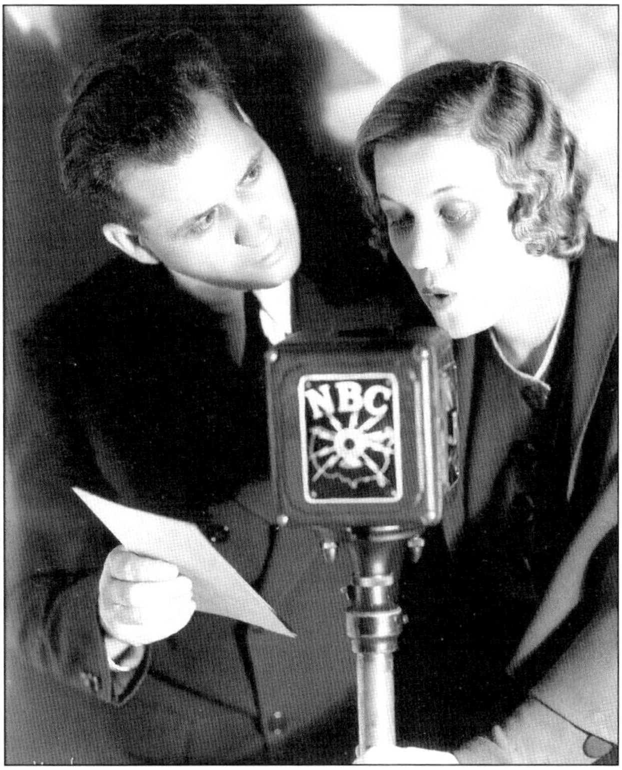

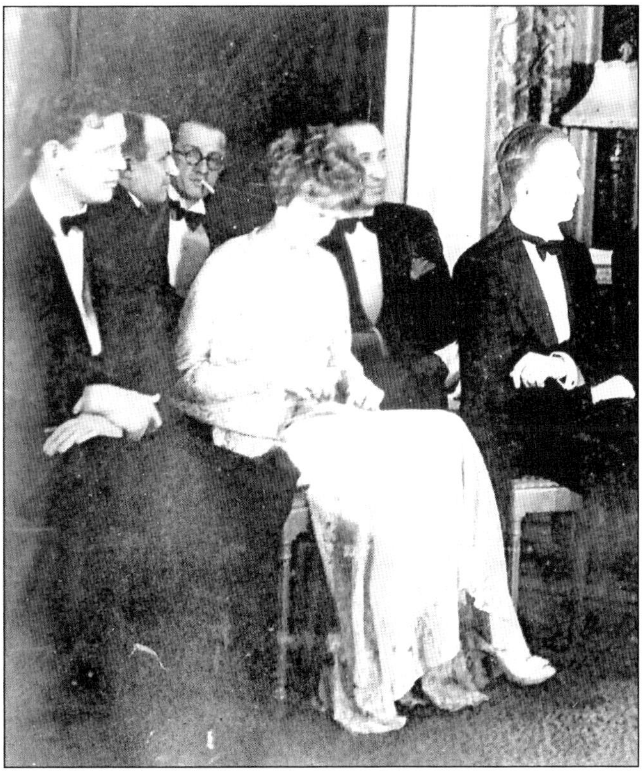

Charles Lindbergh (left) became an international celebrity when he was the first person ever to fly across the Atlantic Ocean, landing in Paris in May 1927. Seen here with his wife, Anne, Lindbergh made a quick publicity tour of the United States soon after his return to America, stopping at only a handful of cities. "Lucky Lindy" stayed at the recently opened Eastland Hotel and spoke to a crowd assembled there. His speech was carried on WCSH Radio.

THE

CONGRESS SQUARE HOTEL COMPANY

REQUESTS THE HONOUR OF YOUR PRESENCE

AT THE OPENING OF

THE EASTLAND

PORTLAND, MAINE

ON WEDNESDAY

THE FIFTEENTH OF JUNE

NINETEEN HUNDRED AND TWENTY-SEVEN

The Eastland Hotel opened with great fanfare in June 1927.

I DESIRE TO RESERVE COVERS FOR THE OPENING DINNER AT THE EASTLAND ON WEDNESDAY, THE FIFTEENTH OF JUNE AT SEVEN O'CLOCK.

DANCING

NAME

ADDRESS

DINNER $10.00 COVER

CHECK ENCLOSED FOR RESERVATIONS

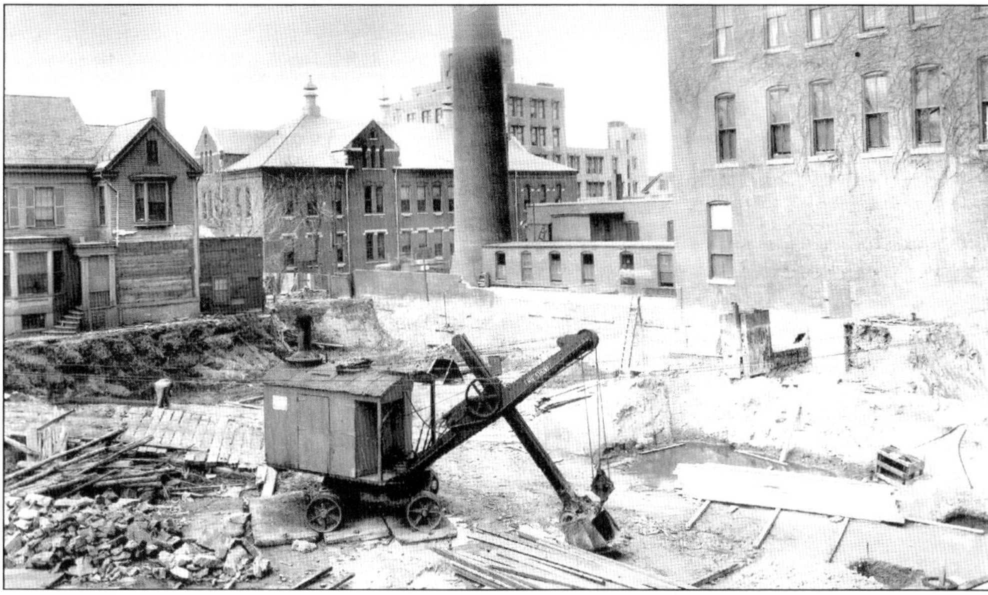

The 12-story Eastland Hotel was built in 12 months, the major construction taking just eight months. Here the ground is being prepared on April 29, 1926. (Collections of the Maine Historical Society.)

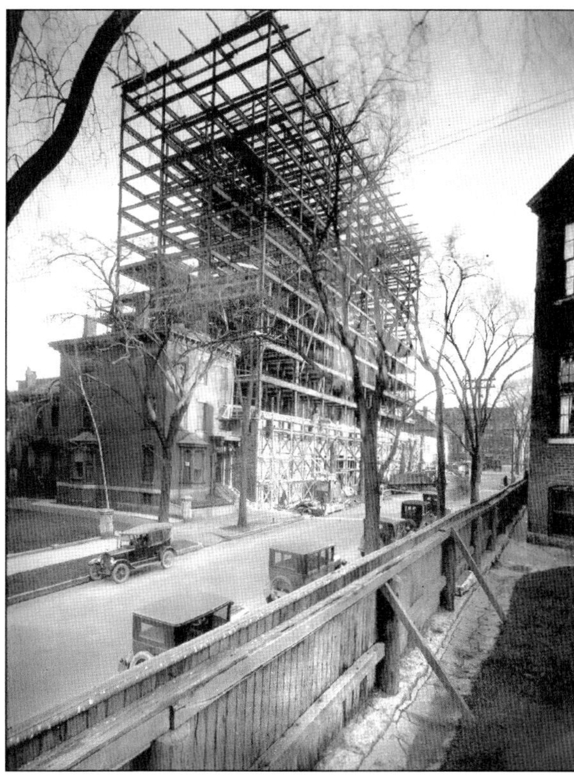

Here is what the construction looked like on November 10, 1926. (Collections of the Maine Historical Society.)

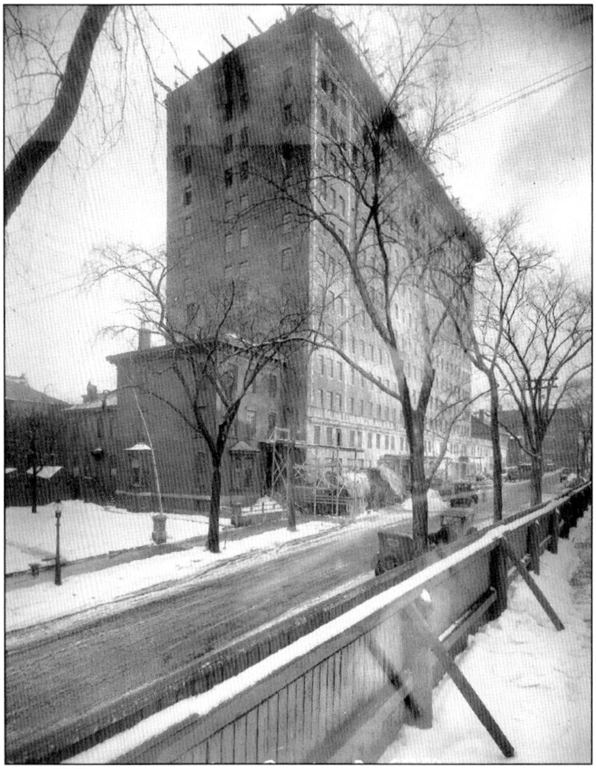

Here is the construction project on December 29, 1926. (Collections of the Maine Historical Society.)

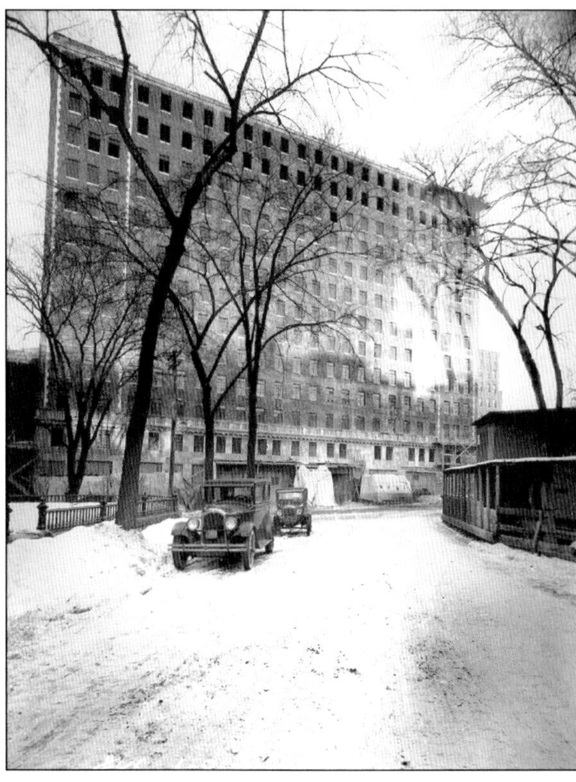

Here is the construction project well along at the end of January 1927. (Collections of the Maine Historical Society.)

The $2 million Eastland Hotel opened its doors in 1927. Located in Congress Square on the corner of Congress and High Streets, the hotel had 369 guest rooms. Of all the rooms, 272 of them had Murphy beds which swung up behind doors for convenient layaway. Every room had radio speakers, directly wired to WCSH Radio, with no off switch, only volume control. Every room had hot, cold, and ice water. (Collections of the Maine Historical Society.)

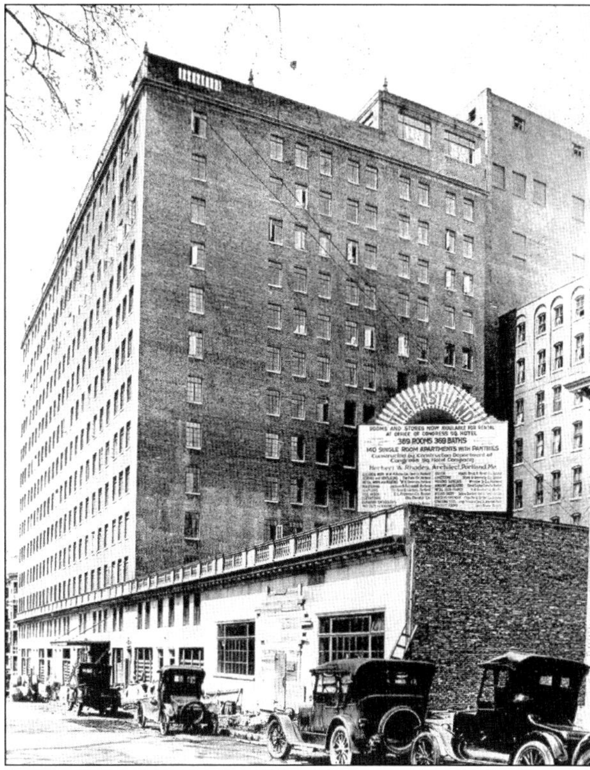

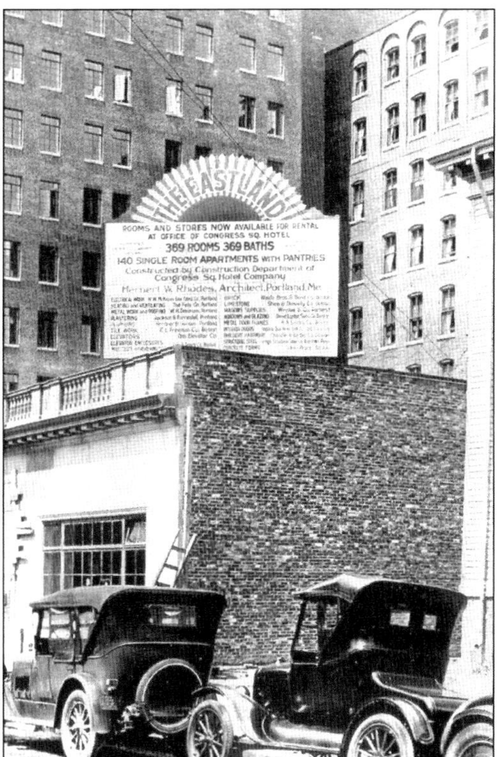

On June 16, 1927, well-known national radio announcer Graham McNamee went aloft in an airplane and dropped a set of hotel keys into Portland Harbor with the promise that the Eastland's doors would always stay open. The marquee on the soon-to-be-opened Eastland Hotel announces 369 rooms with 369 baths. (Collections of the Maine Historical Society.)

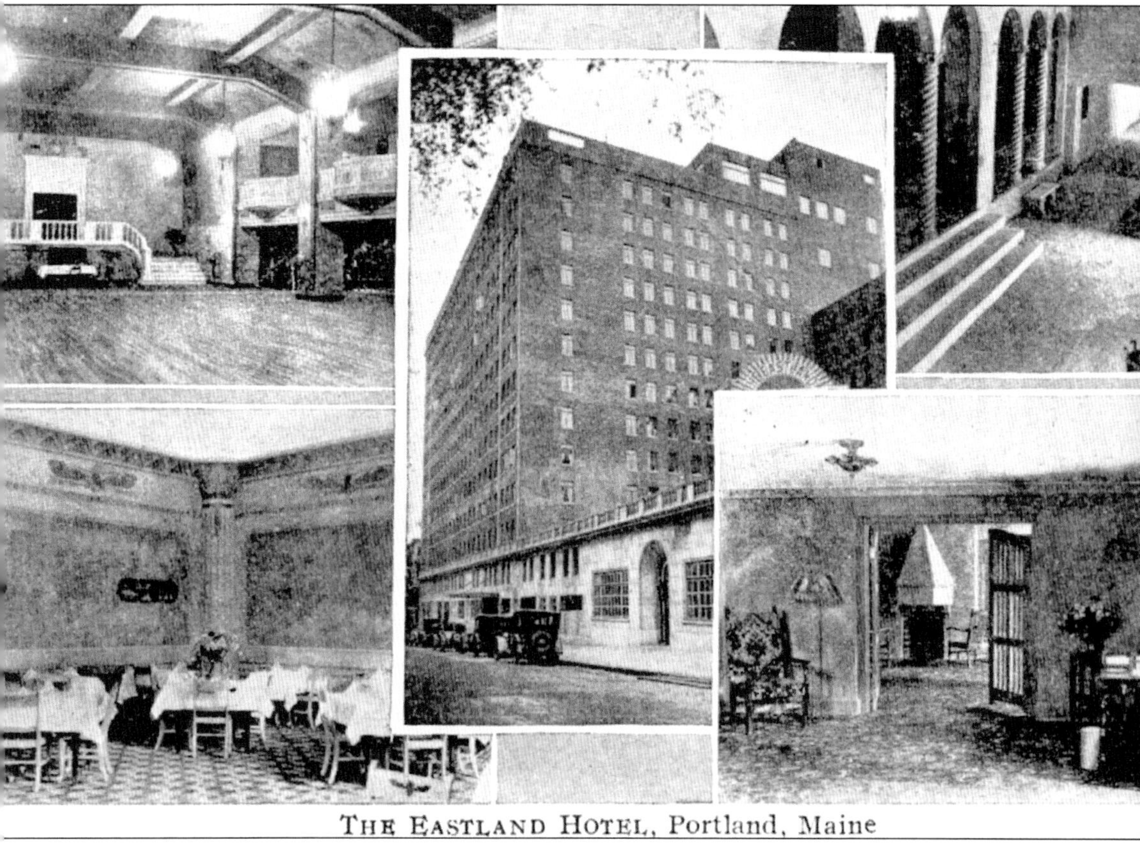

The Eastland Hotel's first postcard featured the beautiful exterior with its grand entrance on High Street and the fine design of the interiors, reflecting the latest European influences.

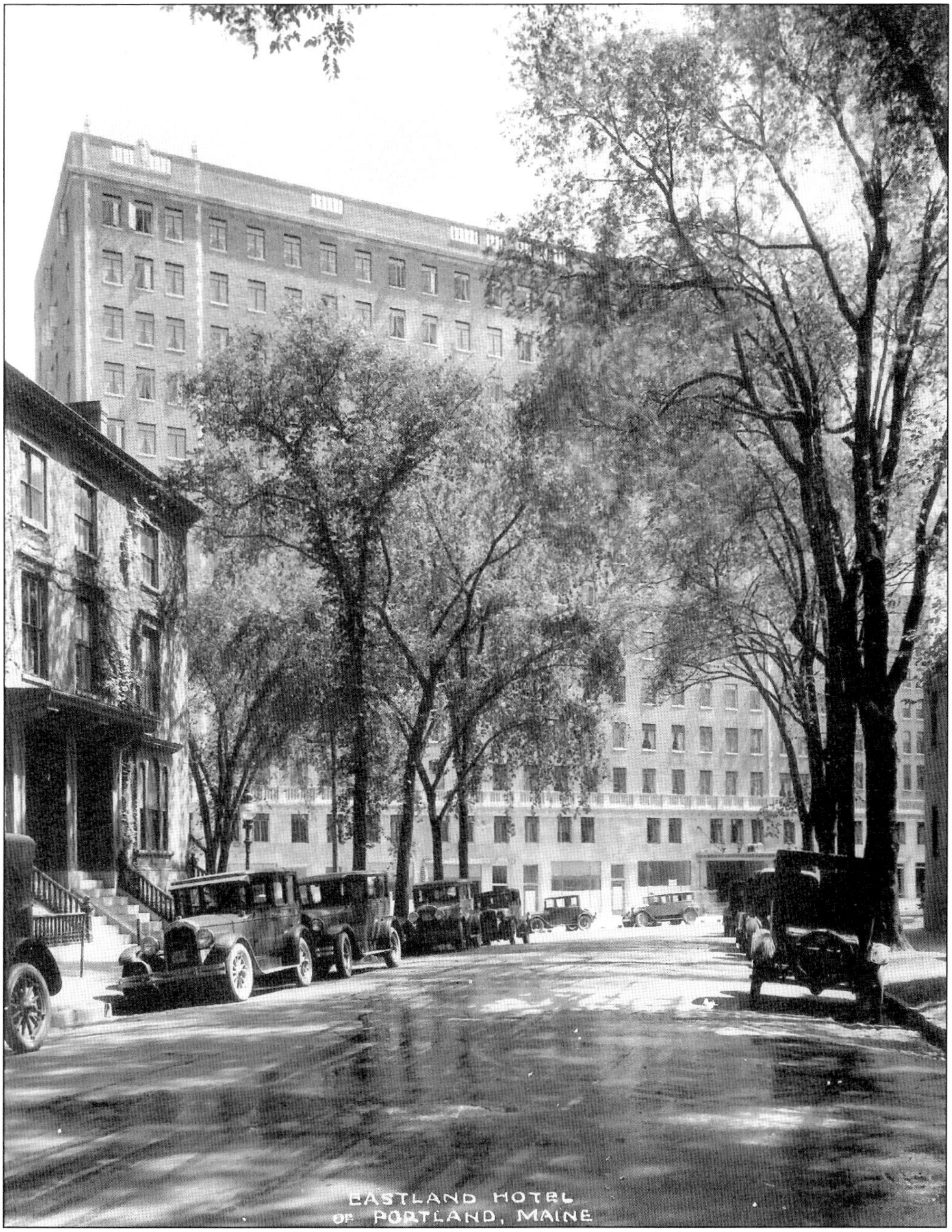

The Eastland Hotel, billed by the local press as "the Forest City's supreme symbol of elegance," opened its doors on June 15, 1927. The $2 million, 12-story Eastland Hotel was heralded as "the most important building project that has ever been carried out in this city."

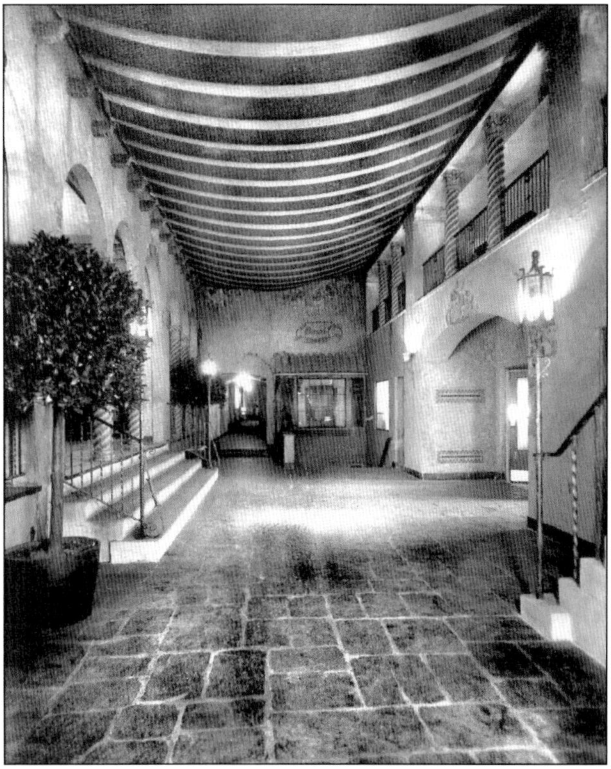

The following series of promotional photographs were taken in 1927 to document the hotel's grand opening. The entrance court of the Eastland Hotel featured the latest Mediterranean appeal, a Spanish motif with Moorish architecture. Benoit's, a sophisticated men's store pictured here, was accessible through the lobby and by High Street. Another store that graced the lobby was Patrick Ahern's men's fashions.

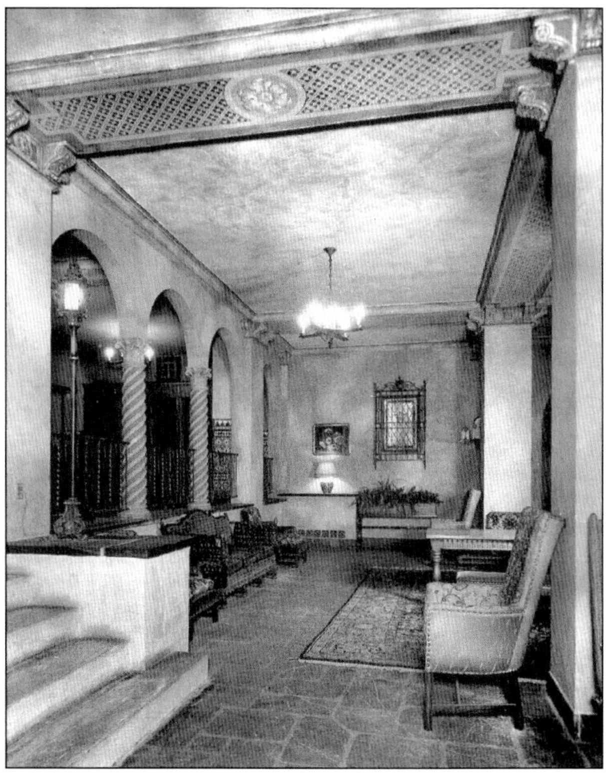

The lower lobby of the new Eastland Hotel allowed for sitting, reading, and chatting with friends.

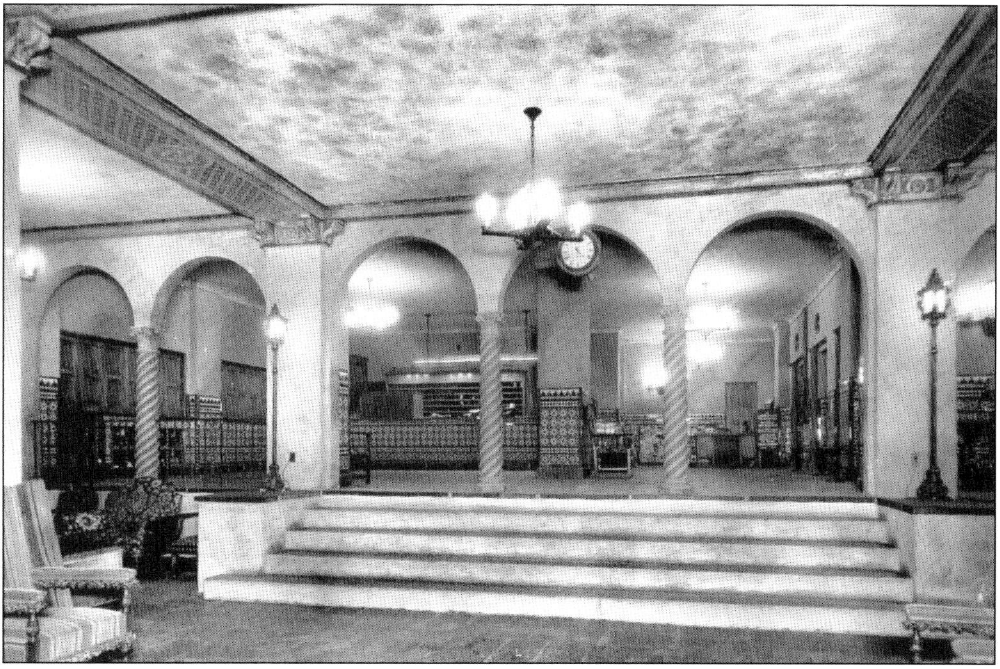

The front desk was located in the upper lobby. A new bank of elevators with uniformed operators lent sophistication to a state that had few elevators in 1927.

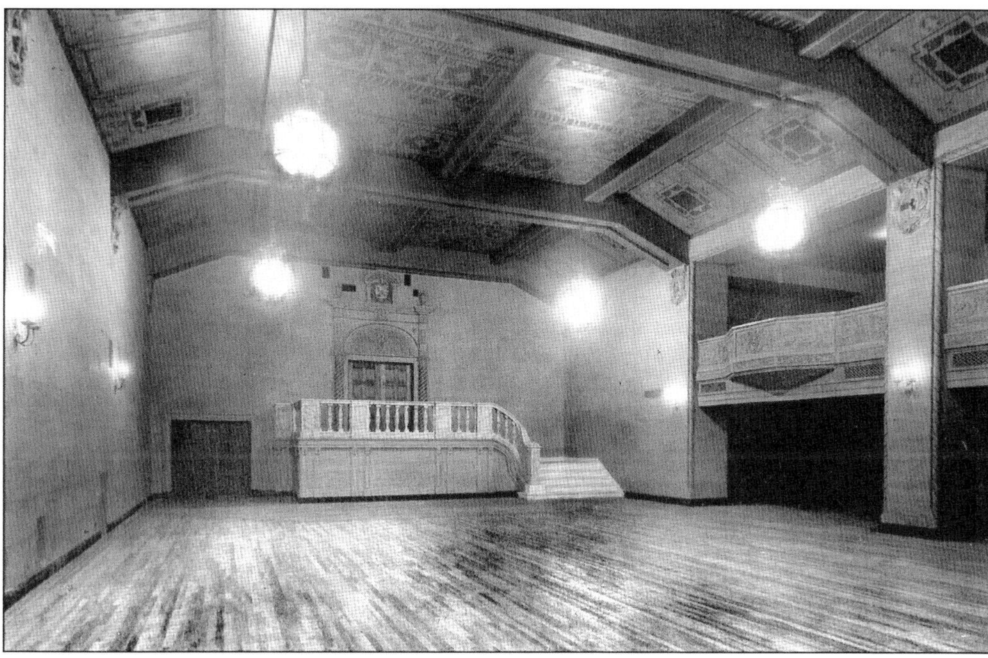

The State of Maine room and banquet hall was available for most every type of function, from weddings and conventions to meetings for service organizations. Many famous people have spoken to audiences here, including Presidential candidates Gerald Ford, George Bush Sr., George Bush Jr., and Bill Clinton, as well as Charles Lindbergh and Tom Brokaw, to name just a few.

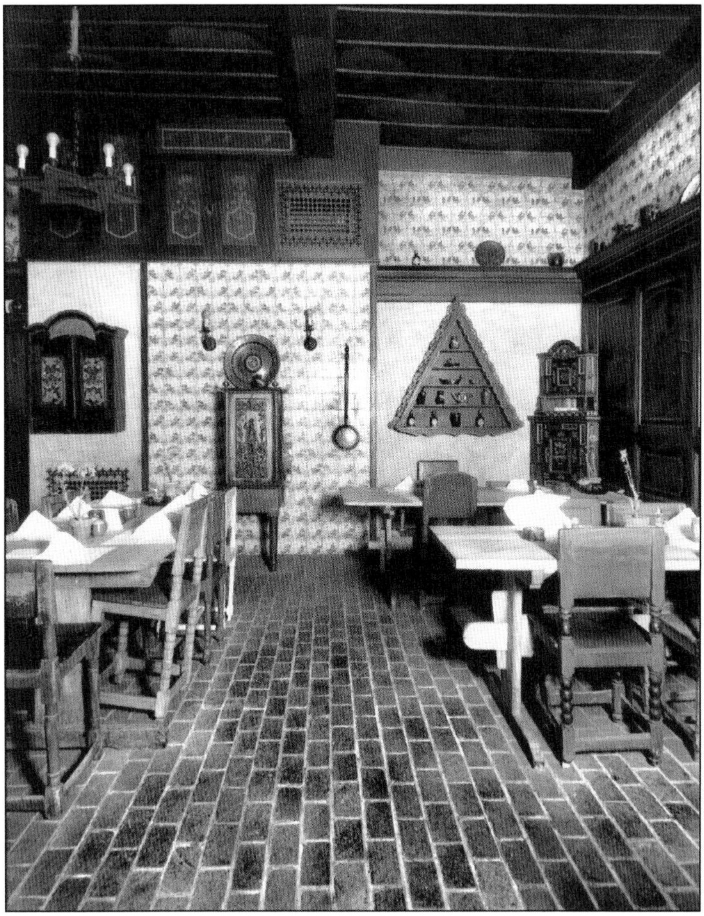

An Eastland Hotel postcard (below) describes the wonderfully appointed Danish Tea Room (above). The Eastland Hotel had several European themes running through it. (Collections of the Maine Historical Society.)

Skenkstuen (Danish Tea Room), Eastland Hotel, Portand, Me. This room is substantially a copy of Skenkstuen (the room where patrons are served) in Weis's Inn in the market place of Ribe, the capital of medieval Denmark, the setting of brilliant court and ecclesiastical life of bygone centuries. The original tavern is several hundred years old, and the last interior decorating as here portrayed, was applied nearly two hundred years ago. Many of the decorative pieces were imported from Ribe especially for this room.

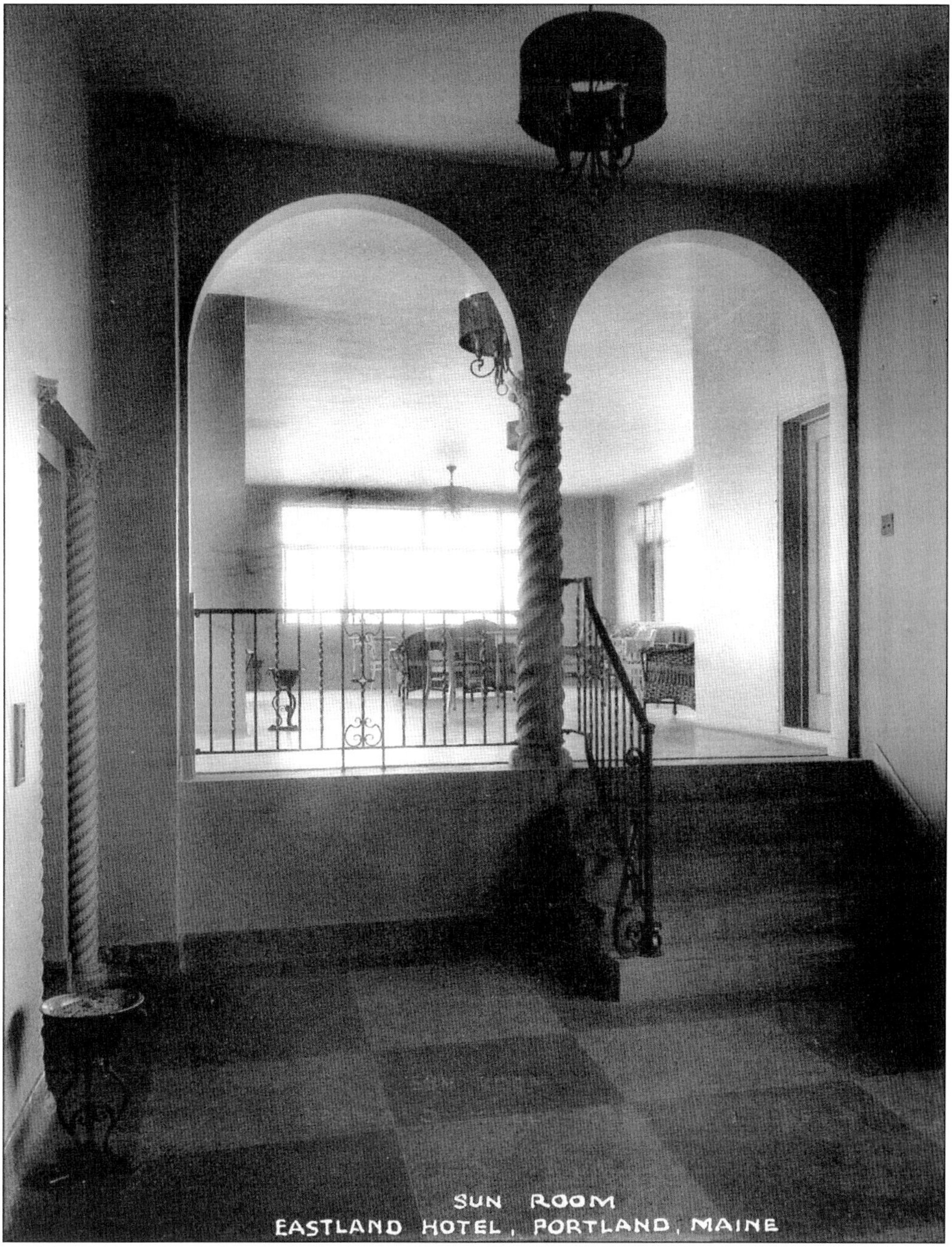

The Sun Parlor on the top of the Eastland was a favorite for many. A 360-degree view allowed residents, guests and hotel visitors a sweeping view of Casco Bay all the way to Mount Washington in New Hampshire. Today visitors to the top of the Eastland will be rewarded with the same breathtaking panorama.

The Eastland

Portland, Maine

EGYPTIAN DINING ROOM

THIS dining room is believed to be the first, if not the only, public dining room of its type in America. The figures on the walls are represented as being carved in stone after the ancient Egyptian manner.

It represents the open air court of Egyptian royalty in the period of King Pepi II. The mural decorating is in true Egyptian, faithful in detail even to the hieroglyphics and hieratic numerals of clock.

The panels represent scenes from the daily lives and activities of royalty in ancient Egypt.

That of the western corner represents the boar hunt with hunters in chariot and afoot. The next beyond depicts the return with the trophy. The third has the preparation of the meal in the royal kitchen. In the panel beyond, King Pepi and Queen Sebek with the royal favorite are at the feast. A dance, not unlike those of the present day, is in progress in the next picture, the King and his harem favorite participating. From there on are domestic scenes in which the Queen and the favorite strive to gain the monarch's favor until the wifely persuasion of Sebek is successful.

The menu cover of the newly opened Egyptian Dining Room describes the atmosphere of the hunt and feast of the pharaoh.

Here are the Egyptian Dining Room menu prices from the 1950s. One can only imagine the prices of food in 1927 when this restaurant first opened.

MAINE SHORE DINNERS

No. 1 ***$2.00***

Steamed Clams
Drawn Butter Crackers Pickles
Fried Clams or Scallops
Hot Rolls Potato Chips
Choice of Dessert
Tea Coffee

No. 2 ***$3.50***

Steamed Clams or Lobster Stew
Crackers Pickles
Fried Clams or Scallops
Lobster Salad
Potato Chips Hot Rolls
Dessert Tea or Coffee

No. 3 ***$4.25***

Steamed Clams, Drawn Butter
Celery Olives
Fried Clams or Scallops or Lobster Stew
WHOLE LOBSTER; Broiled, Boiled or Salad
Choice of Dessert
Tea Milk Coffee

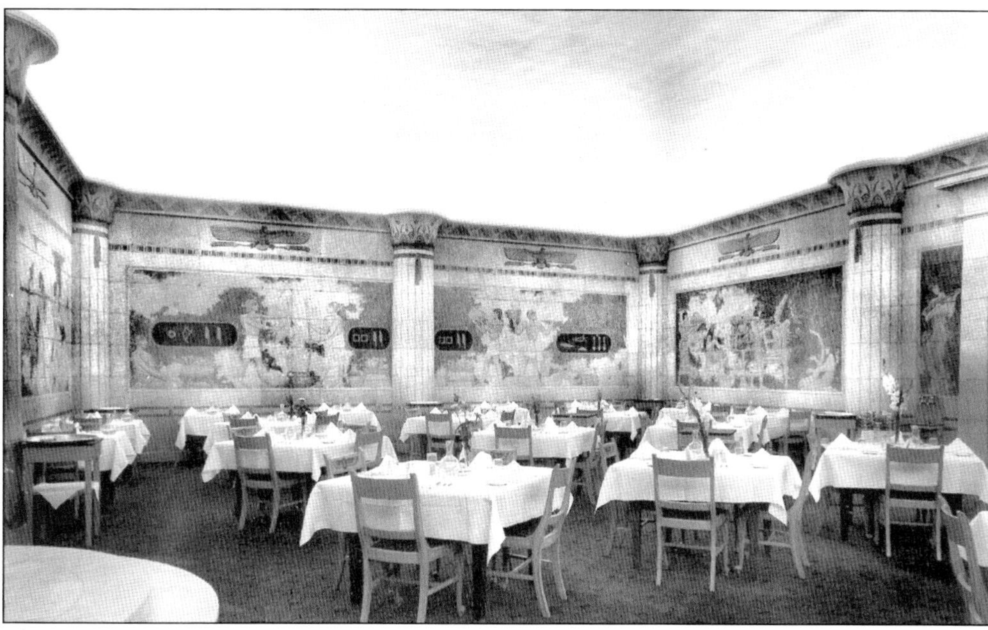

The Egyptian Dining Room was believed to be the first public dining room of its type in America. The figures on the walls depict Egyptian royalty in the period of King Pepi II and Queen Sebek. The mural is authentic in detail even to the hieroglyphics and hieratic numerals of the clock. The motif was an attempt to capture the excitement of the recent archeological discoveries in Egypt and to forget the horrors and sadness of the First World War.

SEA FOOD

Broiled Maine Lobster (1 lb. Av.)	2.35
Broiled Maine Lobster (1½ lb. Av.)	3.50
Lobster Newburg en Casserole	2.25
Broiled or Fried Fresh Haddock	1.20
Fresh Haddock Sticks	1.20
Broiled Halibut Steak	1.30
Fried Clams (Crumbs or Batter)	1.50
Fried Deep Sea Scallops	1.20

Above Served with French Fried Potato and Rolls

SALADS

Maine Lobster	2.25
Diced Chicken	1.30
Fresh Shrimp	1.10
Tuna	1.25
Salmon	1.30
Crabflake	1.30

Above Salads with French Fried Potato and Rolls

Waldorf	.75
Fresh Fruit	1.10
Egg and Tomato	.85
Iceberg Lettuce	.50
Tomato and Lettuce	.60
Chef's Salad, large	.85

Served with Rolls or Rye Krisp

Roquefort Dressing 10c extra

Thursday, September 26, 1957

The Egyptian Room menu offered a variety of seafood dinners.

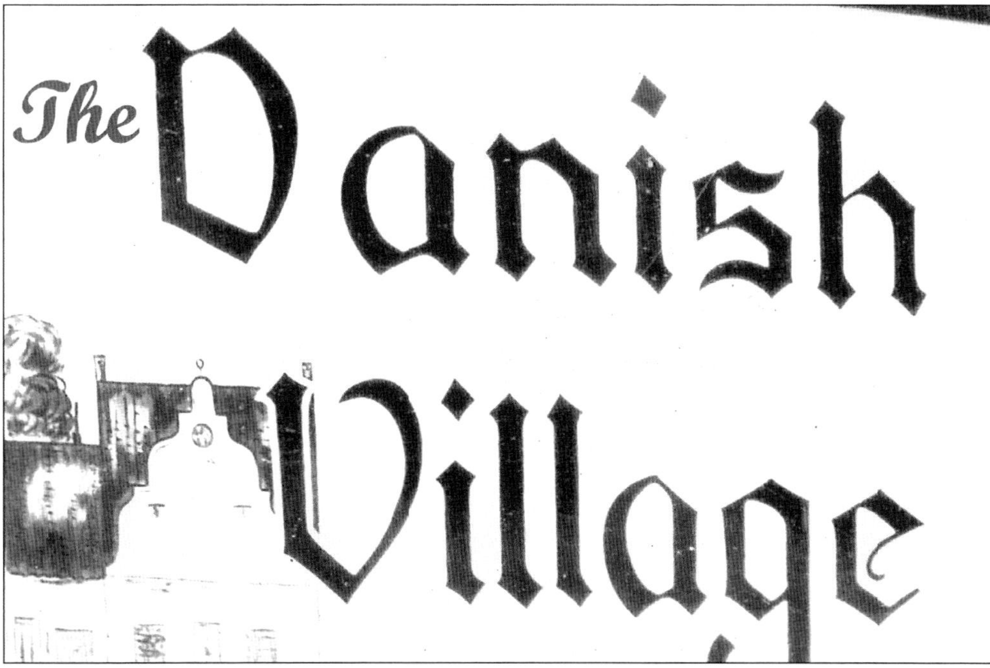

The Danish Village on Route 1 in Scarborough opened with great celebration in the summer of 1930.

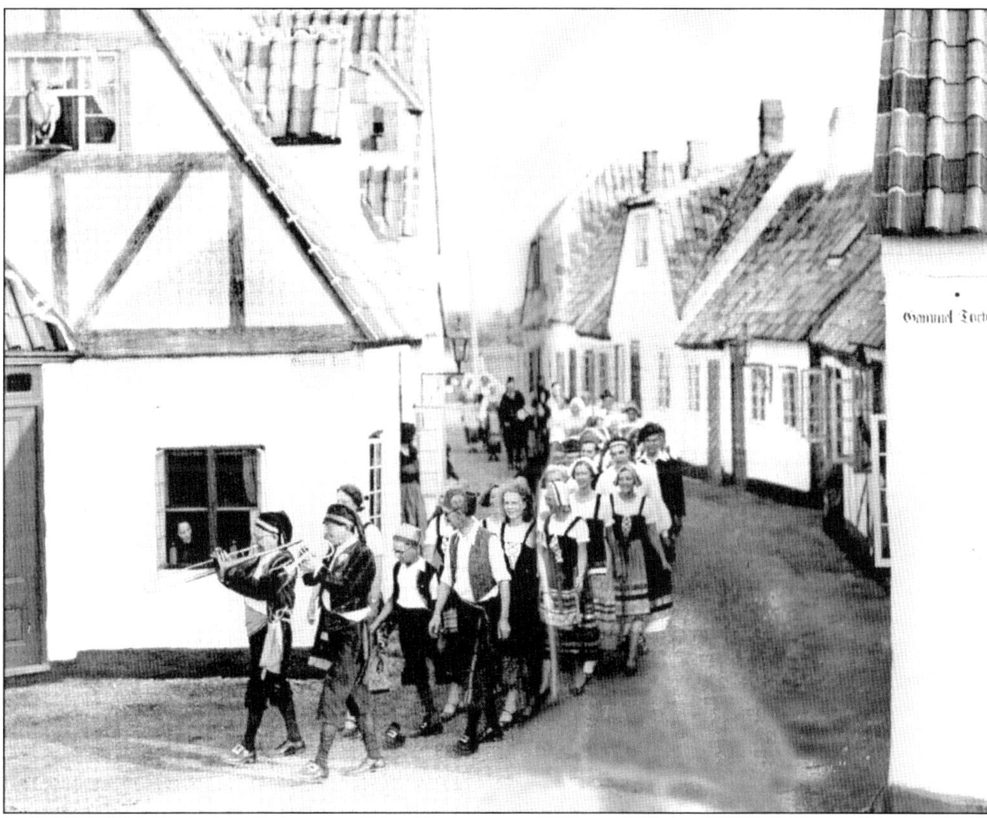

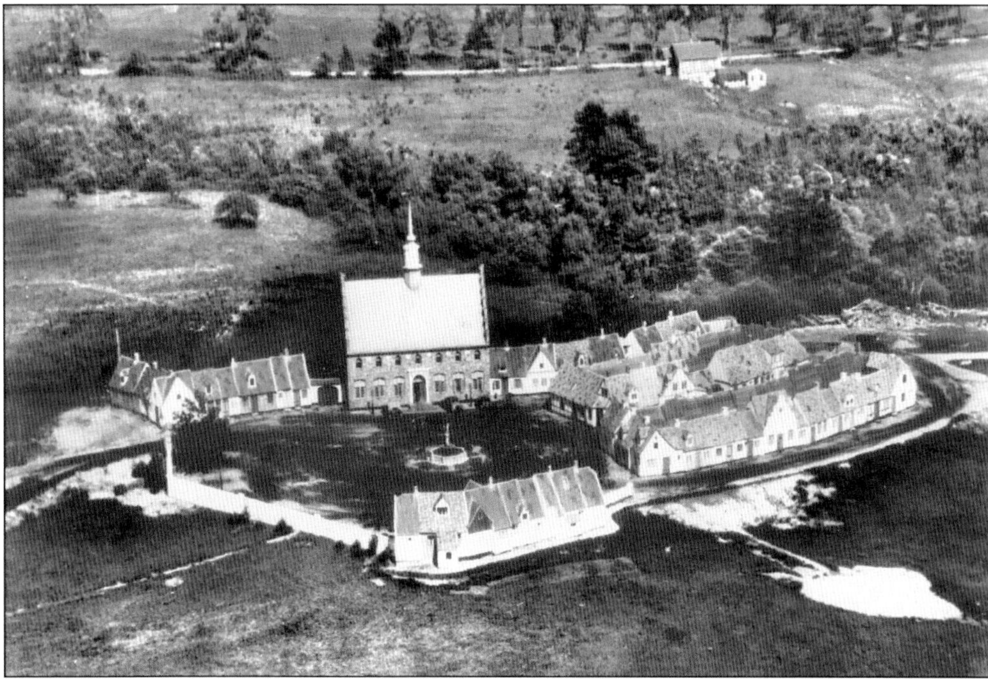

This aerial view of the Danish Village in 1930 gives a sense of its size and layout. It was formerly located next to the present day Big 20 Bowling Lanes in Scarborough, and was considered to be one of the first motels in the United States. Although only open summers, it was popular among visitors to Maine, including Eleanor Roosevelt, wife of the president, who stayed here on her way to Campobello Island, the Roosevelt's summer home in Canada.

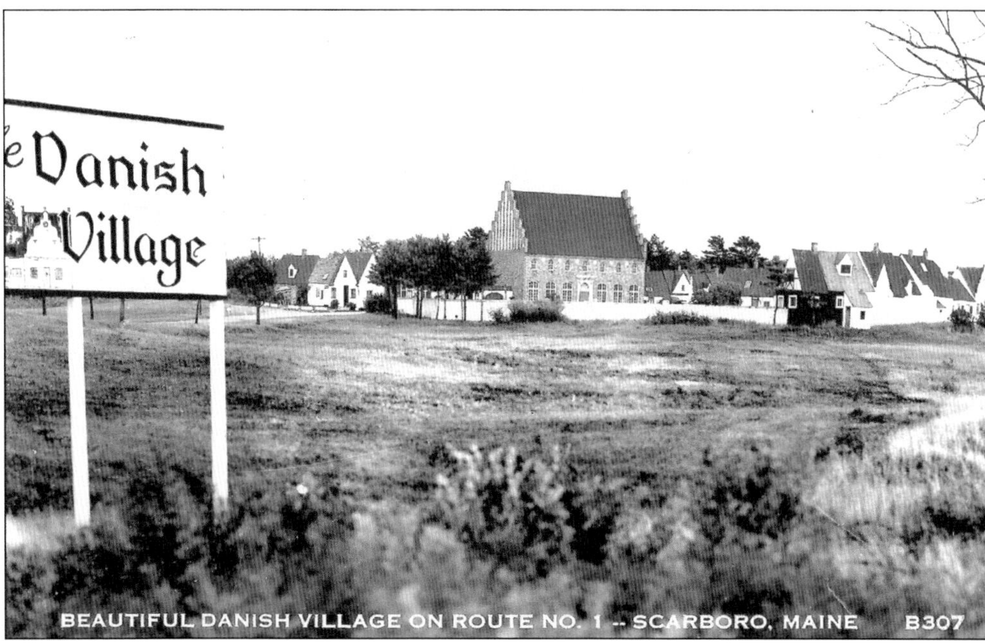

Here is the view of the Danish Village from Route 1 in Scarborough.

The Danish Village with its little narrow streets and crooked buildings was a charming replica of the medieval village of Ribe, Denmark's oldest town. Henry Rines first desired a colonial Williamsburg-type roadside attraction popular to motorists at the time, but was talked into this theme by his Eastland Hotel architect, Peter Holdersen, who was Danish. (Collections of the Maine Historical Society.)

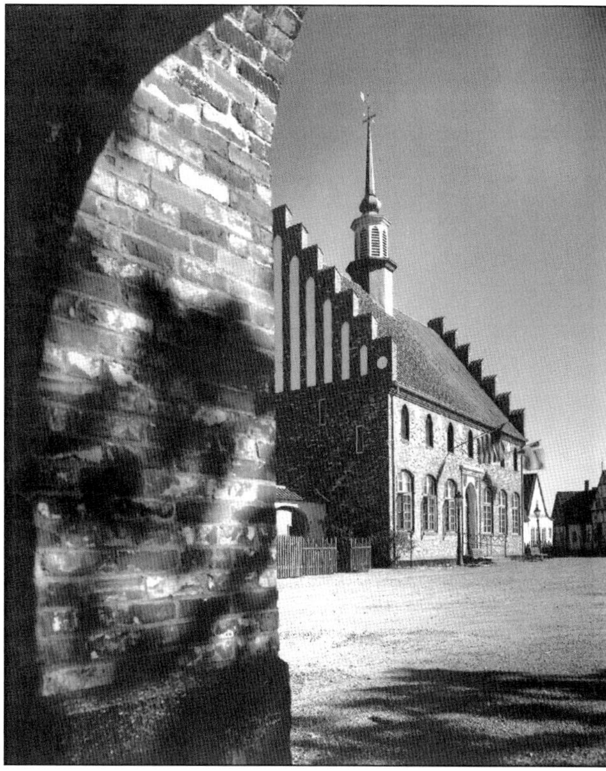

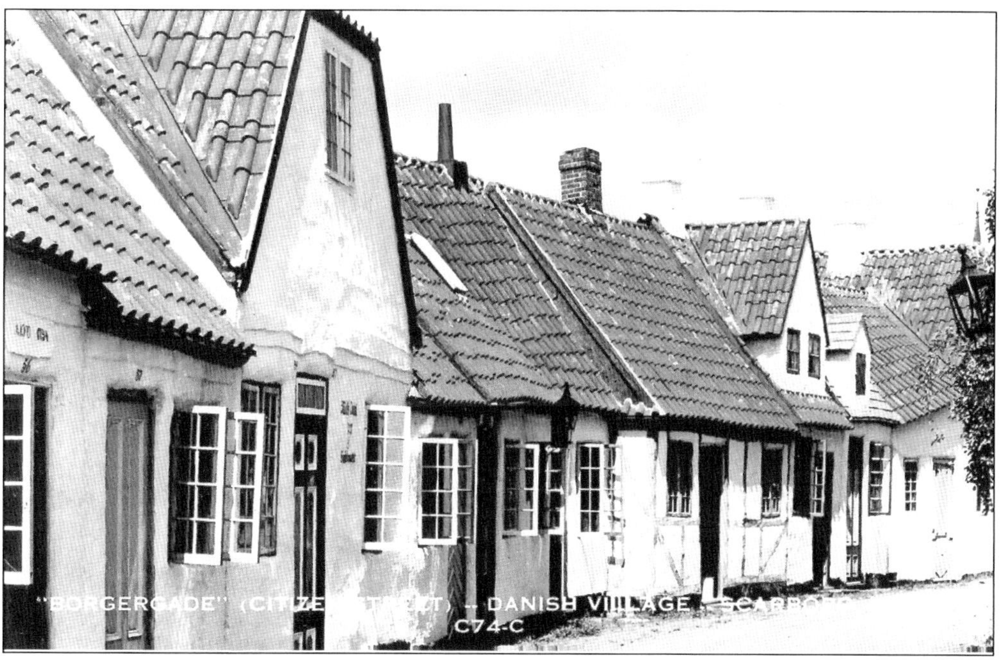

In 1931, the village was the site of an Old World Pageant in which the participants dressed in Danish wedding garb. The Danish Village was featured in a 1937 Paramount Picture movie short featuring Santa Claus. The whereabouts of this movie short is unknown.

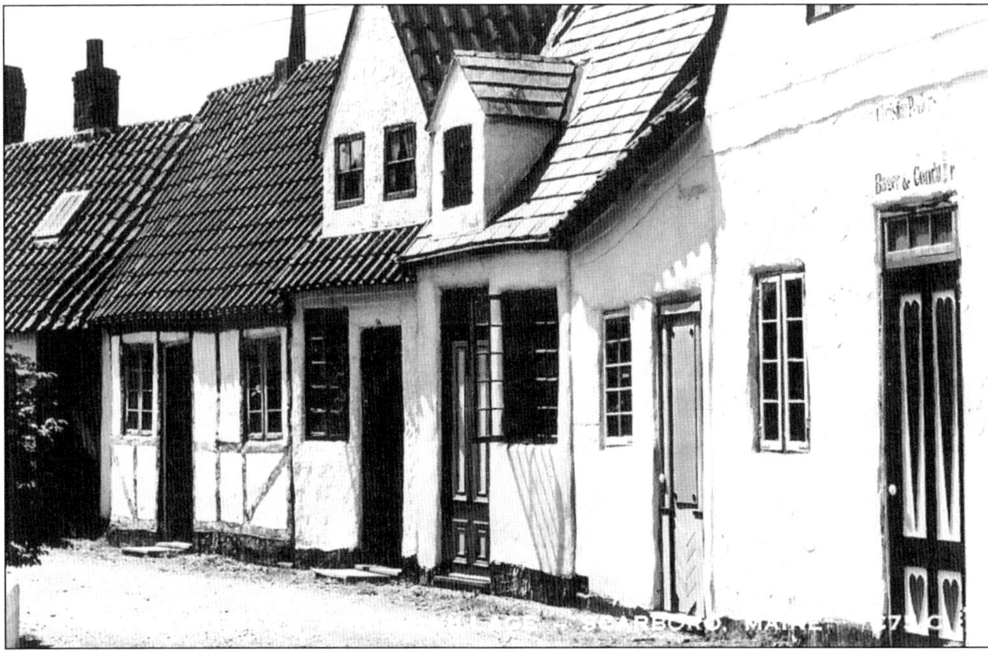

If one were to walk through the medieval town of Ribe, Denmark, today, they would experience this same view as seen here in Scarborough, Maine, in 1930.

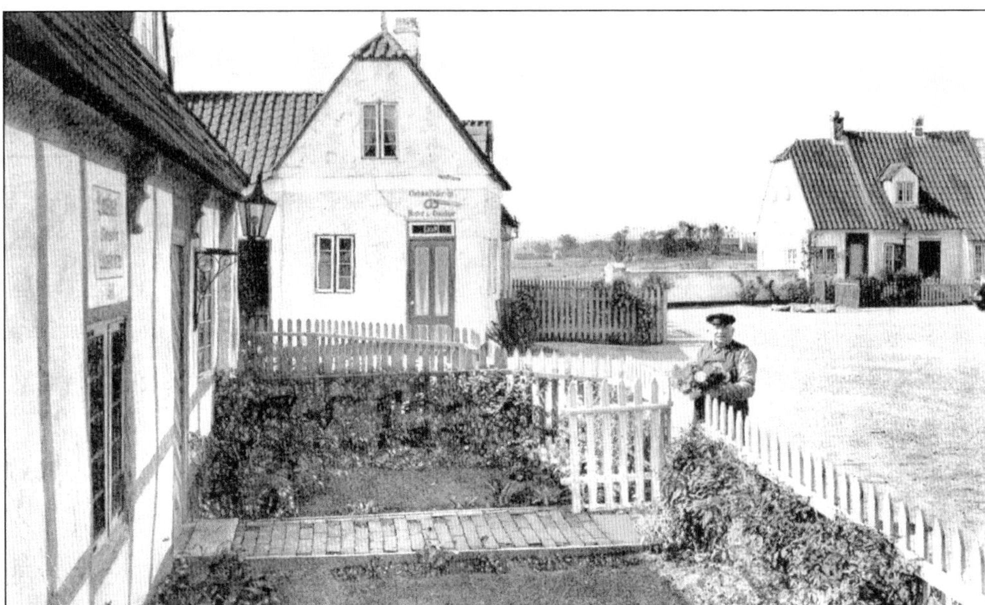

The Danish Village was an attempt by Henry Rines to capitalize on the burgeoning tourist automobile traffic coming to Maine in the 1920s. Concerned that the tourist might drive past Portland and consequently the Eastland Hotel, Henry felt he should go and meet this new class of travelers on the well-traveled Route 1, instead of waiting for them to come to him.

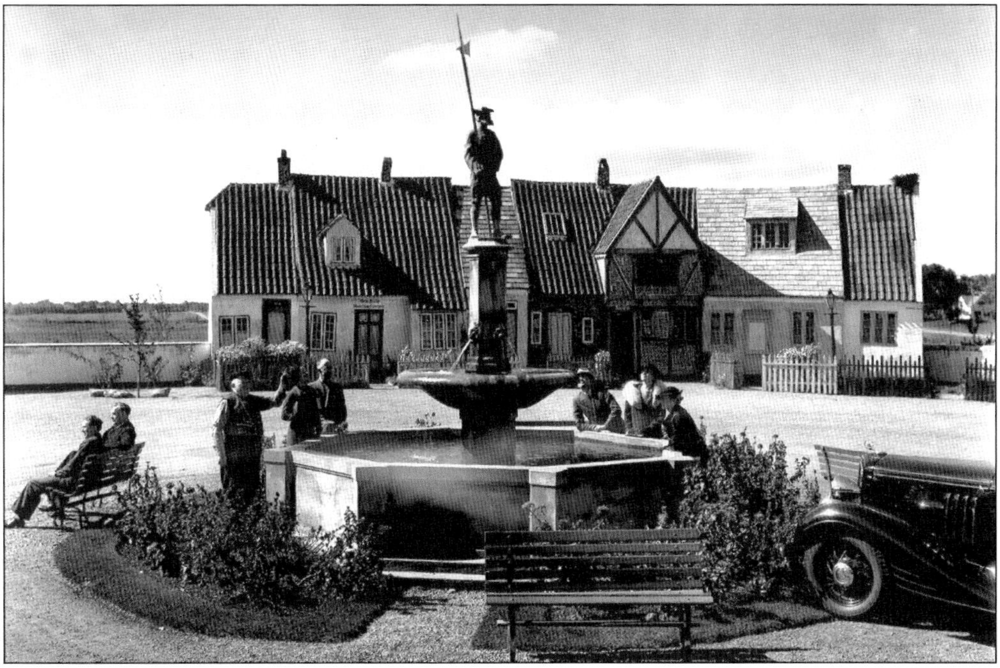

Standing atop the town square fountain was the statue of Niels Ebbensen, a Danish patriot of 1340. (Collections of the Maine Historical Society.)

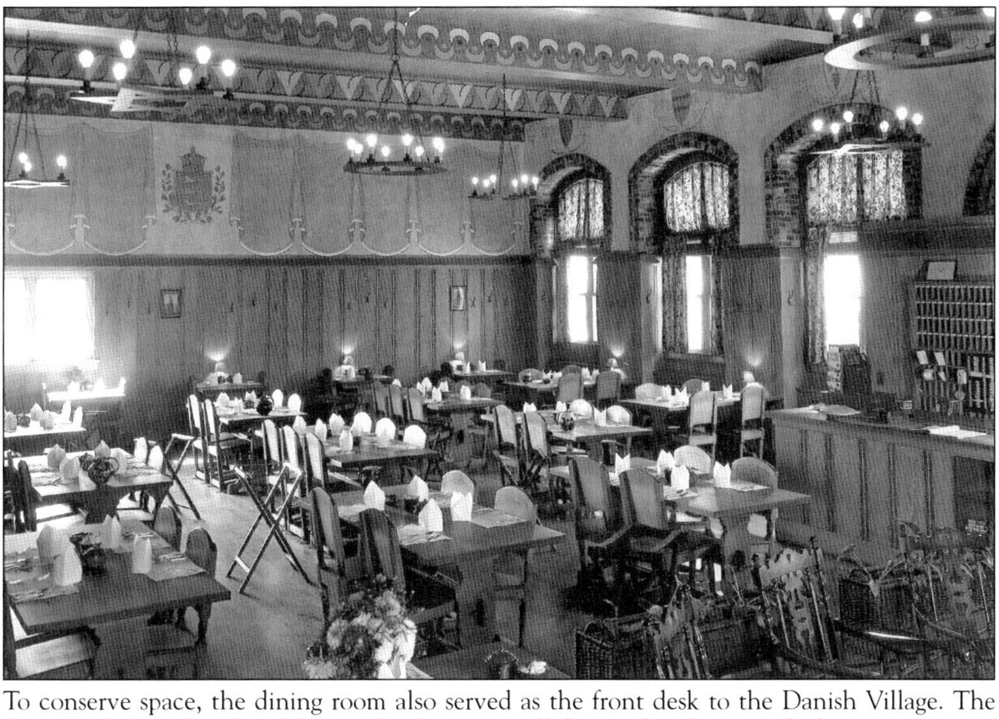

To conserve space, the dining room also served as the front desk to the Danish Village. The décor, including the chandeliers and rafters, were all designed with a Danish theme.

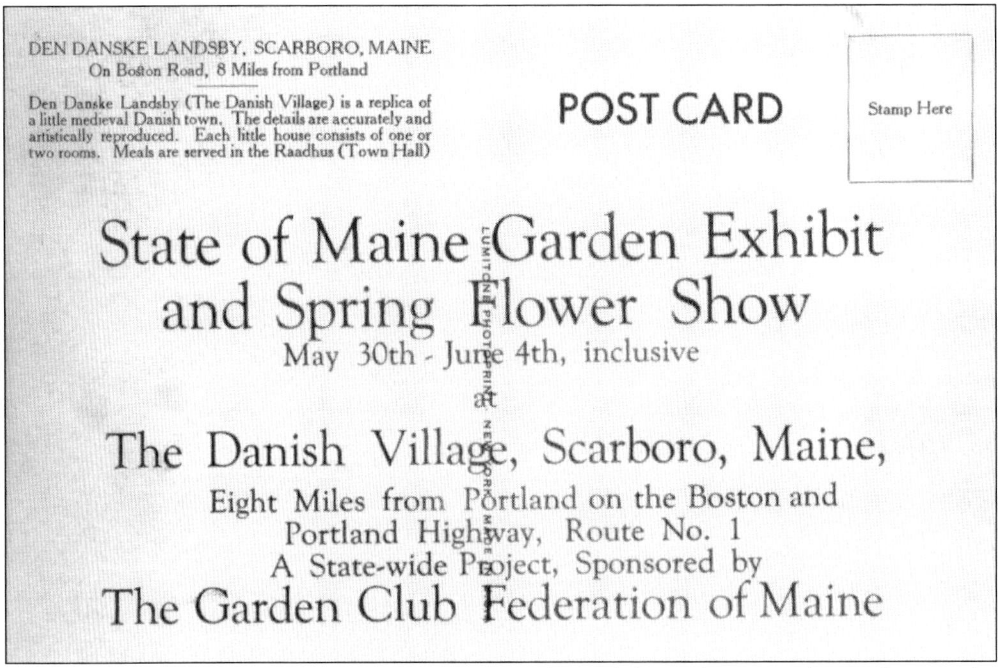

DEN DANSKE LANDSBY, SCARBORO, MAINE
On Boston Road, 8 Miles from Portland

Den Danske Landsby (The Danish Village) is a replica of a little medieval Danish town. The details are accurately and artistically reproduced. Each little house consists of one or two rooms. Meals are served in the Raadhus (Town Hall)

POST CARD

Stamp Here

State of Maine Garden Exhibit
and Spring Flower Show
May 30th - June 4th, inclusive
at
The Danish Village, Scarboro, Maine,
Eight Miles from Portland on the Boston and
Portland Highway, Route No. 1
A State-wide Project, Sponsored by
The Garden Club Federation of Maine

The Danish Village hosted the State of Maine Garden Exhibit and Spring Flower Show in the spring of 1933. (Courtesy of the Maine Historic Preservation Commission.)

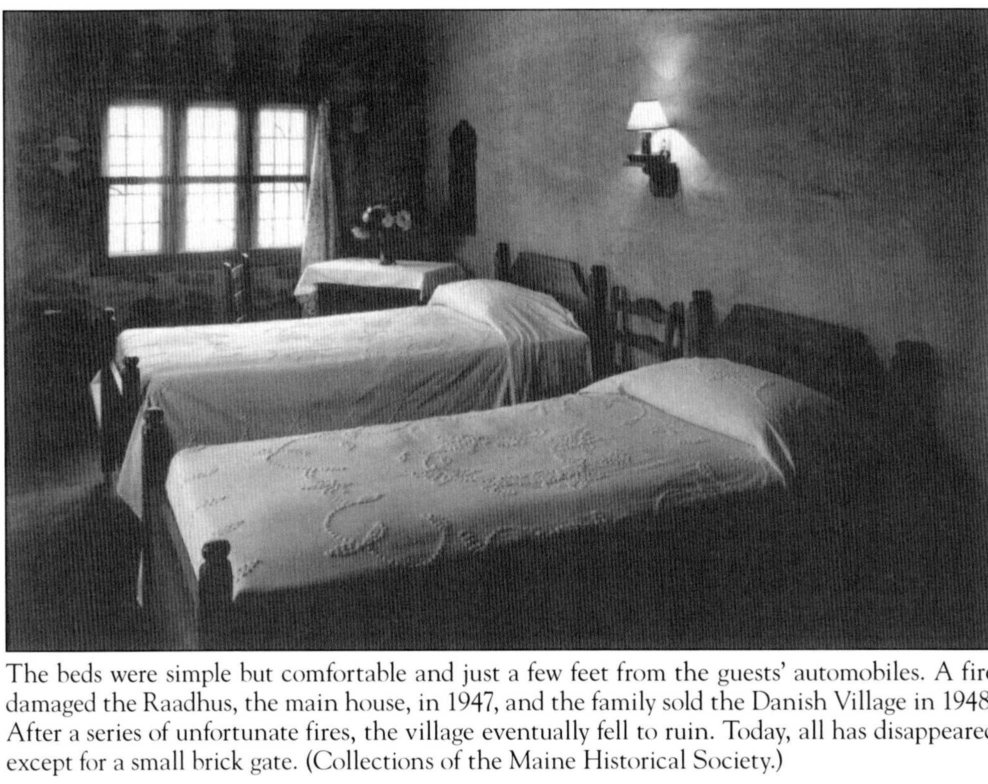

The beds were simple but comfortable and just a few feet from the guests' automobiles. A fire damaged the Raadhus, the main house, in 1947, and the family sold the Danish Village in 1948. After a series of unfortunate fires, the village eventually fell to ruin. Today, all has disappeared except for a small brick gate. (Collections of the Maine Historical Society.)

Henry Rines built and managed the Carpenter Hotel for the Carpenter family in Manchester, New Hampshire, in 1928. Rines felt a radio station similar to WCSH Radio in Portland would work nicely in conjunction with the hotel. In 1932, Rines applied for and received a broadcast license for WFEA Radio, Manchester. WFEA is New Hampshire's oldest radio station. Notice how the hotel has a strong resemblance to the Eastland Hotel in Portland. (Courtesy of Ed Brouder.)

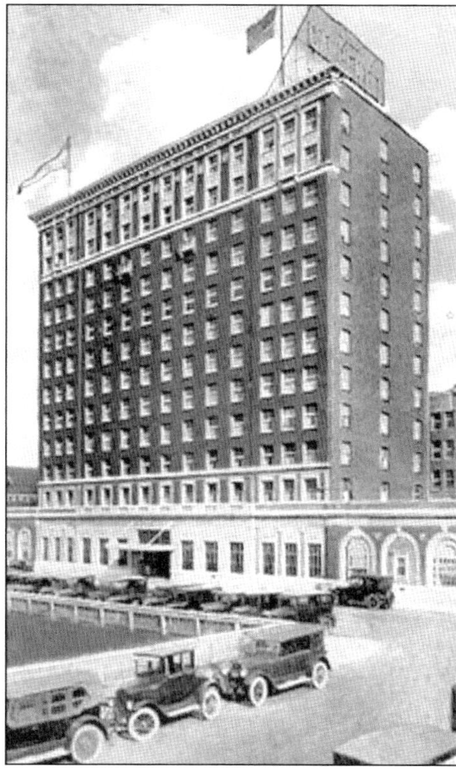

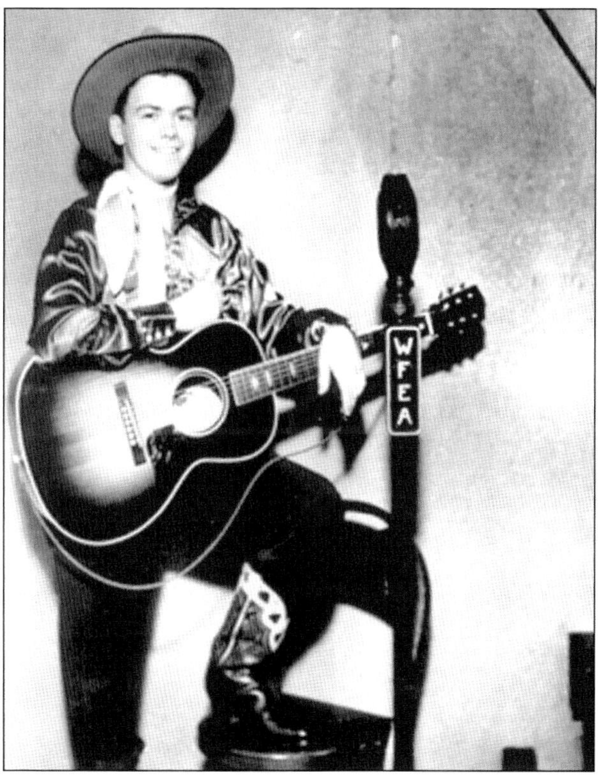

A young Ken Mackenzie, "the country cowboy," a forerunner of today's country musician, started his radio debut on WFEA in 1936. A Concord native, Mackenzie started his own country western group and eventually married Simone Labrie, a Manchester resident in the group. They moved to Portland where they would star on WGAN Radio and eventually WGAN Television, Rines company's competitors. (Courtesy of Ed Brouder.)

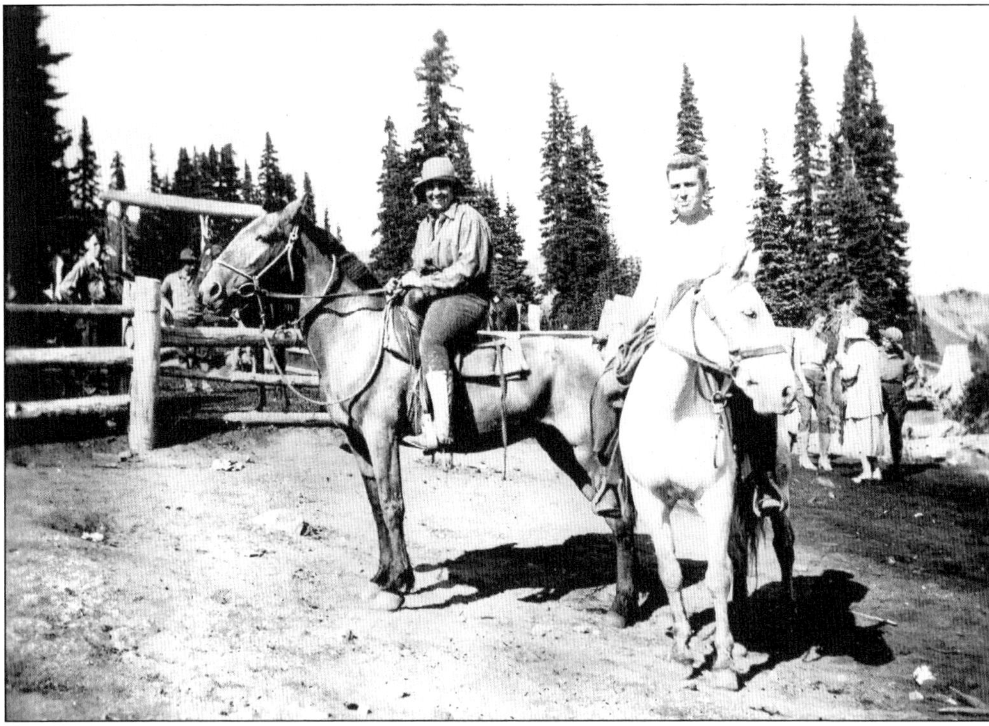

Clinton Rines, Henry's brother, and his wife Marion were skilled horseback riders, a talent they learned while working with their farm animals at Walnut Crest. In the 1930s, Clinton built the Walnut Crest camps just off Route 25 in Westbrook, seen below. (Courtesy of Walnut Crest Farm.)

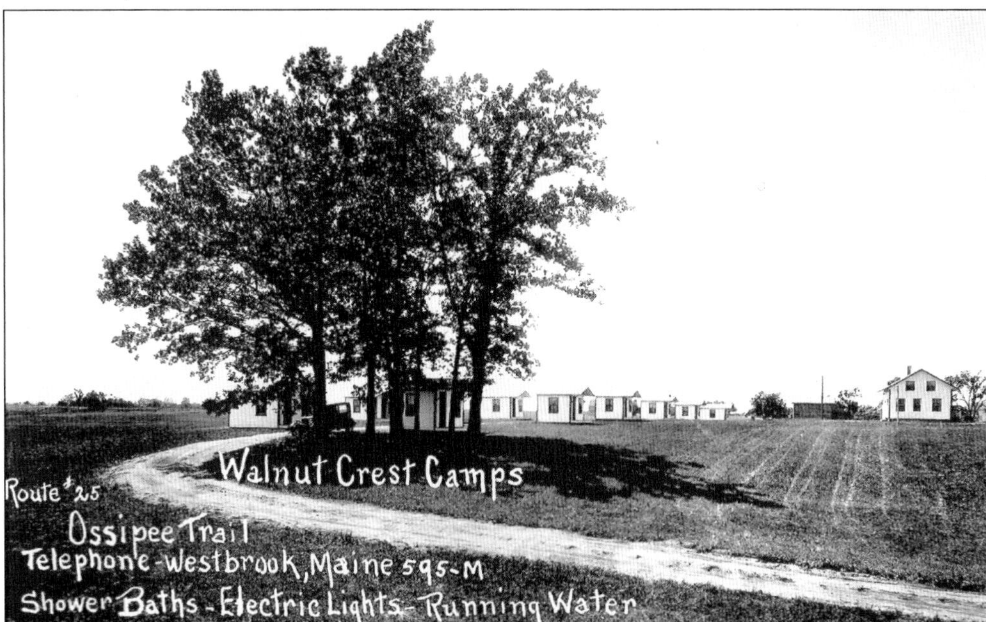

A postcard of the Walnut Crest Camps is shown here located just off Route 25 across the road from the Walnut Crest Farm. (Courtesy of Walnut Crest Farm.)

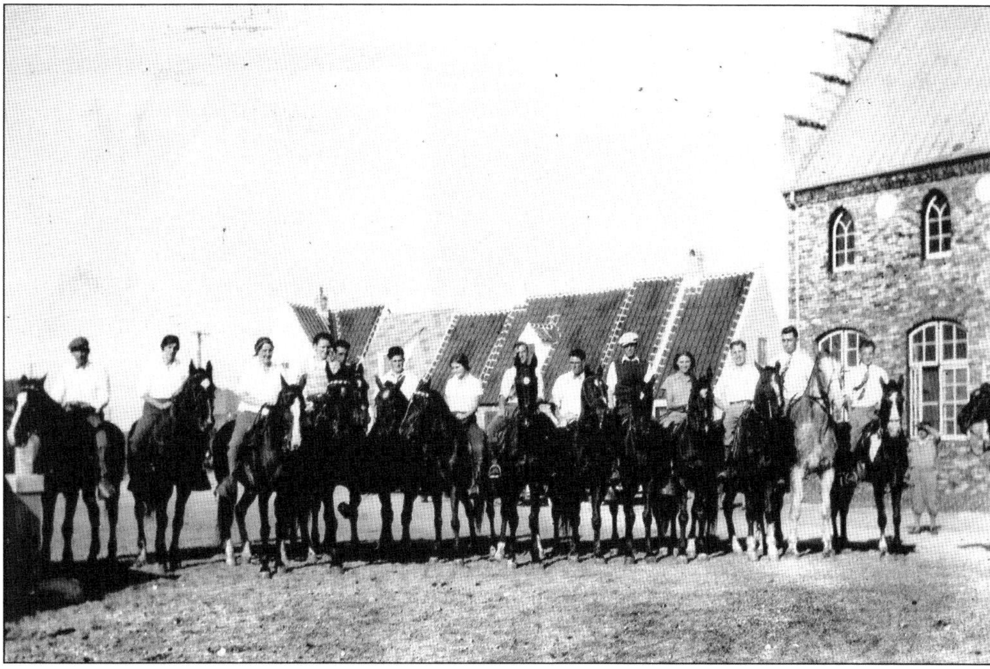

From the camps it was a mere 10 miles to the Danish Village in Scarborough, recently opened by brother Henry in 1930. Clinton Rines, second from the right, is seen here in front of the Raadhus, the main building at the Danish Village. (Courtesy of the Walnut Crest Farm.)

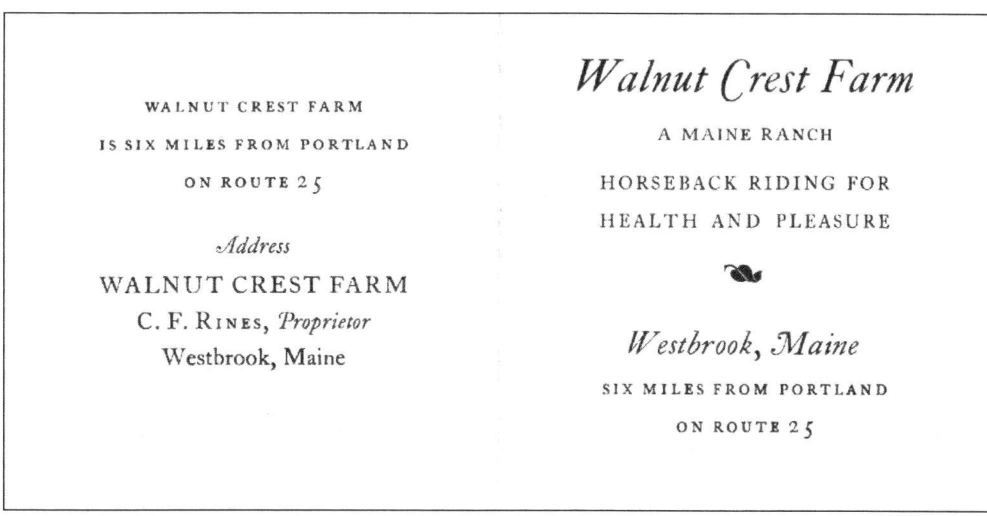

This 1930s flyer promotes the Walnut Crest Riding Camps. (Courtesy of the Walnut Crest Farm.)

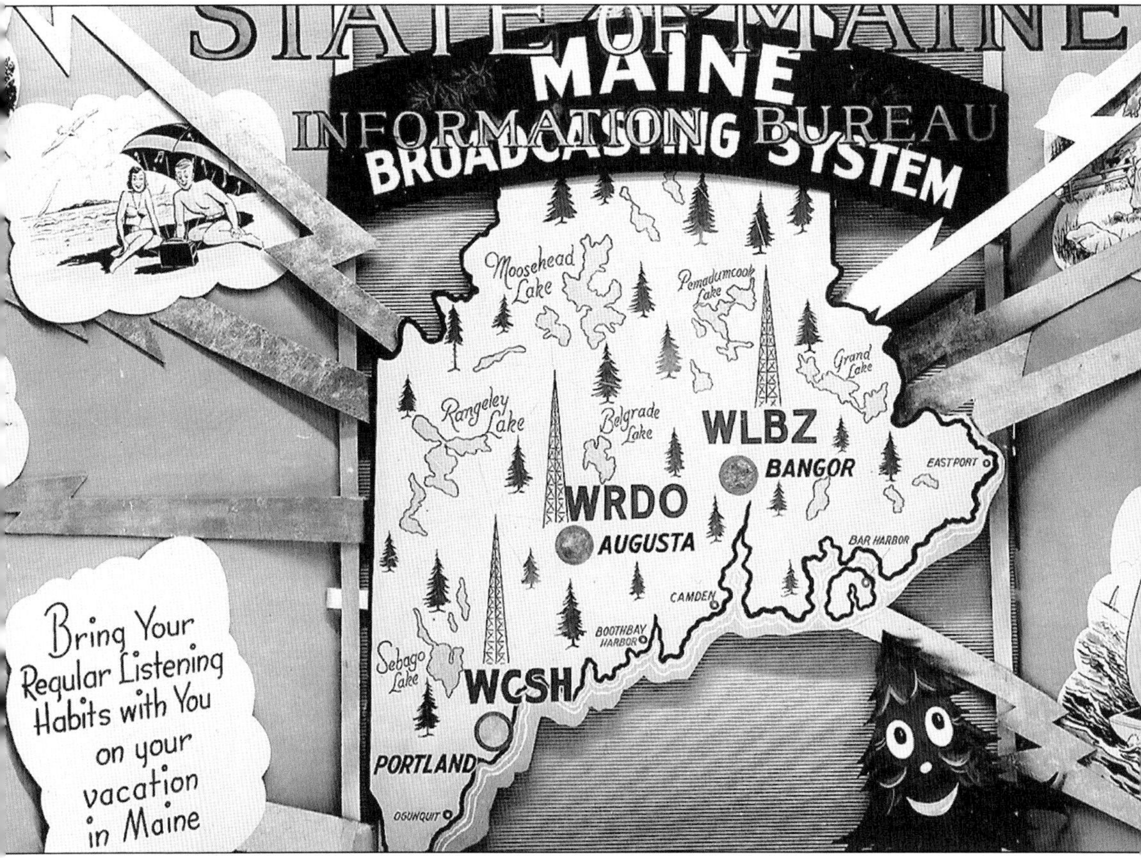

By the beginning of the Great Depression in the early 1930s, Henry Rines began to realize that the radio business was more lucrative than the hotel business with its high capital and labor costs. Networking radio stations together to form pools of programming like the NBC Radio Network resulted in a considerable drop in the cost of radio programming for local stations like WCSH. Consequently, Henry Rines started acquiring radios stations to become NBC affiliates with the intention of forming his own regional radio network throughout northern New England. Eventually Rines would own WLBZ-Bangor; WRDO-Augusta; WCSH-Portland and WFEA-Manchester, New Hampshire. Unfortunately, he barely saw his dream materialize. Shortly after acquiring WLBZ in 1938, Henry Rines died. He was 53.

The revolutionary changes brought about by the automobile and the Great Depression in the 1930s were turning the hotel industry upside down. One of Henry's concerns was what to do with the now aging Congress Square Hotel with its seven stories and 350 rooms. He came up with a novel idea. He would sell the rooms outright to families, many of whom were elderly and could no longer look after their homes or farms. Henry was selling condominiums.

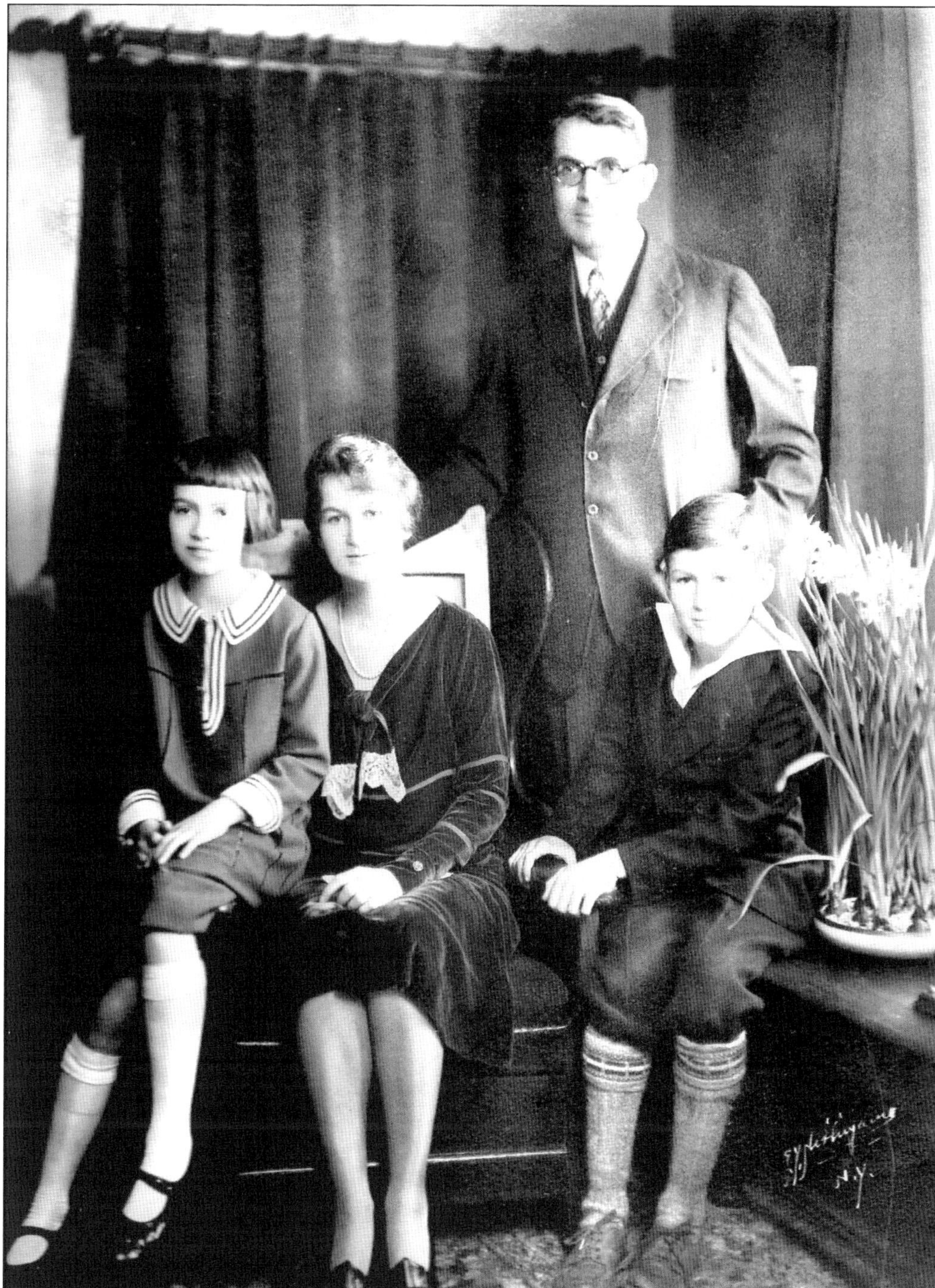

This remarkable photograph depicts a simple family gathering. Shown here, from left to right, Mary Rines (Thompson), Adeline Bond Rines, Henry Pritchard Rines, and William Henry Rines. During their lifetimes, they would each take the role as head of the Maine Broadcasting System.

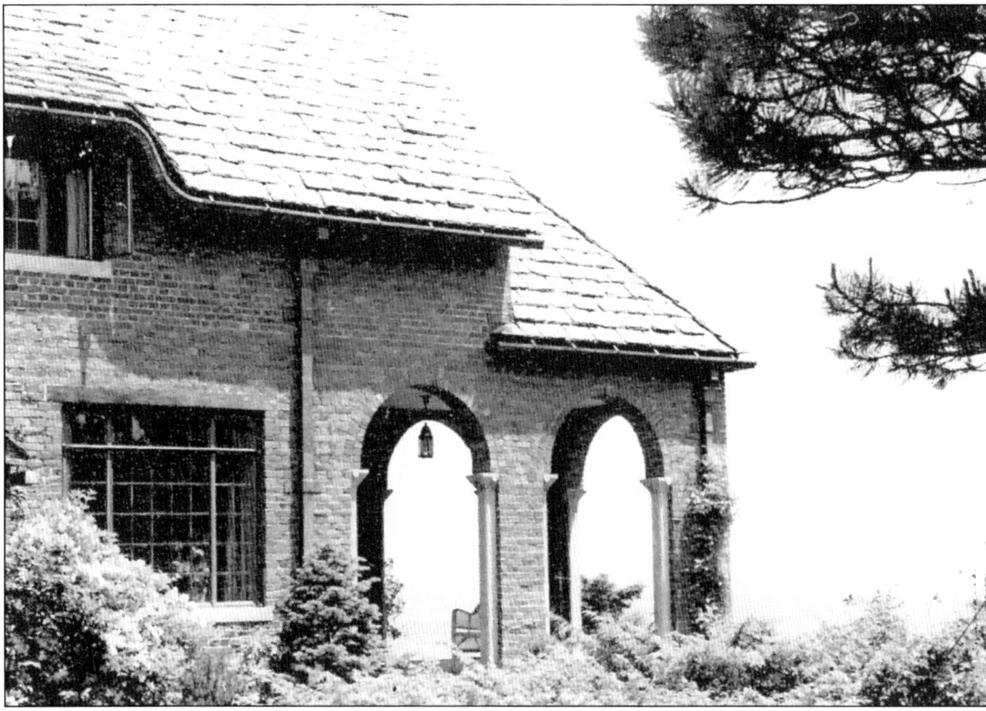

While Henry Rines was building the Eastland Hotel, he had his masons, plumbers, and other craftsmen work on his new home at Cragmoor in Cape Elizabeth. Each May, Rines left the Portland area because of his allergy to ragweed. Never one to use time unproductively, he traveled extensively to acquire new ideas and revitalize. The idea for this home and many of the new concepts used in the Eastland came to him during his travels to Europe.

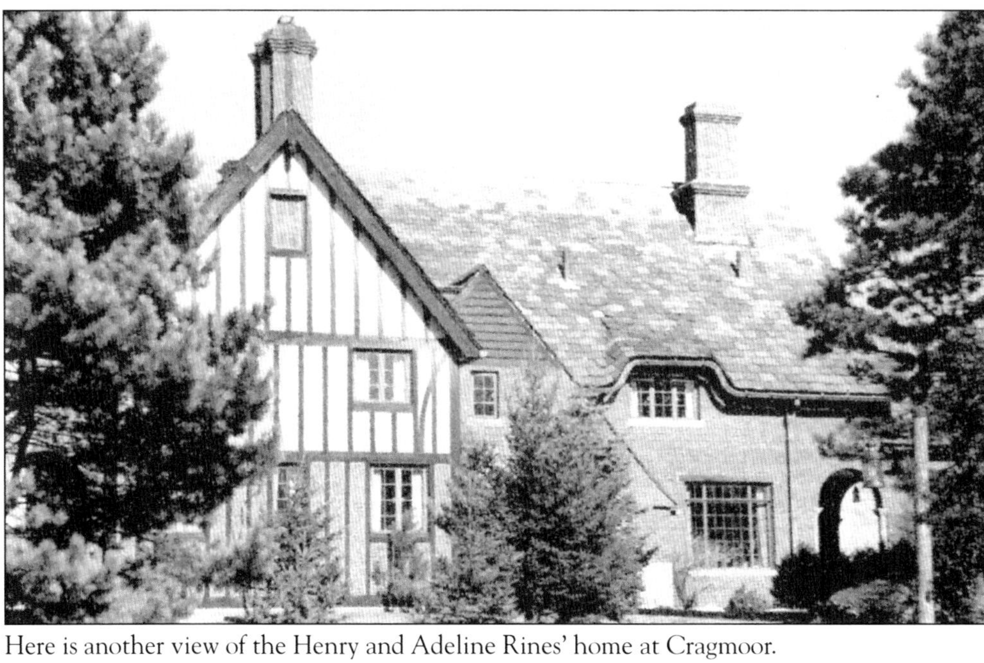

Here is another view of the Henry and Adeline Rines' home at Cragmoor.

Four

William Henry Rines and Images in the Ether

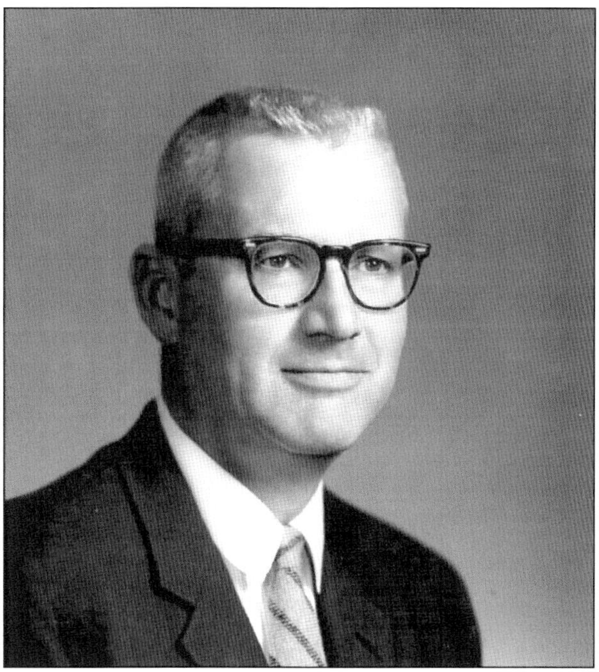

William Henry Rines began work as the station manager in 1941 after his father died. He eventually became president of the Maine Broadcasting System (WCSH-Portland; WLBZ-Bangor; and WRDO-Augusta). These stations were joined by WCSH-TV and WLBZ-TV in the 1950s. People were so excited when television first came to Maine, they would sit and watch the test pattern for half an hour before any programming came on the air.

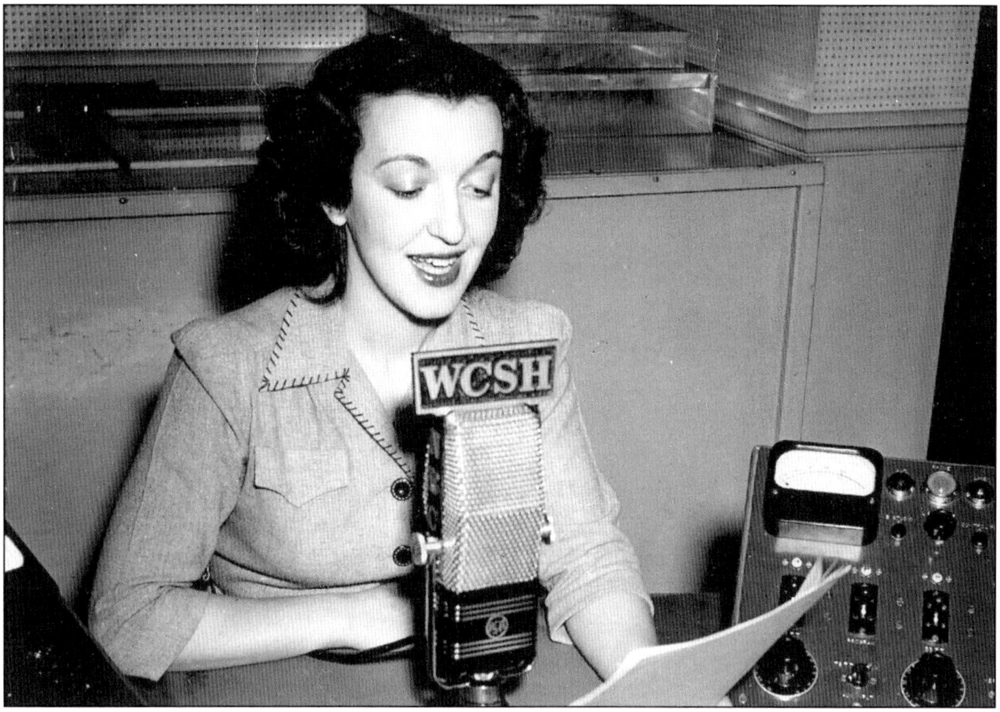

World War II brought many celebrities to Maine to build morale and to promote the war effort. Famous Hollywood star Dorothy Lamour traveled the country to boost America's confidence. Here she reads the headlines on WCSH Radio at the studios in Portland. World-renowned journalist and NBC radio commentator Lowell Thomas (below) also visited the WCSH Radio studios during the war.

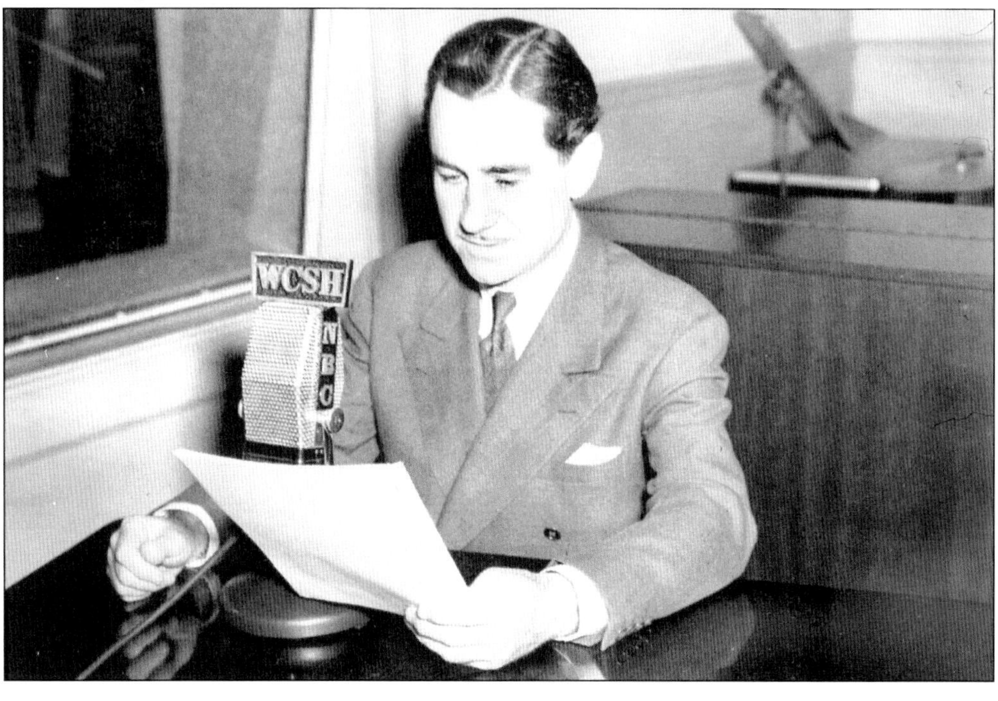

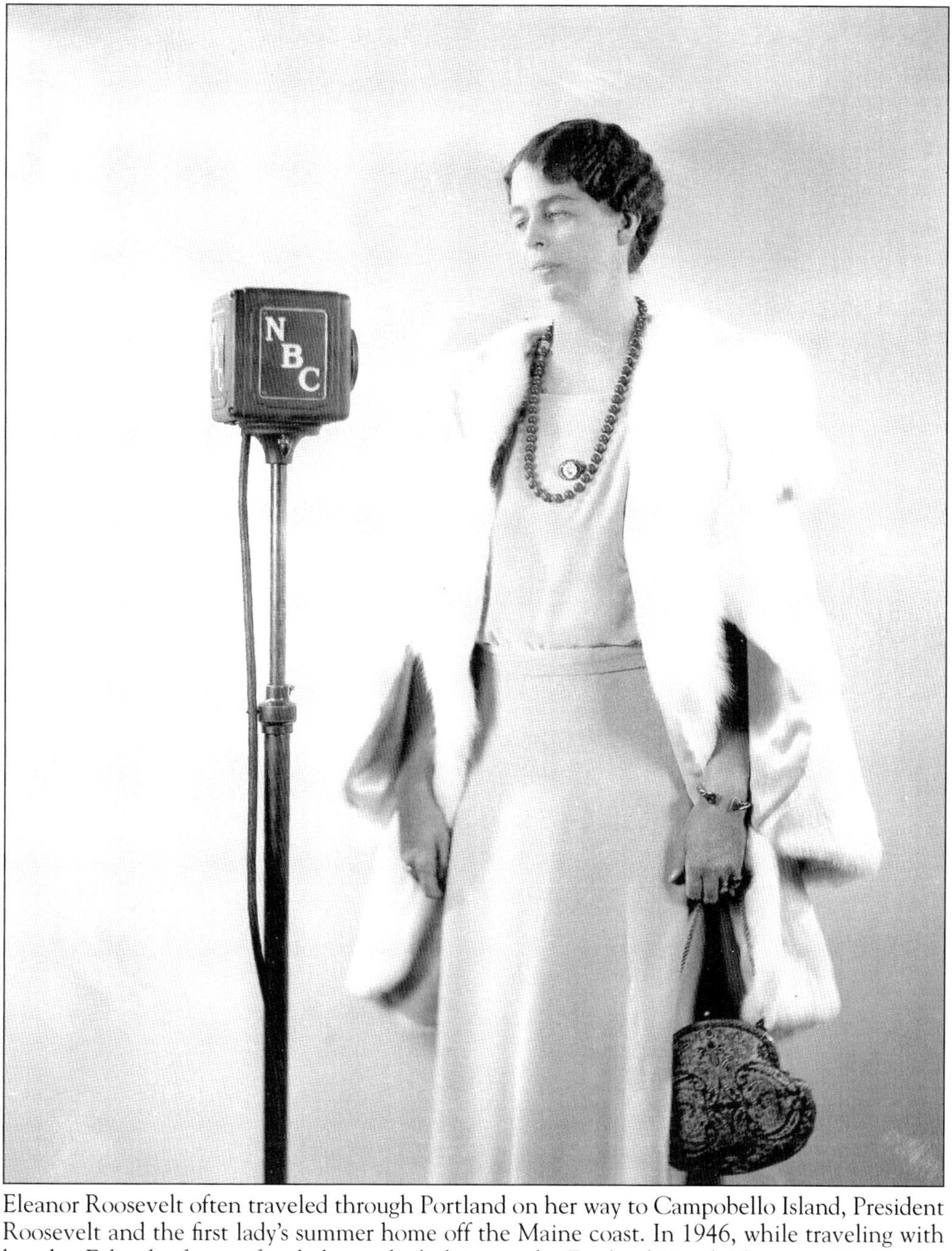

Eleanor Roosevelt often traveled through Portland on her way to Campobello Island, President Roosevelt and the first lady's summer home off the Maine coast. In 1946, while traveling with her dog Fala, the former first lady sought lodging at the Eastland Hotel. She was told that she could stay but that her dog would have to stay in a nearby kennel. She refused to leave her dog and a national controversy ensued. Much was made in the national press of the Eastland management's decision not to allow the president's dog to stay in the hotel. Some papers would claim it was pure politics. Others claimed that the same rules applied to everyone. Roosevelt, Fala, and their chauffeur continued on to the Royal River Cabins in Yarmouth and passed the night there before they resumed their trip to Campobello. The headline in the local paper read; "Dogdom's Greatest Snubbed Here."

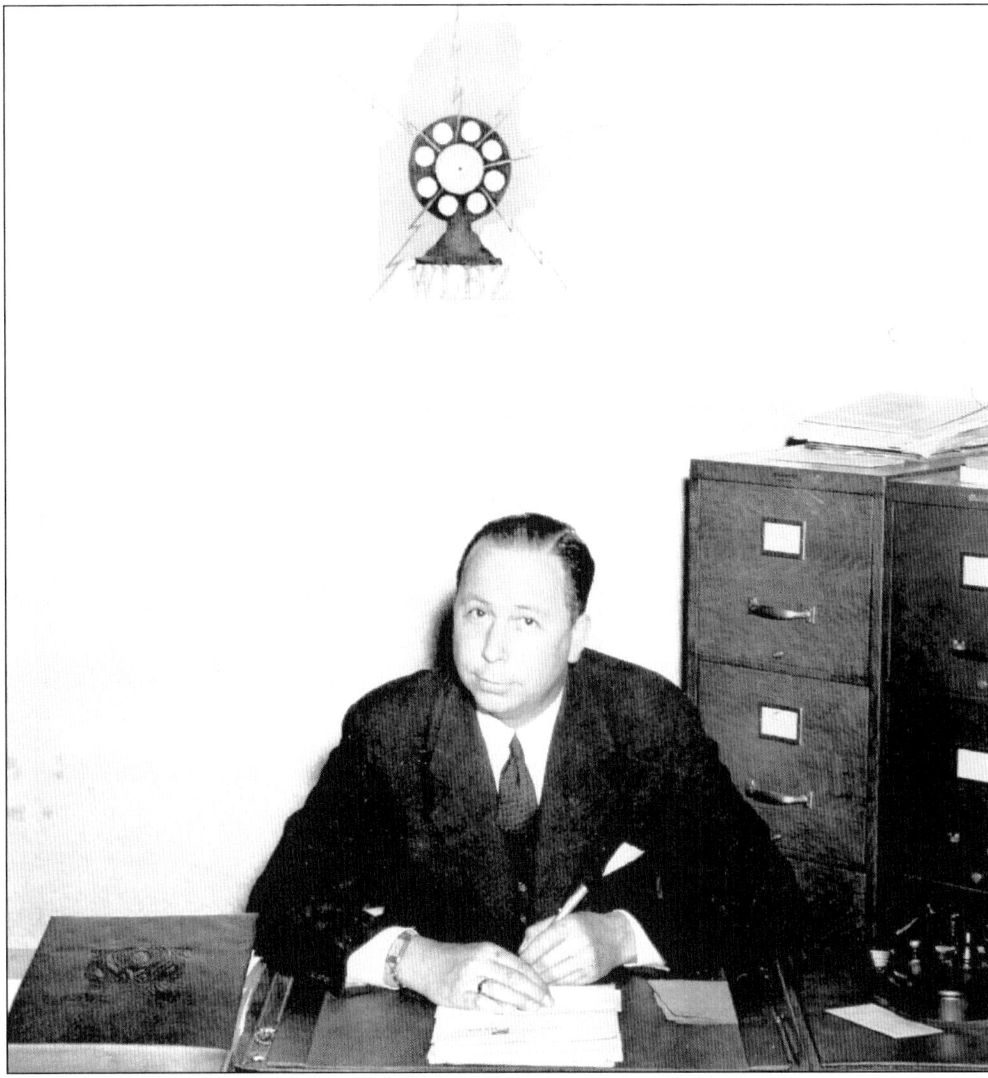

Thompson Guernsey put Bangor's WLBZ Radio on the air in the early 1920s. He eventually sold his interest to the Rines family in 1938. Although he stayed on as general manager, he used his sale proceeds to build Boston's first television station in the early 1940s.

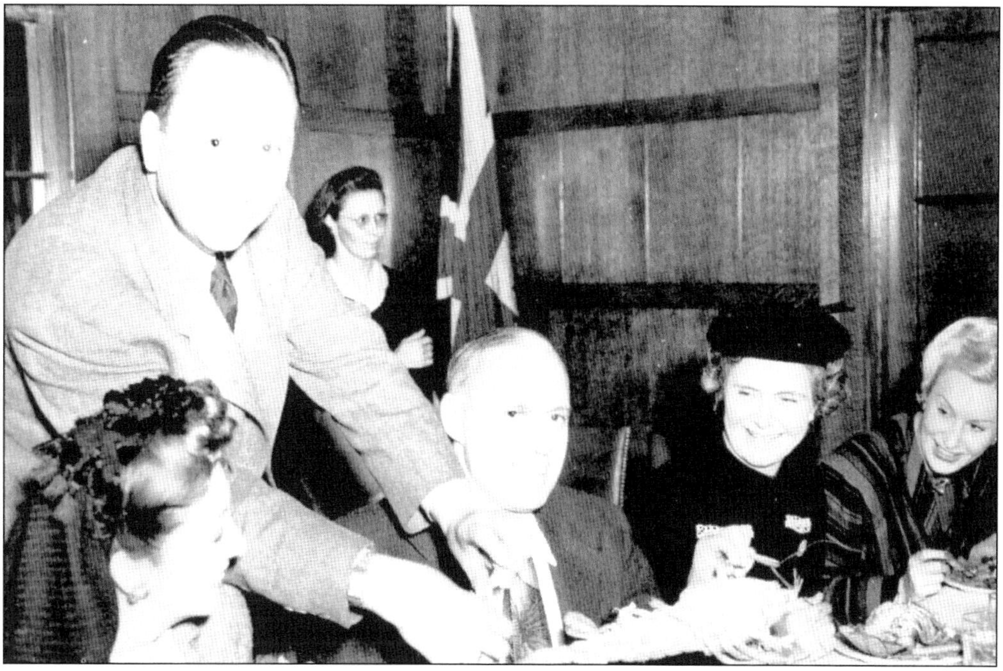

Mary Livingston, Thompson Guernsey (standing), Jack Benny, and friends enjoy a lobster dinner at the Bangor House in 1943. This was prior to the Bangor broadcast of *The Jack Benny Show*, which performed live for the benefit of the airmen of the U.S. Air Force stationed at Dow Field.

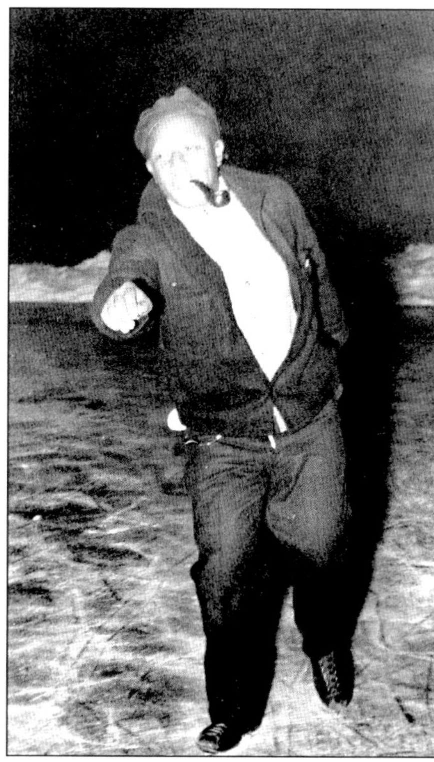

Rochester Van Jones, actor Eddie Anderson, was a popular comedian on the Jack Benny radio show. He is seen here skating on Sebec Lake north of Skowhegan. This was after WLBZ Radio general manager Thompson Guernsey hosted the entire radio program's cast while visiting Bangor in early 1943.

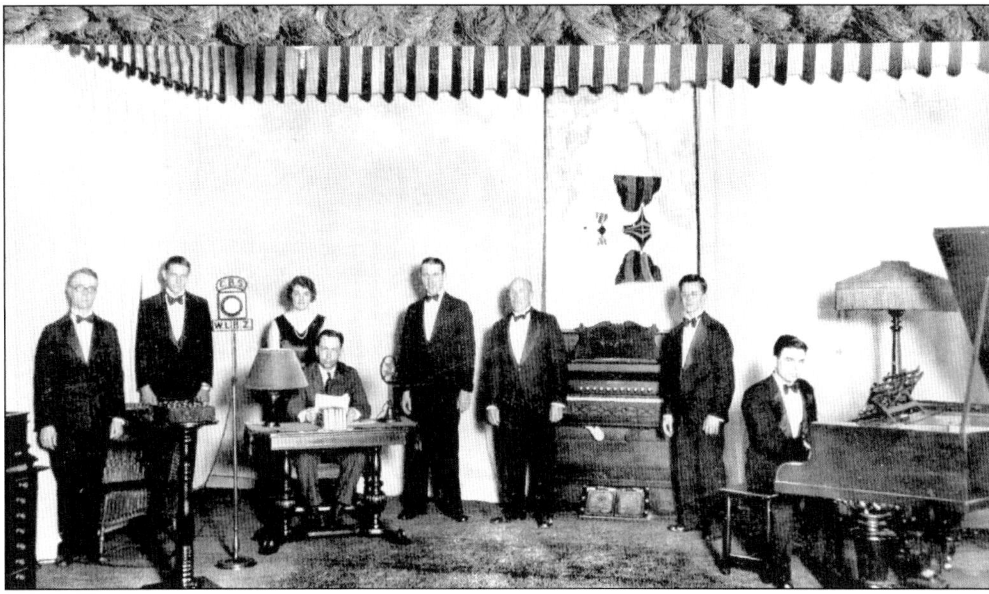

The staff of WLBZ Radio in Bangor is seen here in 1930. Henry Rines started negotiations with WLBZ owner Thompson Guernsey to purchase WLBZ Radio shortly after Guernsey put the station on the air in 1926. In 1940, while still working for the Rines family, Guernsey was given permission by the government to operate an experimental television station in Boston. Future vice president of the Maine Broadcasting System Jack Atwood, who started his career at WLBZ, is seen standing second from the left.

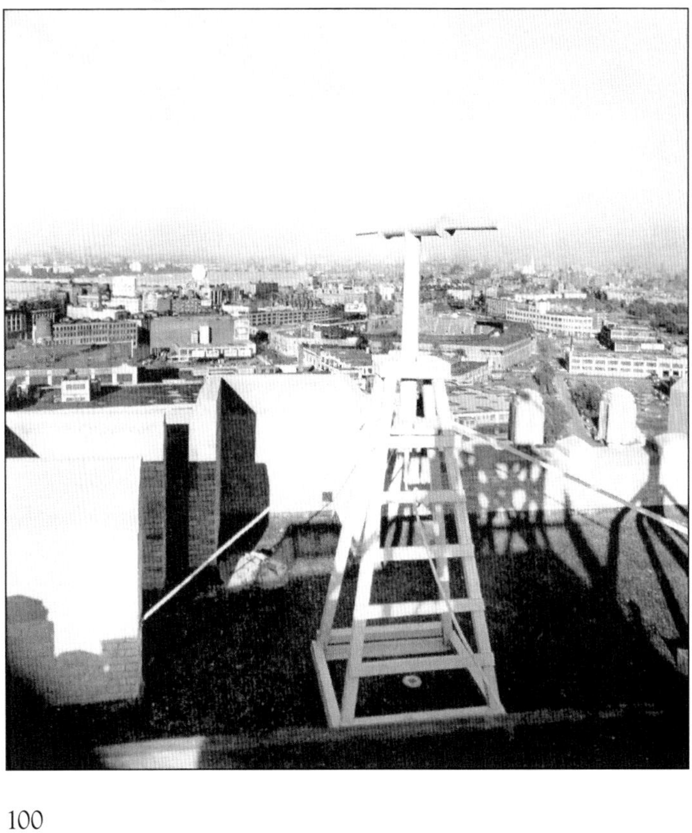

Here is Guernsey's antenna strapped to the top of the Sears Building. Fenway Park can be seen in the background.

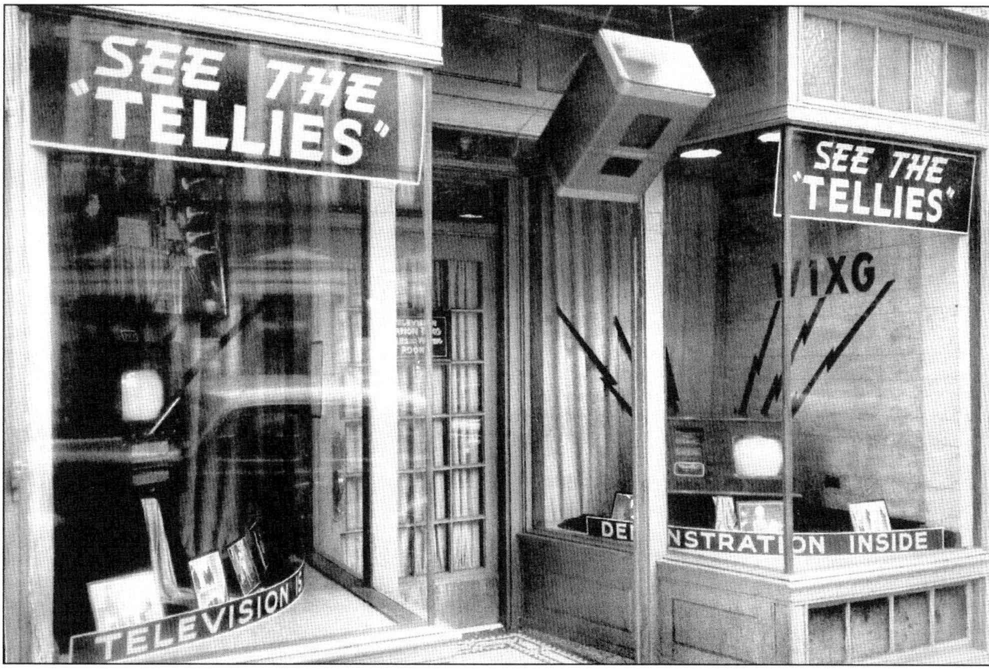

No one in America had television sets in the 1940s, so Thompson Guernsey rented this space on Tremont Street in Boston and invited the public to see what television looked like. The license assigned him the call letters WIXG, which eventually became WBZ-TV, Channel 4, Boston, but not before Guernsey ran out of funds.

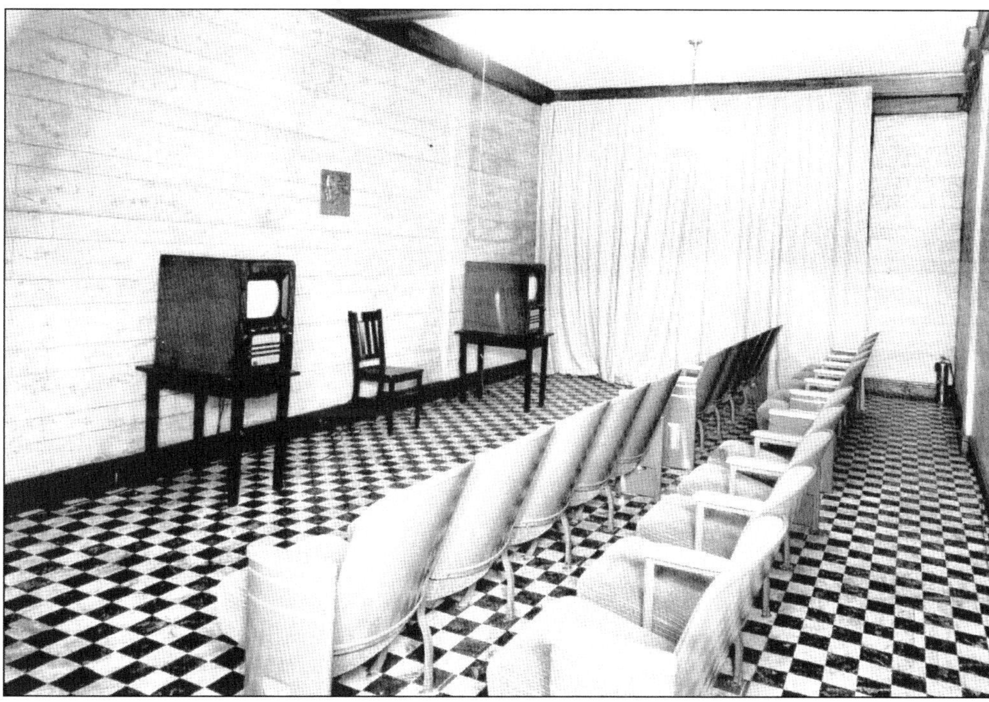

Guernsey allowed the public to come in off the street, free of charge, and watch television on a somewhat smaller screen than we are used to seeing today.

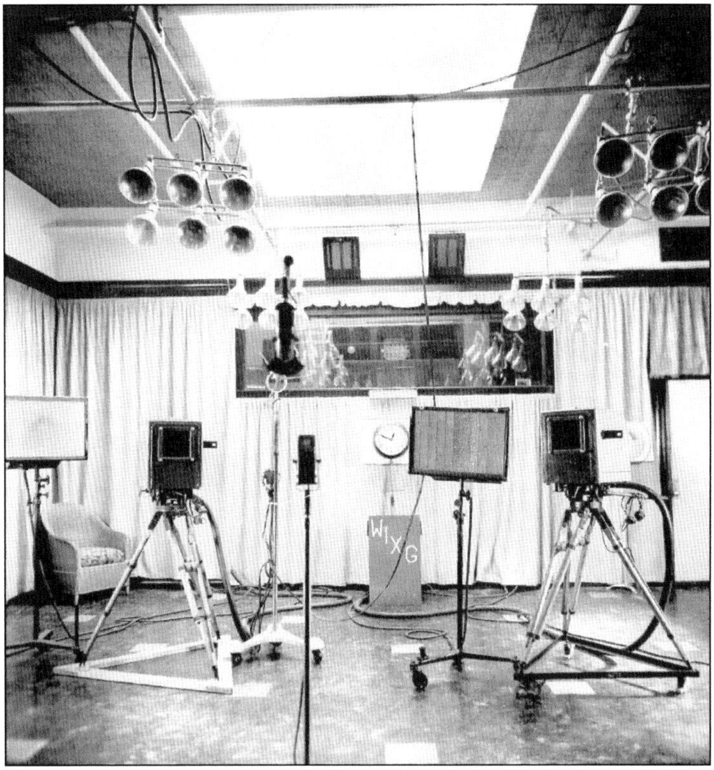

Thompson Guernsey broadcast live from his studios at 70 Brookline Street in Boston. Television was first shown to the public at the 1939 World's Fair in New York. The cameras seen here were purchased from RCA after their pavilion closed at the end of the fair. They were the world's first production model television cameras.

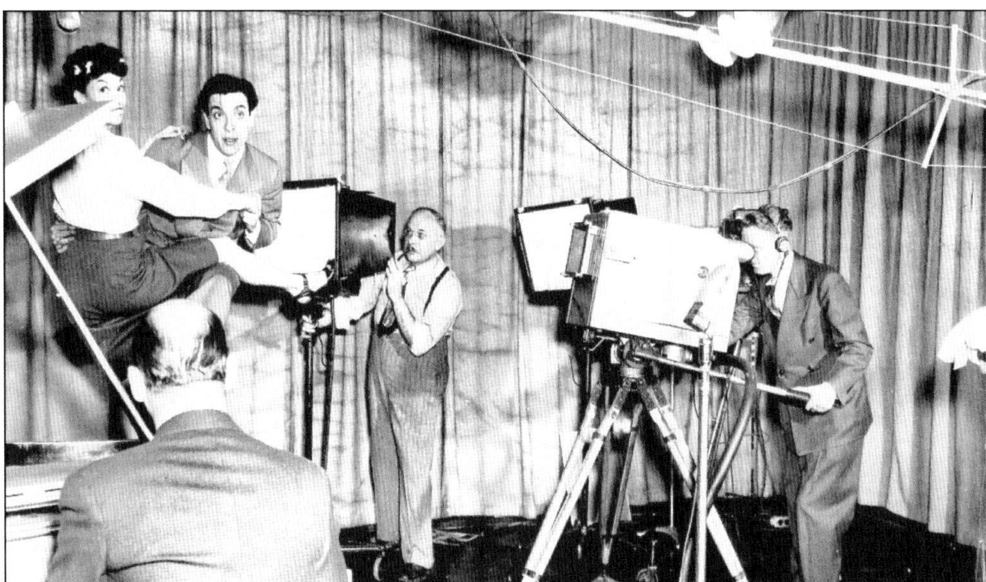

Pictured here is a forerunner of American Band Stand and MTV. Thompson Guernsey abandoned the idea of broadcasting television programming from Boston after he ran out of funds in 1944. He brought some of his equipment back to Bangor where he still managed WLBZ Radio for the Rines family. The equipment was abandoned there until 1997, when the Rines family donated the television camera, seen here, to their employees at WLBZ2 in Bangor. It is the only World's Fair camera known to exist.

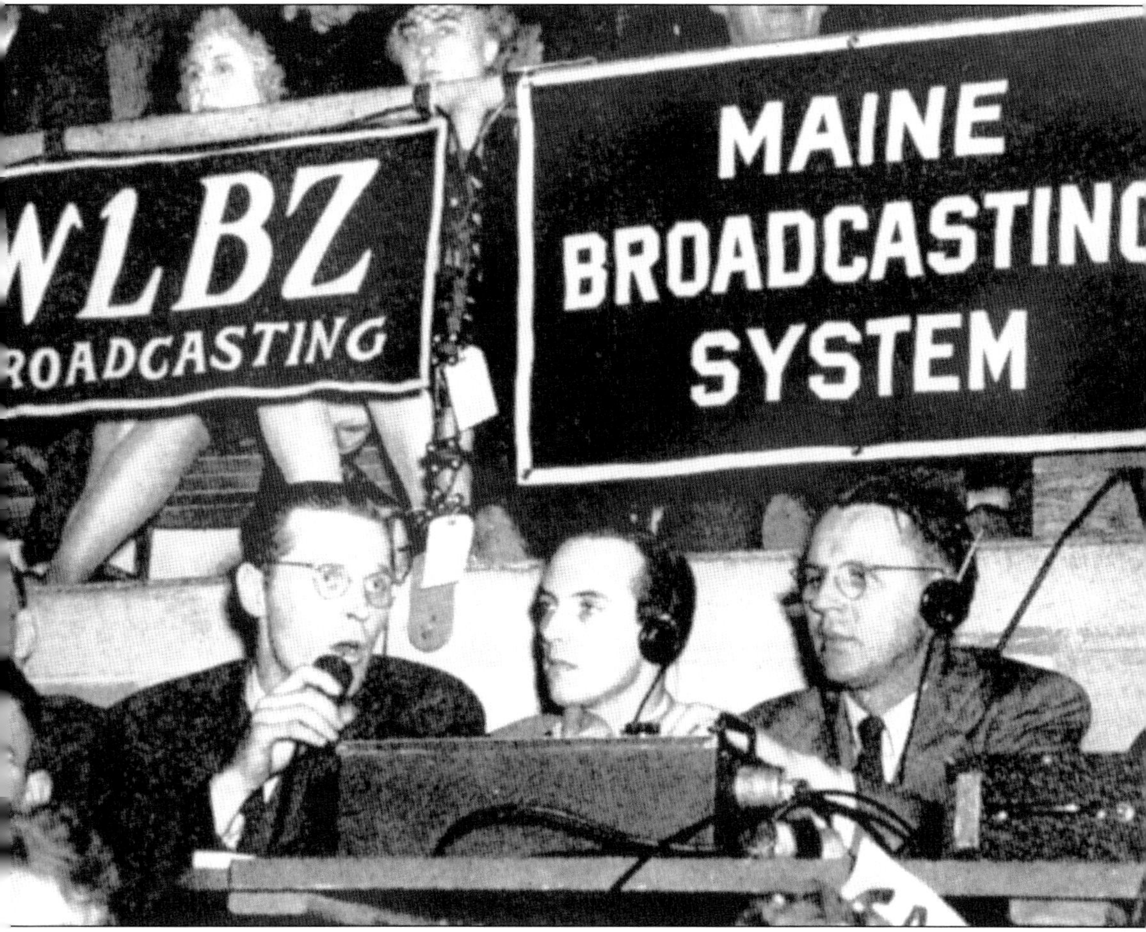

John McKernan Sr. gives the play-by-play on WLBZ Radio during the action between South Portland and Waterville High Schools for the state basketball crown at the University of Maine gymnasium in 1949. Joining him are announcer Eddie Owen and engineer John Wibby. McKernan died in the early 1950s. His love of sports survived in his son, "Jock," a high school and college athlete who became governor of Maine in 1986.

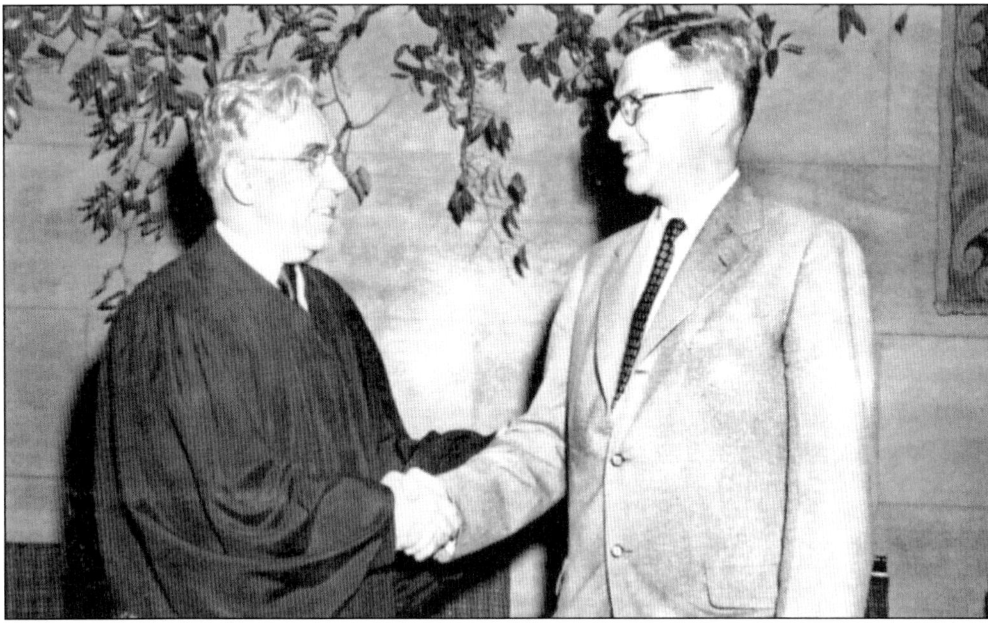

William H. Rines (right) General Manager of WCSH Radio, congratulates Rev. Howard O. Hough on the 25th anniversary of the First Radio Parish Church of America on April 18, 1951. Premiering on WCSH Radio in 1926, it is the oldest continuously broadcast religious program in the country. It is currently in its 80th year and airs daily on two television stations in Maine, WCSH6-Portland and WLBZ2-Bangor.

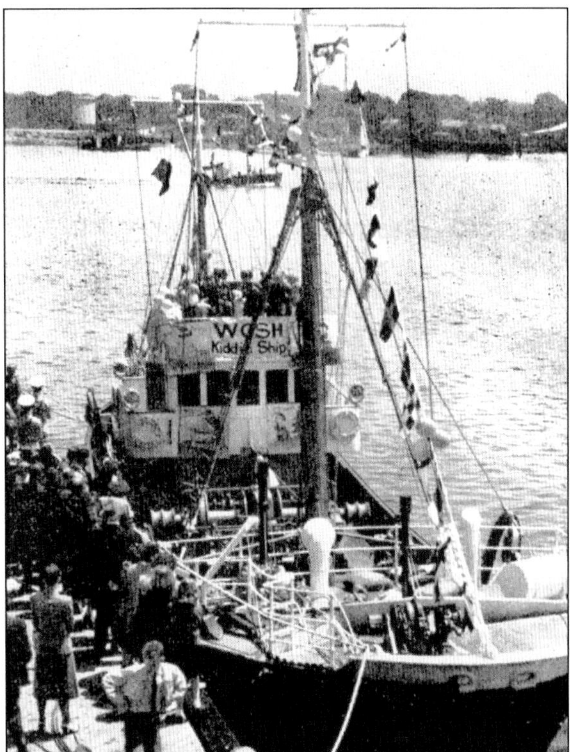

After World War II, Europe was in turmoil and Mainers were willing to give a helping hand. Organized by WCSH Radio and coordinated by 20 Maine Rotary clubs, 30 tons of food, clothing and toys were sent to France on a fishing trawler from Portland in July 1948. The send-off ceremonies were broadcast to France live by WCSH Radio announcer Ellis O'Brien, who spoke French fluently.

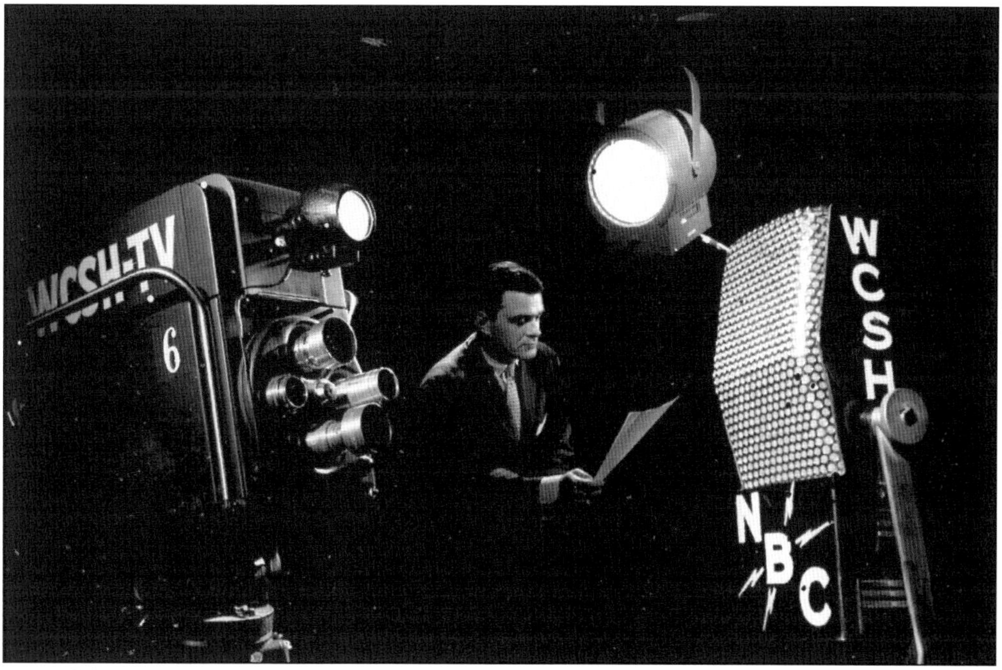

One of the more familiar faces in Maine Broadcasting was Clif Reynolds, seen here surrounded by the WCSH logos for radio and television. Clif was a station break announcer, the host of *Weekday*, a commercial talent, and a news anchor. His television career covered four decades.

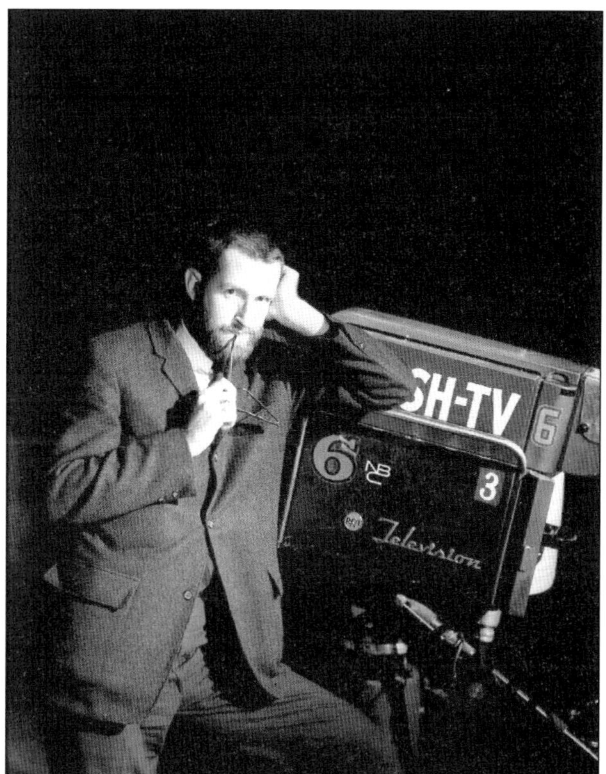

Lew Colby started his career as the WCSH-TV weatherman in the early 1960s. His quick wit and lively delivery garnered him an enthusiastic following of viewers. His humorous references to the people in the fictitious town of Hannibal's Crossing became his trademark. Throughout his career he was promotion manager, program director, station manager and general manager. By 1995, Colby had become the executive vice president of the Maine Broadcasting System.

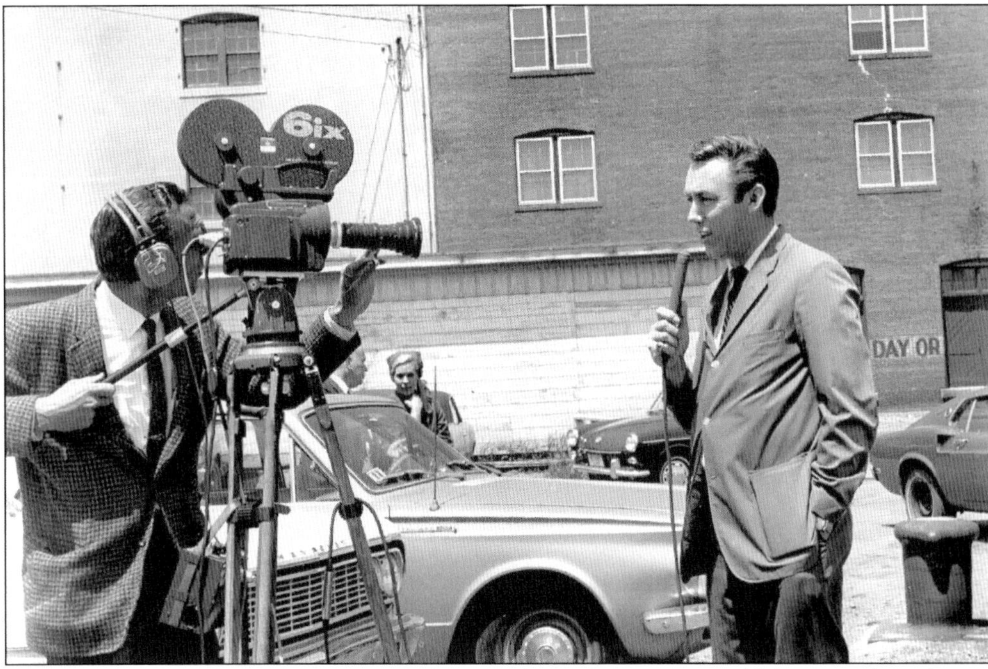

Fred Nutter, a popular news correspondent in the early 1960s, would become the editorial director. Don Sturtevant is the photographer.

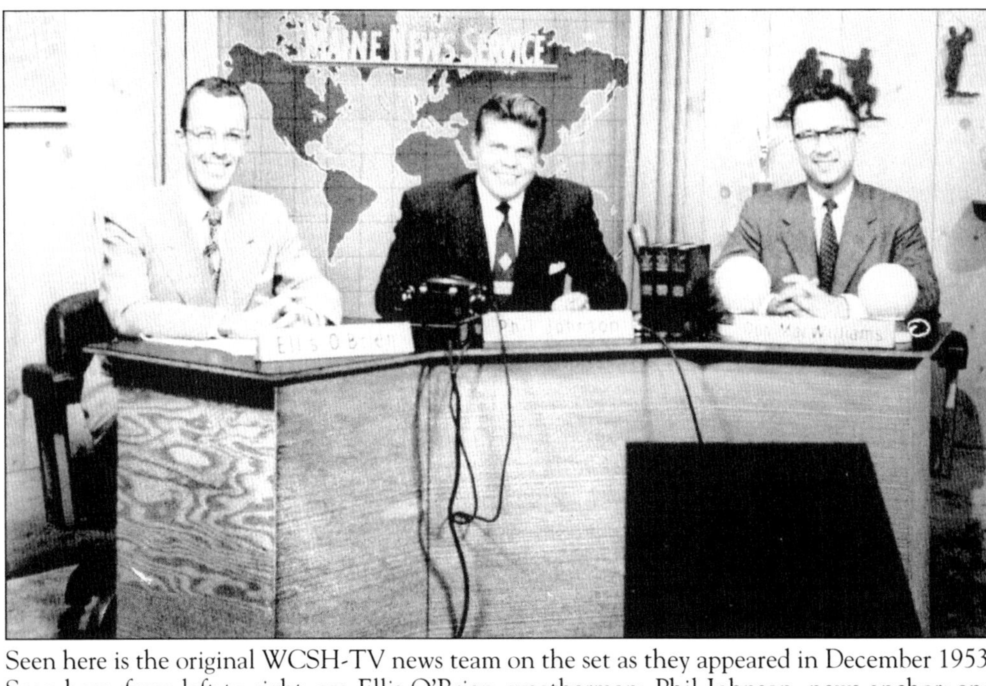

Seen here is the original WCSH-TV news team on the set as they appeared in December 1953. Seen here, from left to right, are Ellis O'Brien, weatherman; Phil Johnson, news anchor; and Don McWilliams, sportscaster. This news team stayed together for several years.

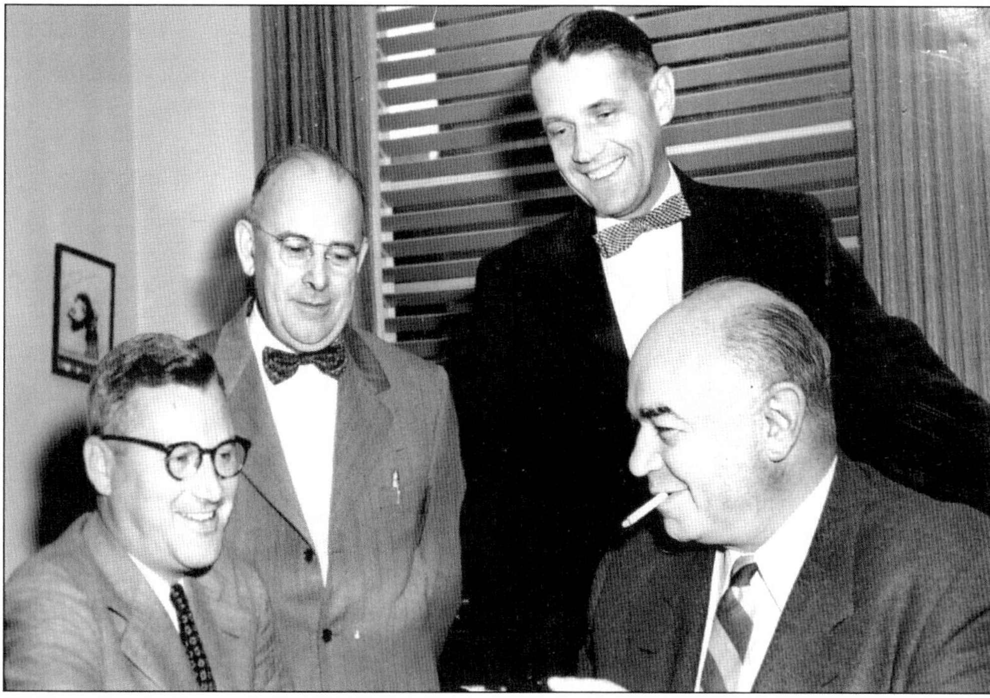

William Rines (lower left) president of the Maine Broadcasting System and Jack Atwood (upper right) executive vice president and general manager, watch as Henry Bannister signs the agreement affiliating WCSH Television with the NBC Television Network.

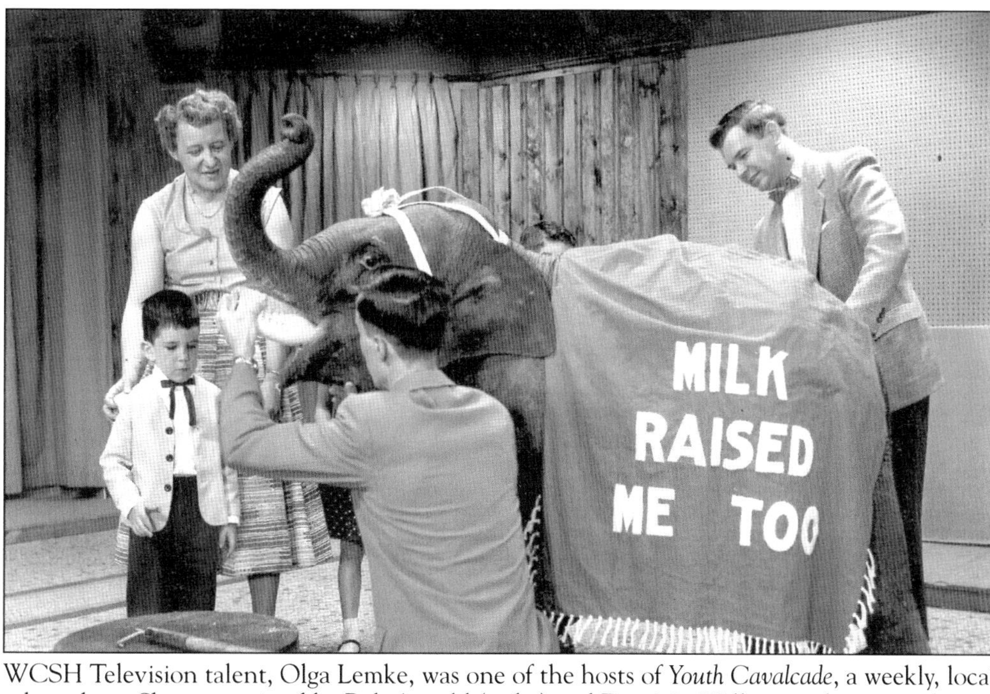

WCSH Television talent, Olga Lemke, was one of the hosts of *Youth Cavalcade*, a weekly, local talent show. She was assisted by Bob Arnold (right) and Don MacWilliams, who is not shown. Lemke was the only woman in America to have a doctorate of television at the time.

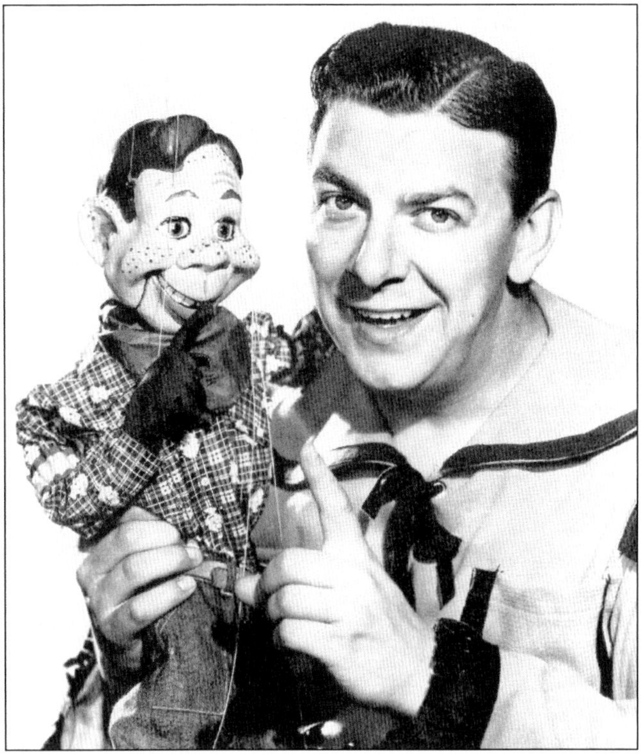

Howdy Doody and "Buffalo" Bob Smith were favorites with audiences in the early days of television and seen on WCSH-TV. Seeking escape from the brightness of the national spotlight, Smith bought a home in Maine. He liked it so much he purchased three Maine radio stations as well, WMKR-Millinocket, WHOU-Houlton and WQDY-Calais.

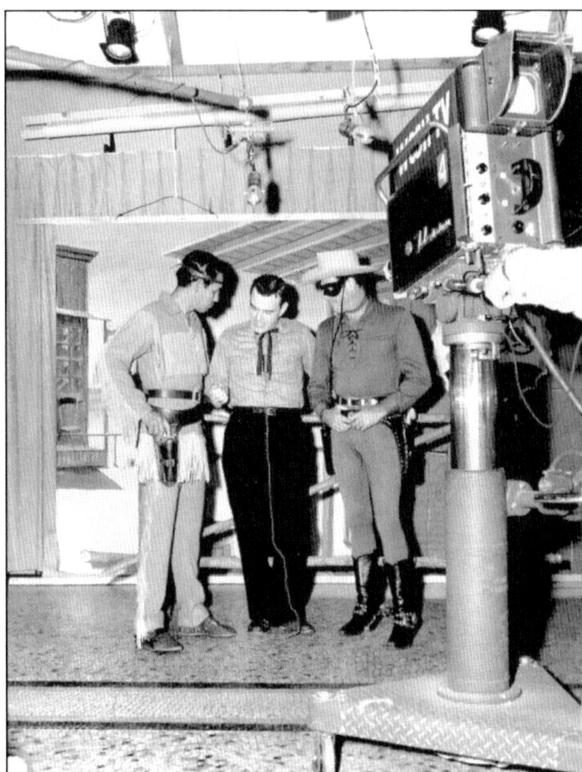

Clif Reynolds gives some friendly advice to the Lone Ranger and Tonto, Clayton Moore and Jay Silverheels. Early television programs like *The Lone Ranger* were very popular and drew large ratings in the early days of television for many affiliates. Clif would often announce the local commercial cut-ins live.

Romper Room was a popular children's program on WCSH-TV in 1962. Area children were brought to the studios each day to make up a new "class."

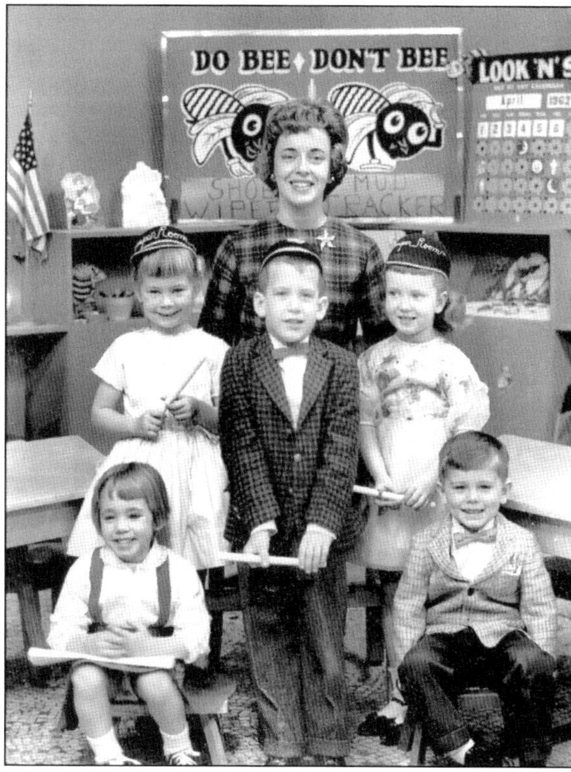

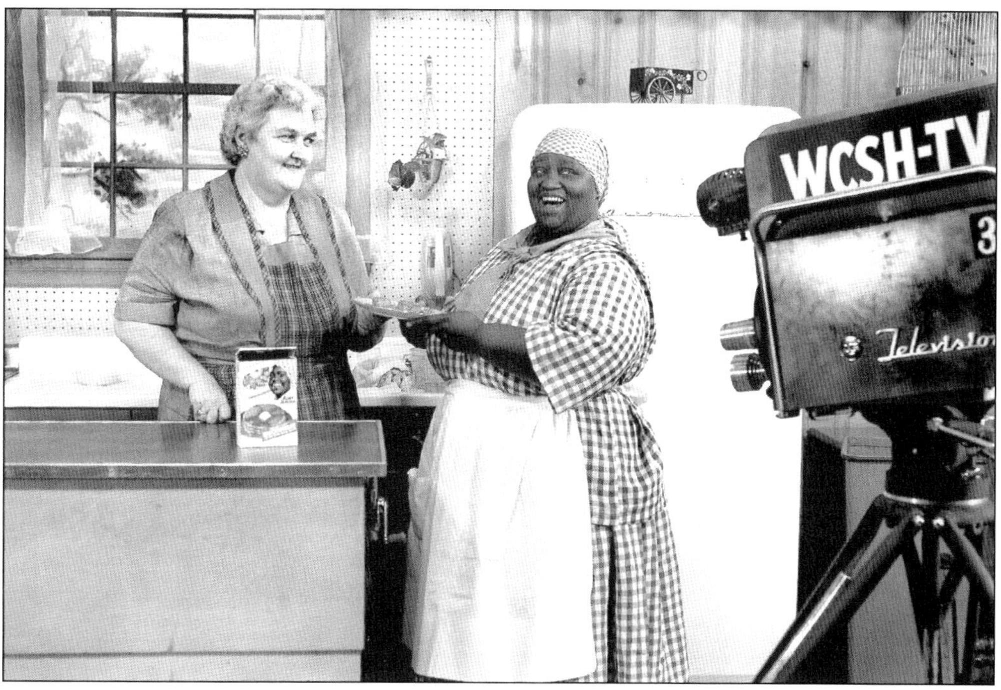

Aunt Jemima, who was on tour promoting her well-known pancake products, visits Agnes Gibbs. Gibbs (left) was the host of a popular cooking program on WCSH-TV in the 1950s and 1960s.

Clif Reynolds started working at WGUY Radio, Bangor, before moving to WCSH-TV Portland in 1955. He anchored the morning news continually for 33 years before he retired on December 30, 1988. During the early days of television, Clif would memorize 60-second commercials and rattle them off live several times an hour. Here Clif promotes the products of the Pepsi-Cola Bottling Company of Auburn.

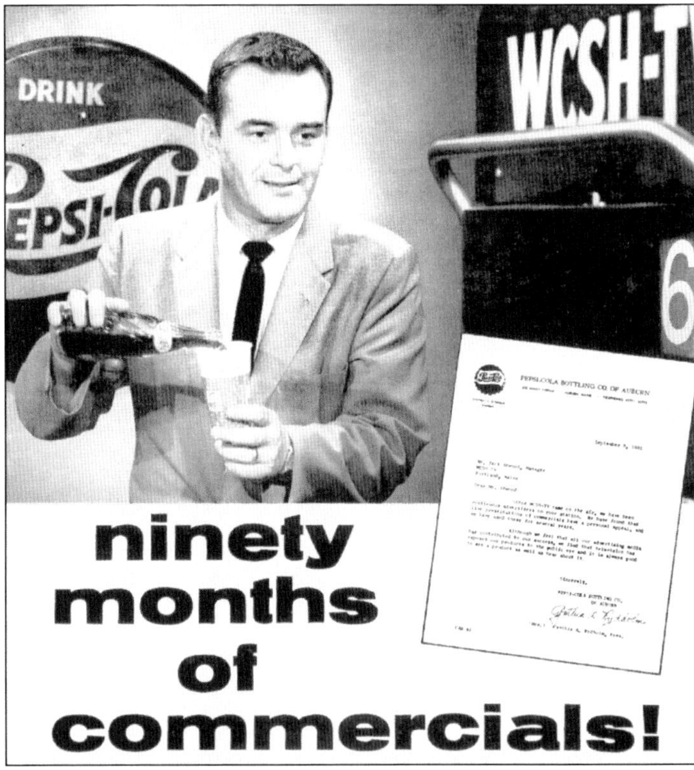

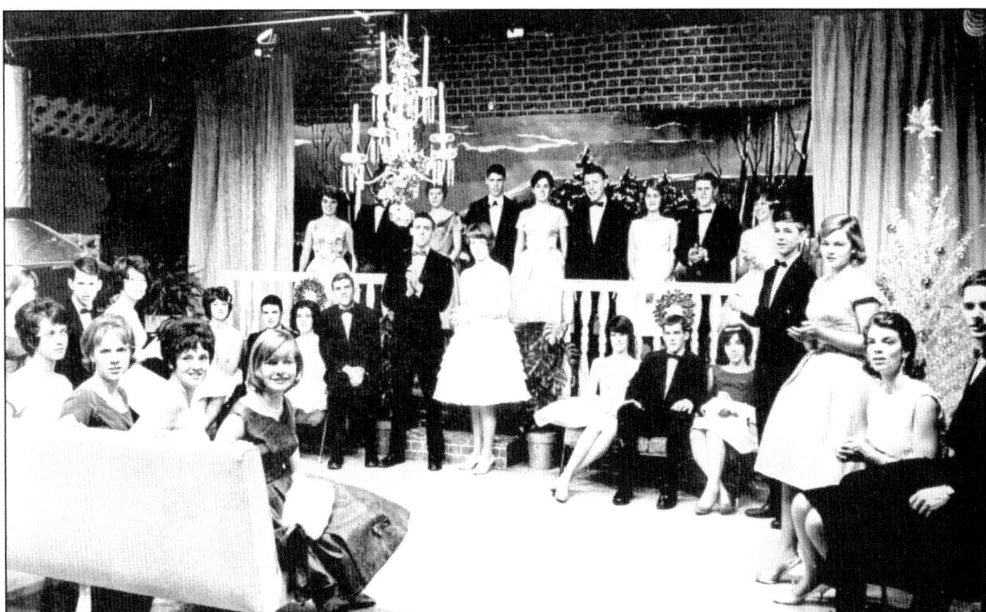

Anyone who attended high school in southern Maine in the late 1950s and early 1960s would recognize the set of *The Dave Astor Show* on WCSH-TV. Joining his regular performers were students from area high schools. The dance party aired live Saturday afternoons and featured young people dancing to records and lip-synching songs of popular recording artists. Quite innovative for its time, Astor's program was a tremendous personal effort.

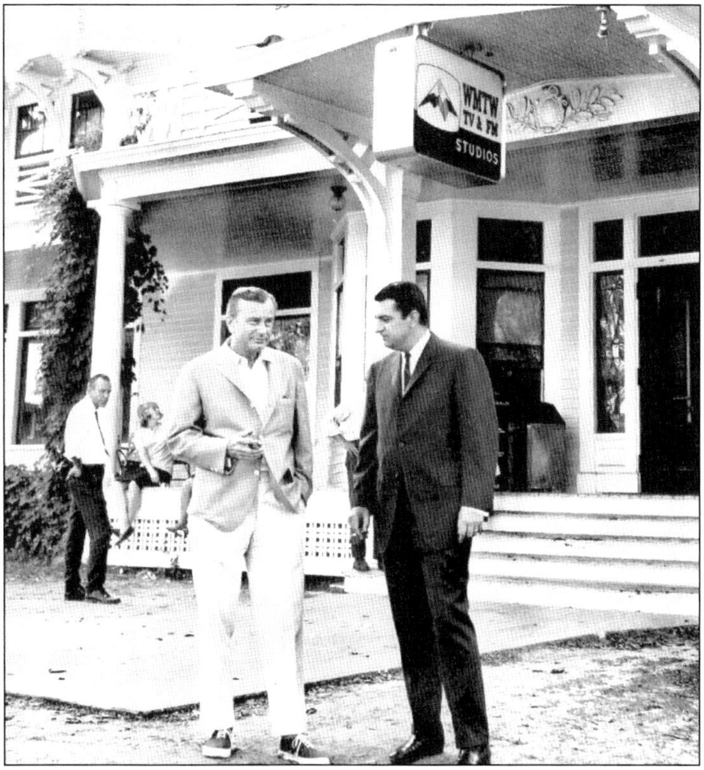

Jack Paar (left) and Lee Nelson discuss station matters under the WMTW-TV studio sign in 1965. Paar, a popular network television talk-show host, purchased WMTW-TV, channel 8 in Poland Spring, in the early 1960s. Lee Nelson had a lengthy career in broadcasting. He became Maine's first television announcer on WABI-TV in 1953 before working as the news director at WMTW-TV from 1960 to 1966. Lee's son, Lee Nelson Jr., became a television reporter in 1989 and is seen today on WCSH6-Portland and WLBZ2-Bangor.

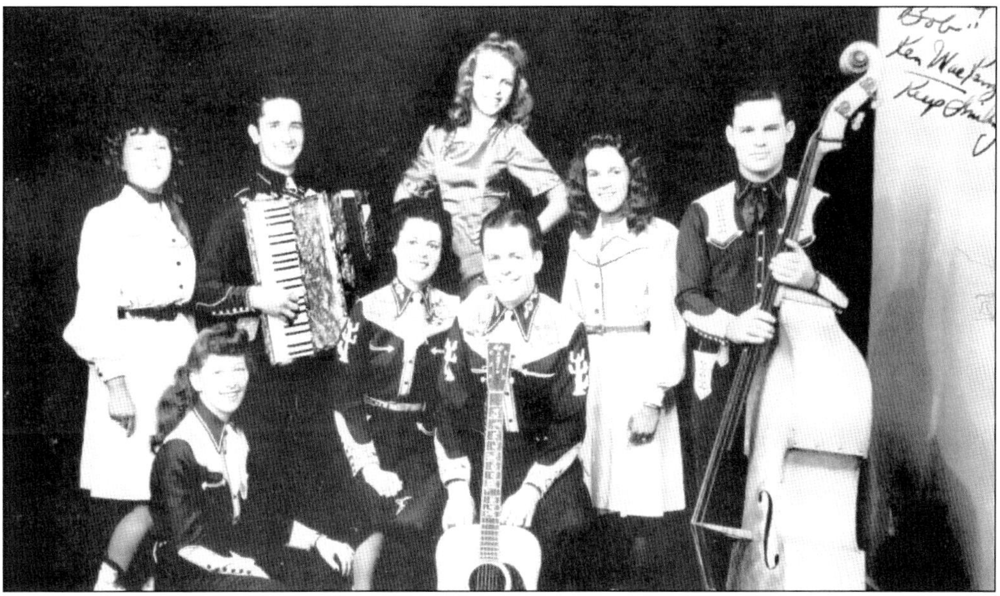

Stars of one of the most popular local programs appeared on WGAN Radio and later on WGAN-TV. Country-western singer Ken MacKenzie and his band are shown here in 1936. He always referred to his lovely wife as "Simone the Mrs." Ken had some talented members in his band, including Betty Gribben (lower left), the original singing cowgirl comic. MacKenzie started working full-time for WGAN Radio and Television in 1951, retiring in 1983. He started his broadcasting career on Henry Rines' radio station WFEA in Manchester, New Hampshire.

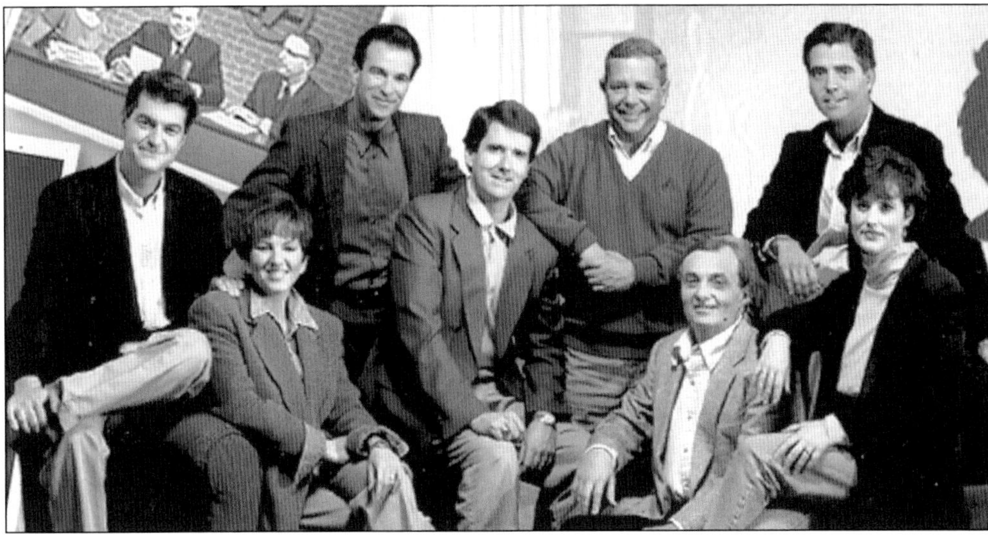

Here is the WCSH news team in 2005. Lee Nelson, Cindy Williams, Joe Cupo, Pat Callahan, Bruce Glasier, Kevin Mannix, Rob Caldwell and Sharon Rose (seen here, from left to right) have been together for over fifteen years. In 1998, the Rines family sold the television stations of the Maine Broadcasting System to the Gannett Corporation of Arlington, Virginia. Gannett, another longtime broadcasting company, recognized a quality company like itself and saw little need to change the on-air product and superb talent.

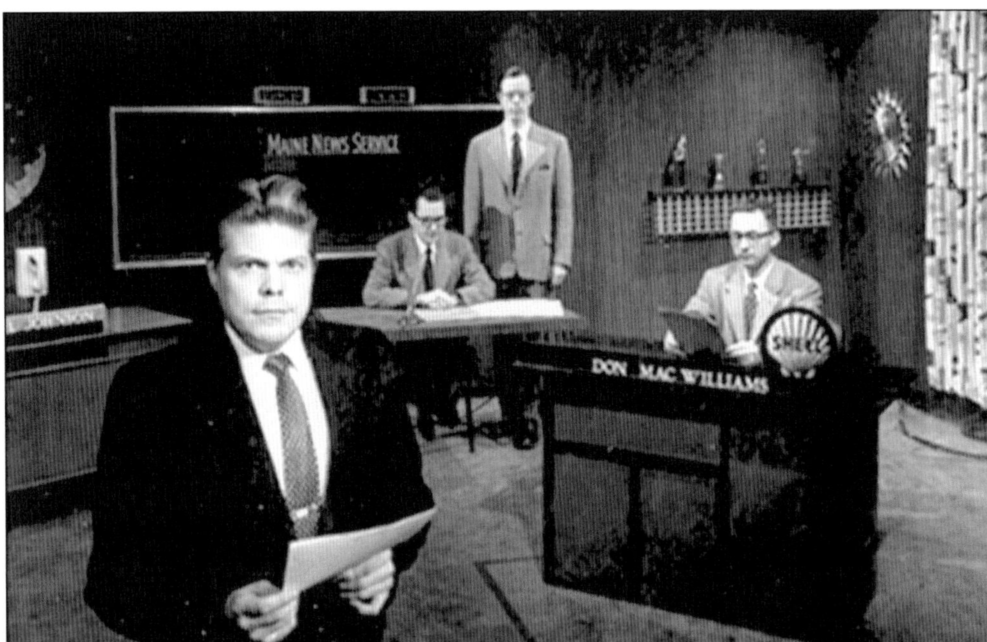

Pictured here is the first Channel 6 news team in 1953, made up of Phil Johnson, Larry Garrity, Ellis O'Brien and Don MacWilliams.

Five

Two Women of Enduring Grace

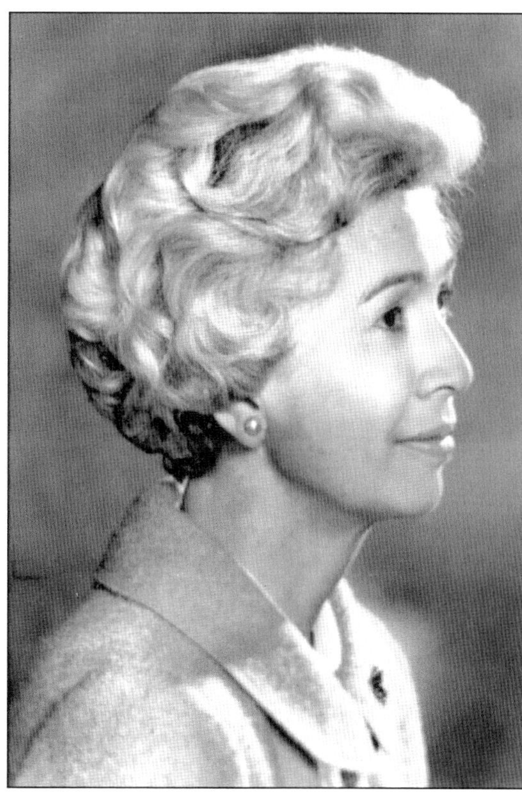

Adeline Bond Rines and Mary Rines Thompson (seen here) shared many things as mother and daughter. Nothing tested their abilities more than when the patriarchs of the family died suddenly. They were forced to play a role unfamiliar to most women at the time, that of business executive. Adeline did so in 1939 when her husband Henry died and Mary followed in 1970 when her brother William died. Both excelled.

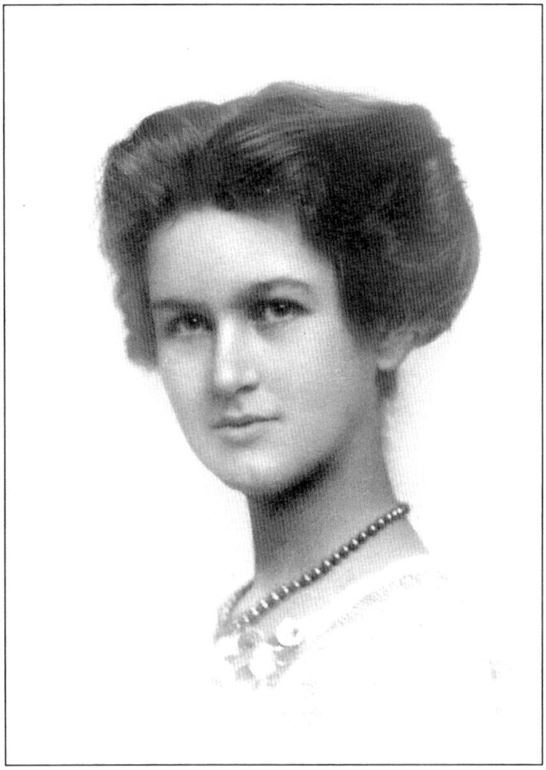

Adeline Rines was Cumberland County's first female attorney. She was admitted to practice before the courts of Maine on February 14, 1914. When her husband died suddenly in 1939, Adeline stepped in and watched over the operation of three hotels and four radio stations.

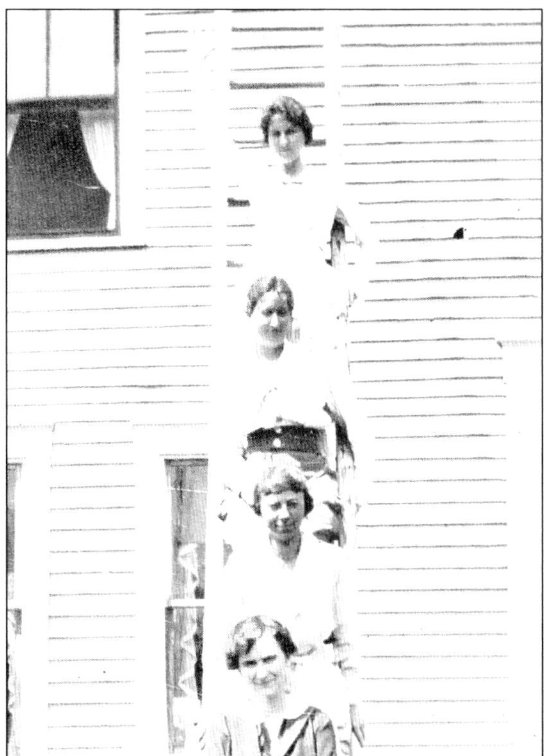

Here Adeline, with her sisters and friends, stands atop a ladder in front of her parents' home on Cumberland Avenue around 1910. Ironically, this house was located directly across the street from 769 Congress Street where Joseph and Anna Rines lived. Adeline would eventually move into 769 Congress Street with her husband Henry. She would give birth to two children, William and Mary, in their home. A few years later that home would become the Roma Restaurant.

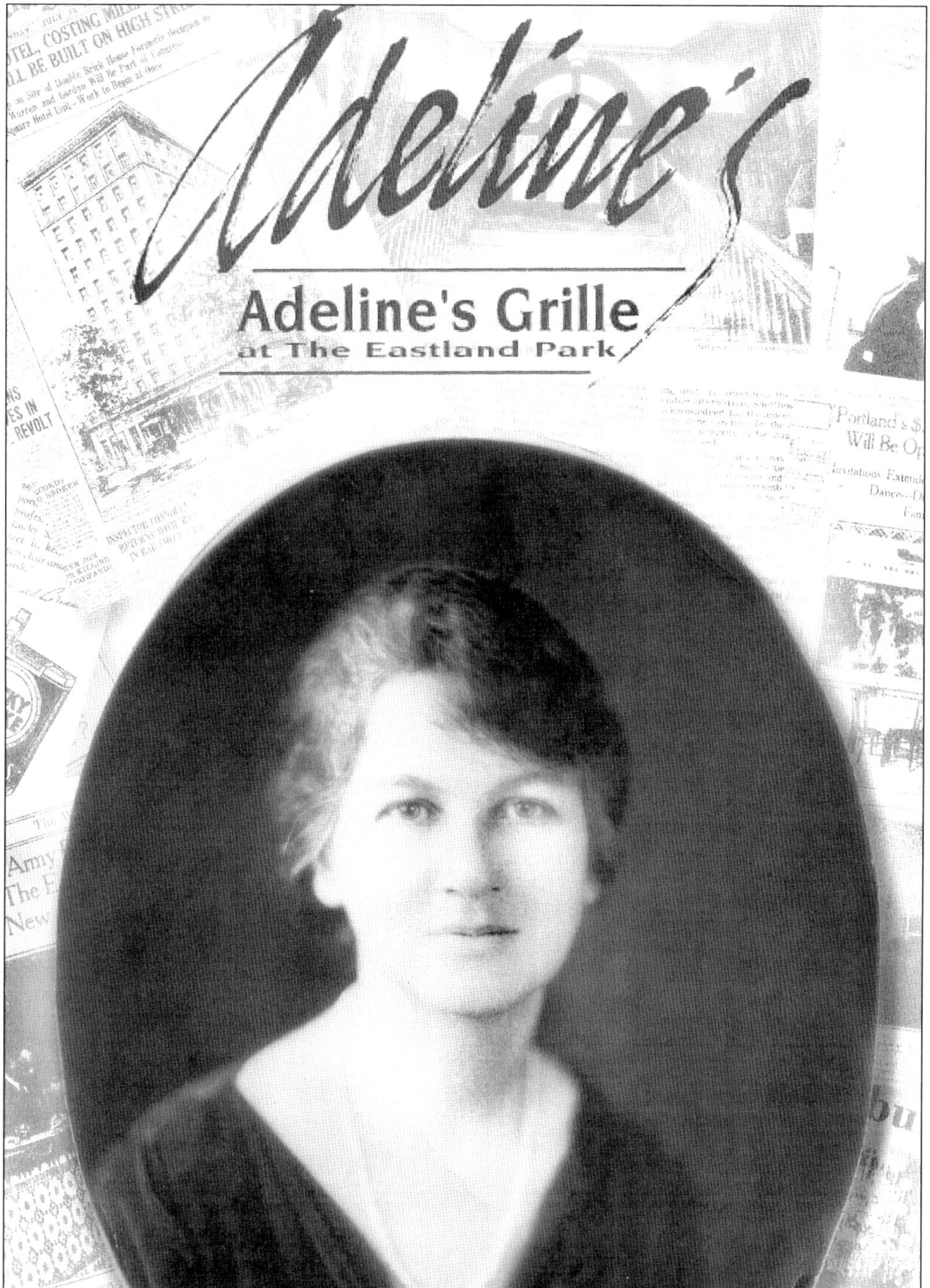

To honor Adeline in her role as female pioneer and hotel owner, the Eastland Park Hotel's new management named their premiere restaurant in her name. Adeline's Grille is located in the former Egyptian Court dining room, and is well worth a visit. (Courtesy of the Eastland Park Hotel.)

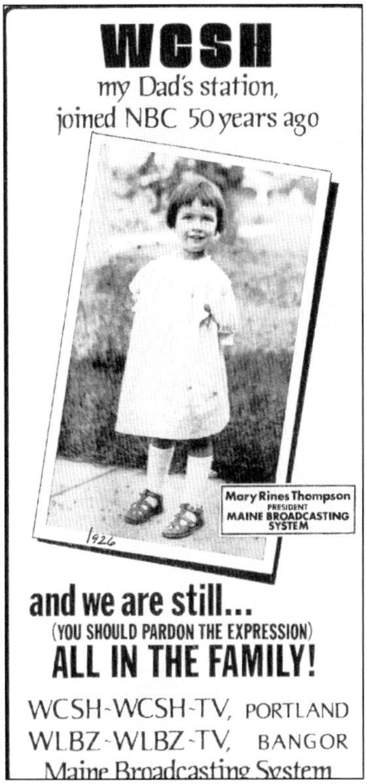

Mary Rines Thompson, sister of William H. Rines, took over as chairman of the board of the Maine Broadcasting System in 1970. She maintained the position until she retired in July 1983. Mary was one of only a few female executives in America to run a major media company. The Rines/Thompson family had the longest running ownership of an NBC affiliate in the country, dating back to when NBC and WCSH Radio first formed the network in 1926.

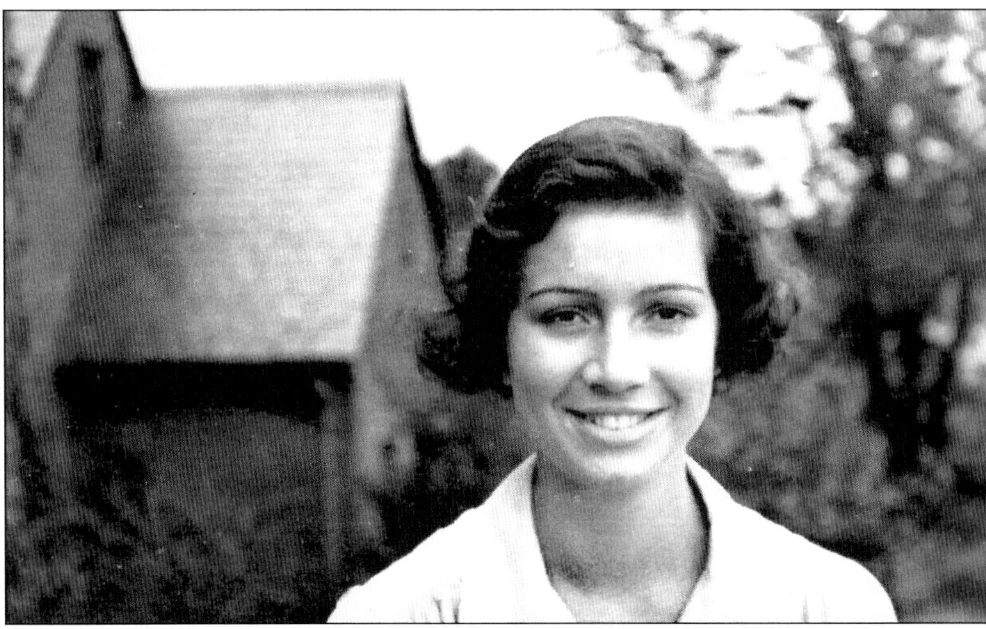

Mary Rines studied biology in college with the intention of becoming a physician. World War II forced her to reconsider. However, she did teach biology at Westbrook College during the war. Having six children and working as a very active public volunteer gave her a great deal of satisfaction. When Adeline asked her to run the family business upon the death of her brother in 1970, Mary did it without hesitation.

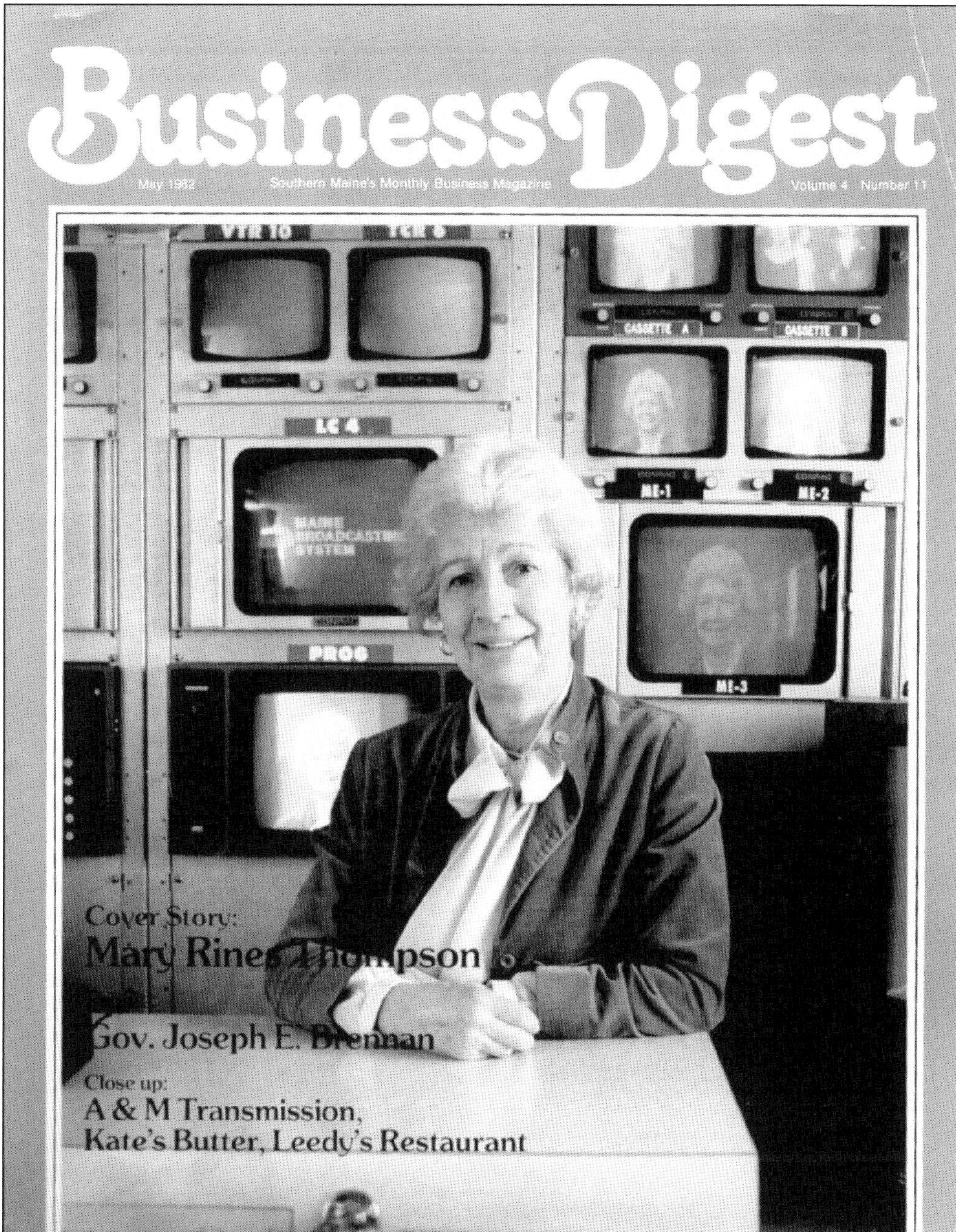

Mary Rines Thompson is featured on the cover of *Business Digest* in May 1982.

★ MARY RINES THOMPSON
1918 - 1992
Past President, WCSH - TV
Past Chairman of the Board,
Maine Broadcasting System

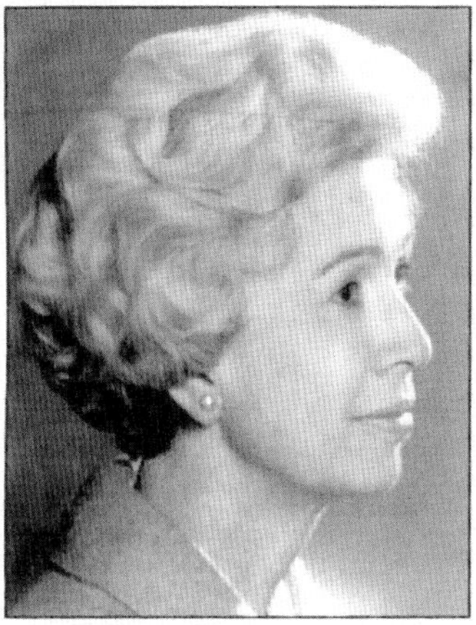

CAREER
Mary Rines Thompson was devoted to her family, business involvements and volunteer work in the community. She committed her life to raising her six children and serving her community. She was introduced to the broadcasting business through her family. Mary's father, Henry P. Rines, was involved in the hotel business. Henry had the Eastland Hotel (now the Sonesta Hotel) constructed and his father built the Congress Square Hotel. They were in need of advertising, thus the Maine Broadcasting System and WCSH were formed.

Mary joined the family business after her brother's death in 1970. Though previously uninvolved in the operation of the station, she took over the reins without hesitation. "I never gave it a second thought, it seemed like something I should do. It has always been a family-run station, and I thought it should remain that way," stated Mary during a 1982 interview. She continued to operate the Maine Broadcasting System for seventeen years, serving as President and Chairman of the Board from 1970 - 1982. It was Mary who created the climate and provided the leadership that helped to define the stations' corporate responsibility to the community. WCSH is NBC's oldest network affiliate and at one time Mary was one of the very few women in the country to head a large broadcast operation. When she retired in 1983, she was succeeded in her post by her son, Frederic Thompson.

COMMUNITY SERVICE
Mary was an active volunteer and served on many boards and committees including the Board of Directors of United Way, Board of Visitors of the Maine Youth Center, Board Member for the Greater Portland Chamber of Commerce and various positions with the University of Maine. Mary was one of the original founders of the Center for Voluntary Action in Portland. In recognition of Mary's service, The Center for voluntary Action gives the "Mary Rines Thompson Award" every year in her honor. In 1983 she was honored with the 40th annual Distinguished Service Award from the Kiwanis Club of Portland, and in 1987 Mary received the TWIN Award (Tribute to Women & Industry Emerita Award) from the YWCA of Portland in recognition of her many business and community involvements.

We honor Mary Rines Thompson tonight as an outstanding leader in the business community. She devoted her life to her children and serving her community.

MAINE BUSINESS HALL OF FAME

Mary Rines Thompson was the recipient of the Maine Business Hall of Fame Award in 1988. Another award presented annually by the Portland YWCA to businesswomen who demonstrated extraordinary professional leadership is the YWCA TWIN Award. The TWIN Emerita was only given once, to Mary Rines Thompson in 1984.

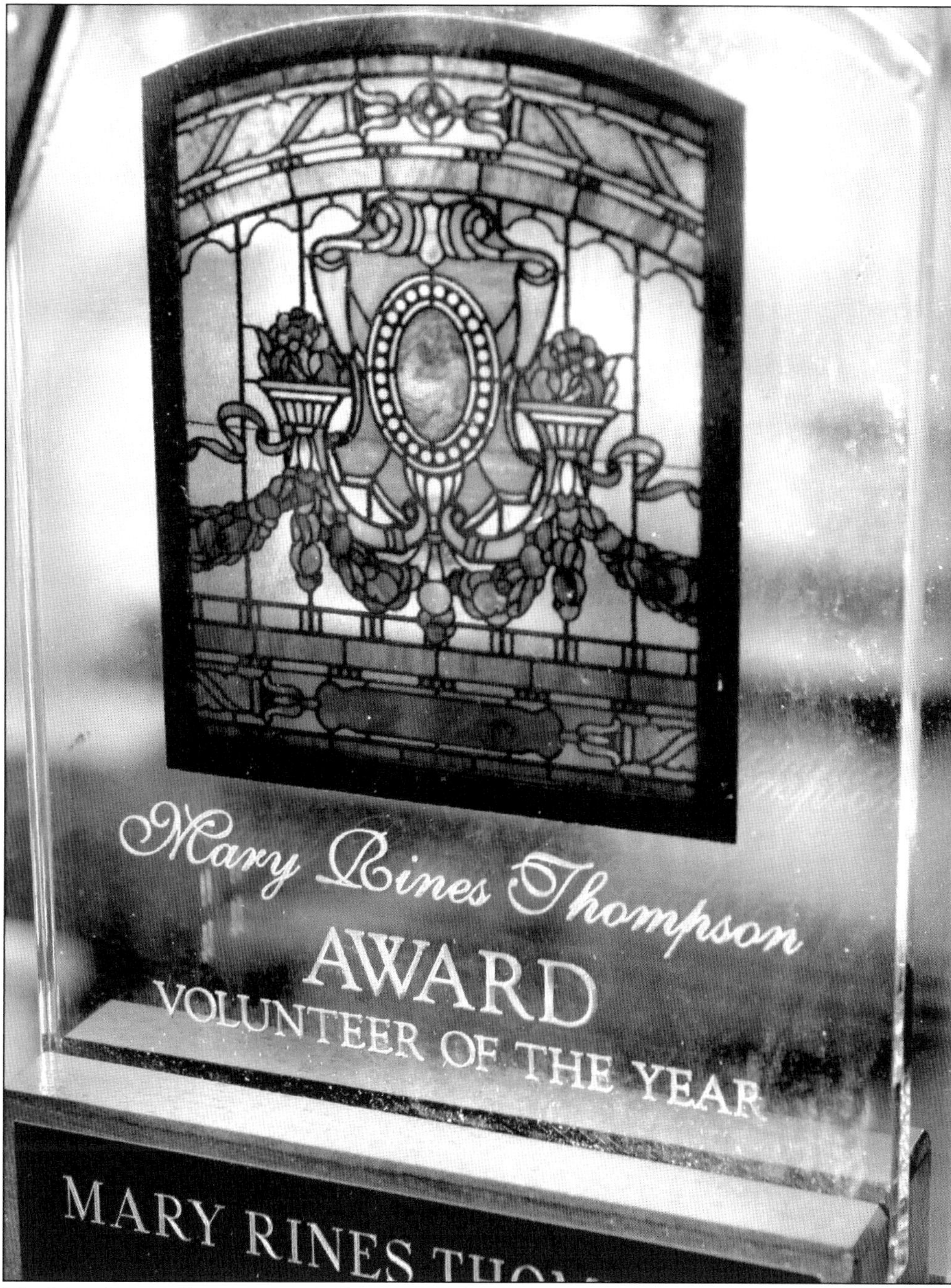

The Mary Rines Thompson Award is presented annually by the United Way of Greater Portland and WCSH6 to that person who shows an unselfish dedication to helping others. The stained glass image embedded in the award is a reproduction of the windows that Mary's grandfather, Joseph, had installed in his Congress Square Hotel dining room in 1896.

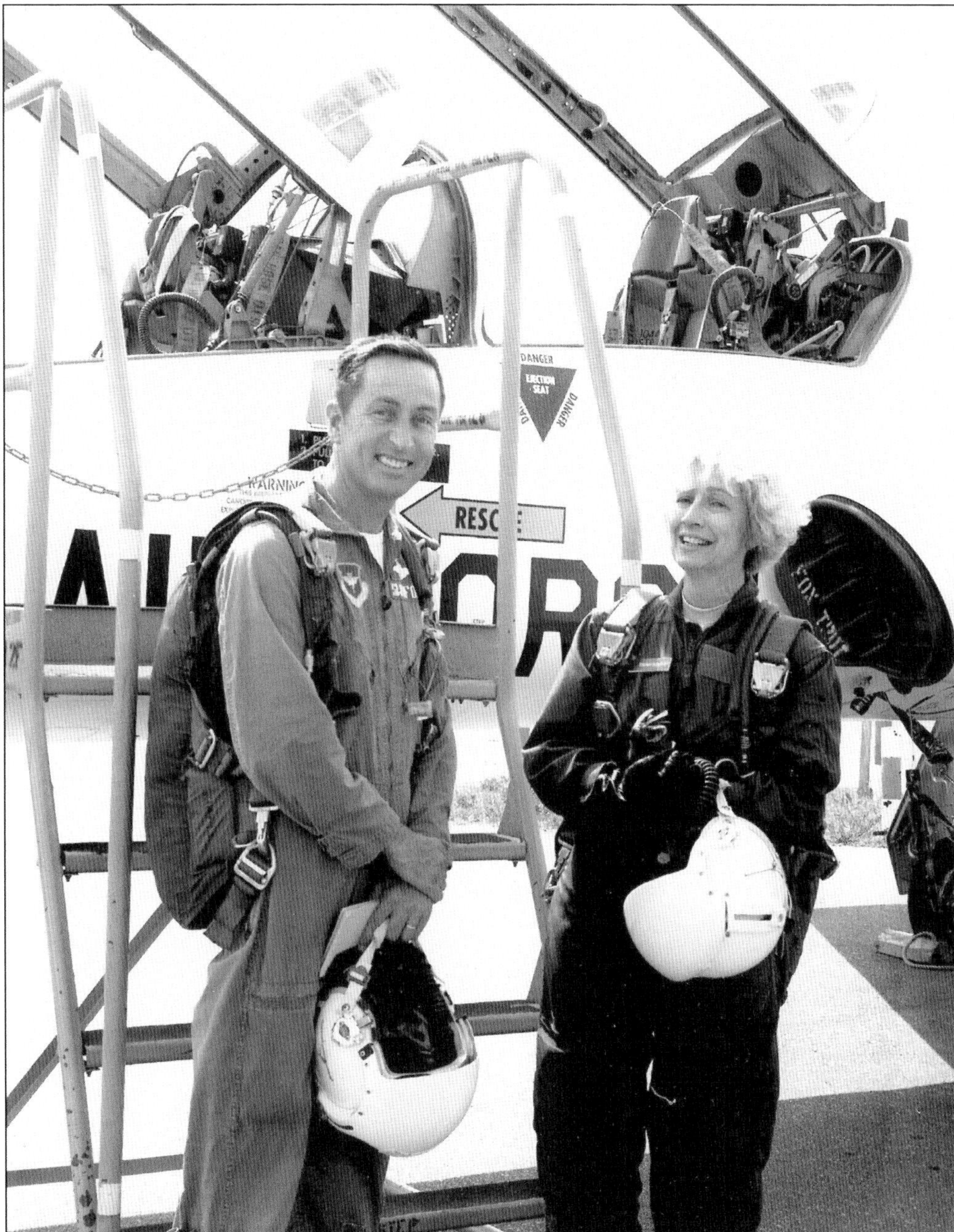

Mary Rines Thompson was a friend of U.S. senator Margaret Chase Smith of Maine, and was appointed by independent governor James Longley to be a member on the Commission for Maine's Future. Senator Smith had a lot of influence at the pentagon. When the senator was asked if a businessman from Maine would like to visit Maxwell Air Force Base in Alabama, the senator said, "No, but I do know a woman." Anyone who knew Mary would think this was very much out of character, but she was thrilled to fly in a military jet.

Six

The Rines Family Legacy

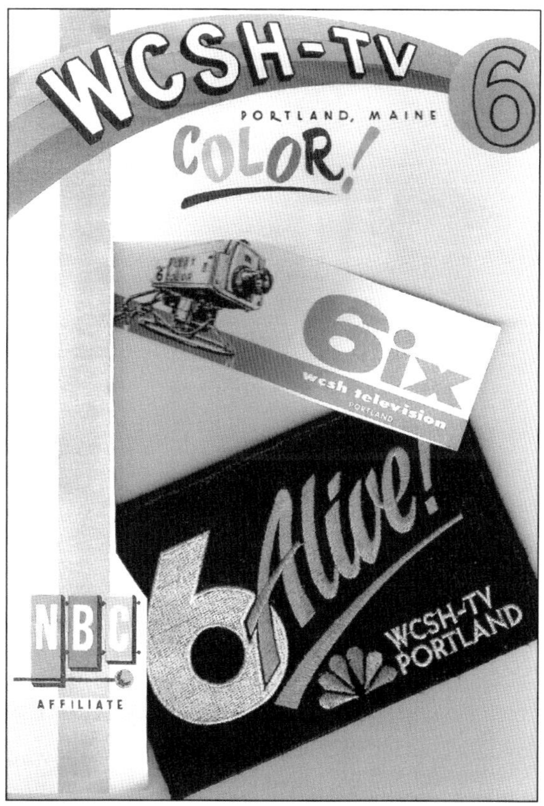

The Rines Brothers Company Store is gone. The Congress Square and Columbia Hotels are gone. The Danish Village is no longer, and the family sold the Eastland Hotel in 1960. The radio stations were sold in 1979 and the television stations were sold in 1998, but Portlanders will frequently come across the Rines' name. Whether they hear guest speakers at the Portland Public Library in the Rines Room, see the televised Mary Rines Thompson Award given away every year by WCSH6 and the United Way of Greater Portland, or apply for funding for their favorite charity or civic organization from the Rines/Thompson Fund of the Maine Community Foundation, the legacy of the Rines family will live a long time in Maine.

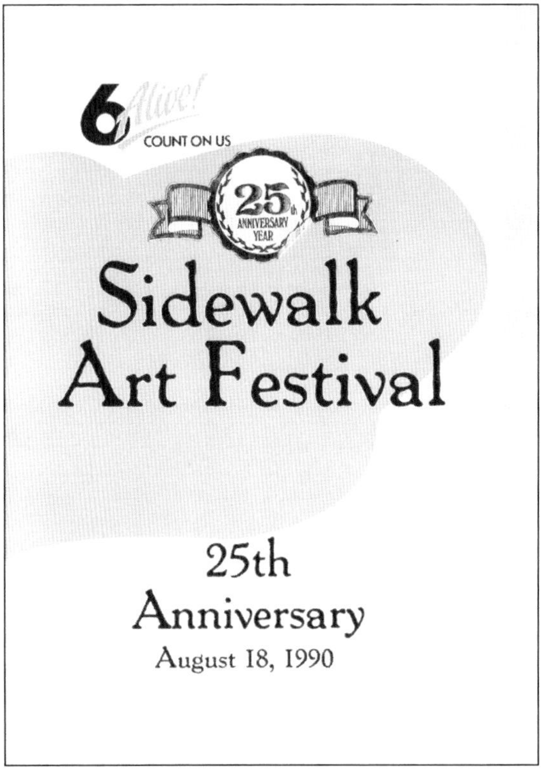

WCSH-TV employees Lew Colby and Arthur Hahn came up with the idea for the WCSH Television Sidewalk Art Festival in 1965. Then as now, it is the largest single one-day art festival on the east coast with over 350 artists displaying their work along Congress Street in late August. The event draws over 40,000 people to downtown Portland and 2005 marks its 40th anniversary.

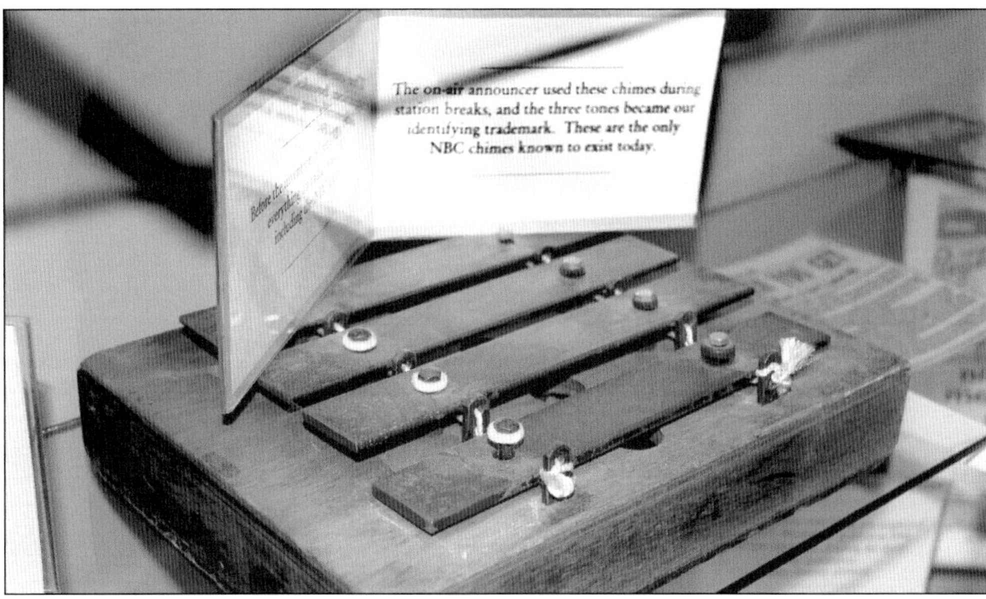

The dinner chimes seen here were given to WCSH Radio in 1926 to signal the NBC Radio Network of pending station breaks through the 1920s and 1930s. They are the only original NBC chimes known to exist and belong to the WCSH6 museum showcase. The notes for the famous chimes were G, E, C which stood for the first co-owner of the NBC Radio Network, the General Electric Corporation. Ironically, several owners later, the General Electric Company once again owns the NBC Television Network.

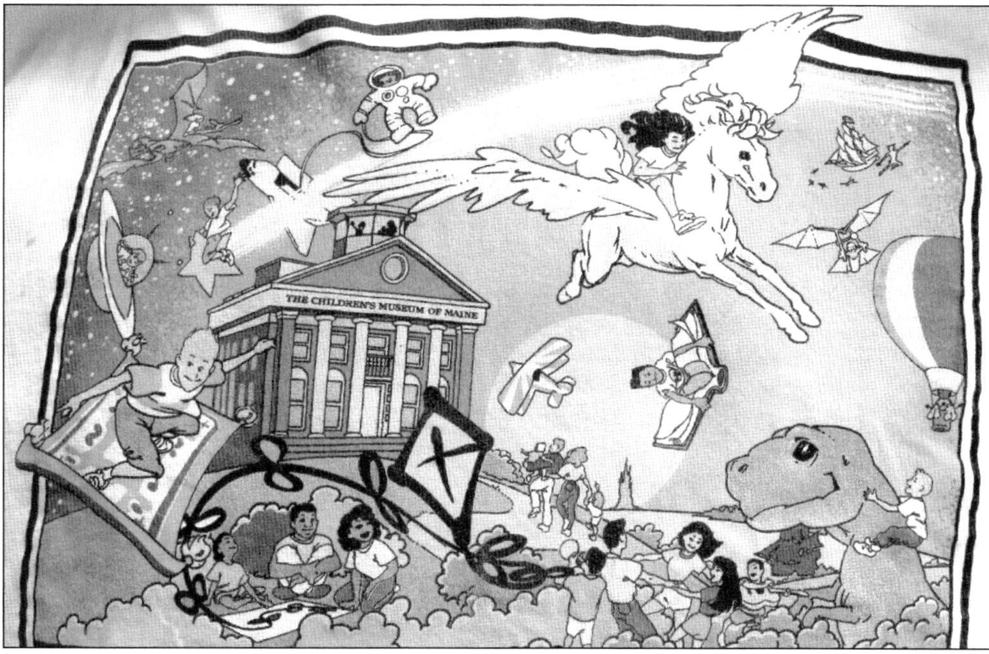

In 1990, WCSH6 led the campaign to bring the Children's Museum of Maine to the former Chamber of Commerce building in downtown Portland (seen below in 1920). The Children's Museum is considered one of the best in the country. The museum's camera obscura, designed by Kodak, is the finest in the world.

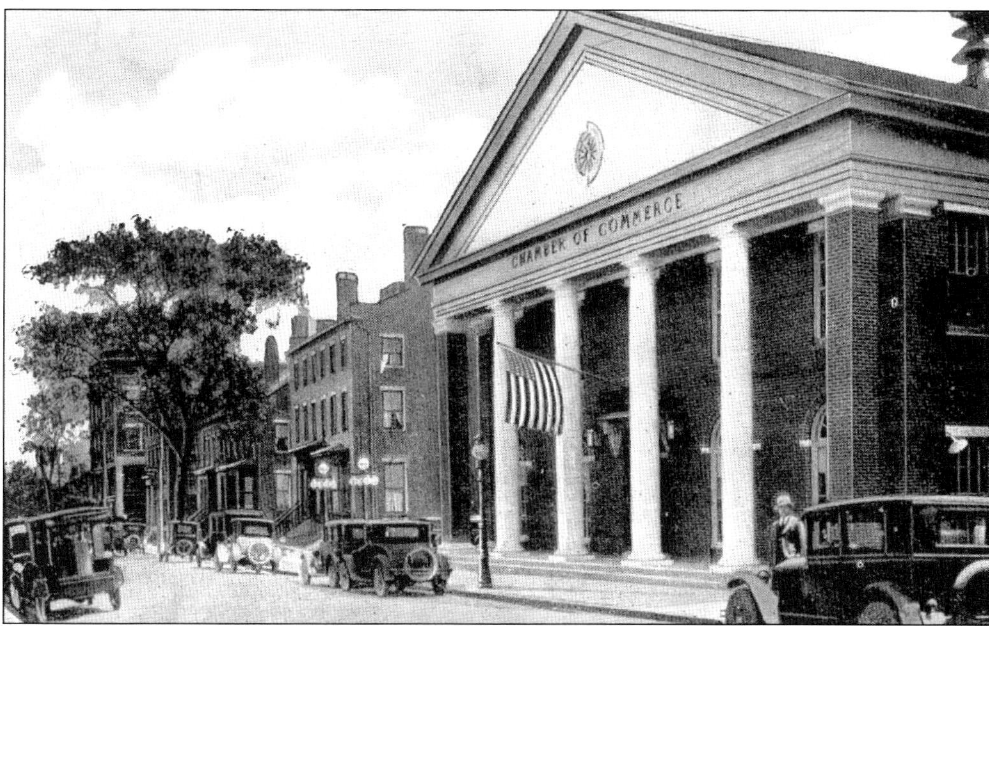

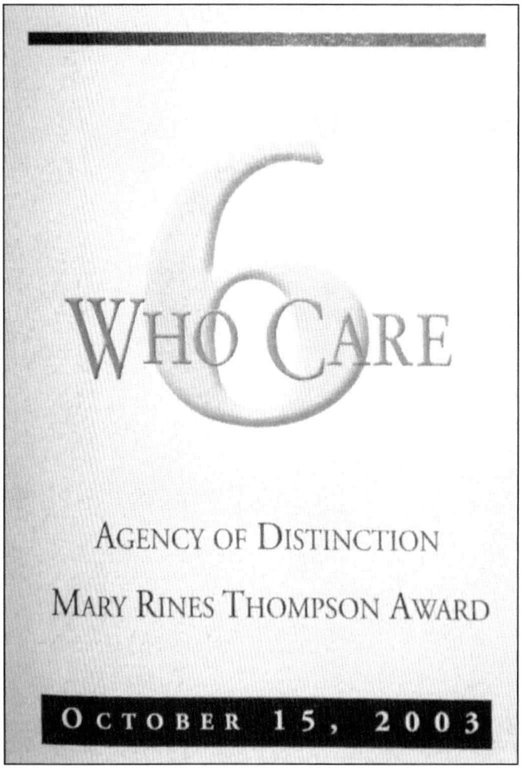

WCSH6 and the United Way of Greater Portland celebrate the 6 Who Care Awards every year. Six individuals are given awards for their commitment to charitable work or public service. The recipient who receives the most votes by the judges is given the Mary Rines Thompson Award for unselfish dedication to others. An Agency of Distinction Award is also given to the social organization that the judges deem to have performed the most outstanding public service.

MAINE COMMUNITY FOUNDATION

Fulfilling the promise of giving

245 Main Street, Ellsworth, ME 04605

The Rines/Thompson Fund of the Maine Community Foundation gives away over $100,000 every year to greater Portland charitable and non-profit organizations. Information about the Maine Community Foundation and the Rines/Thompson Fund can be found on the Maine Community Foundation Website.

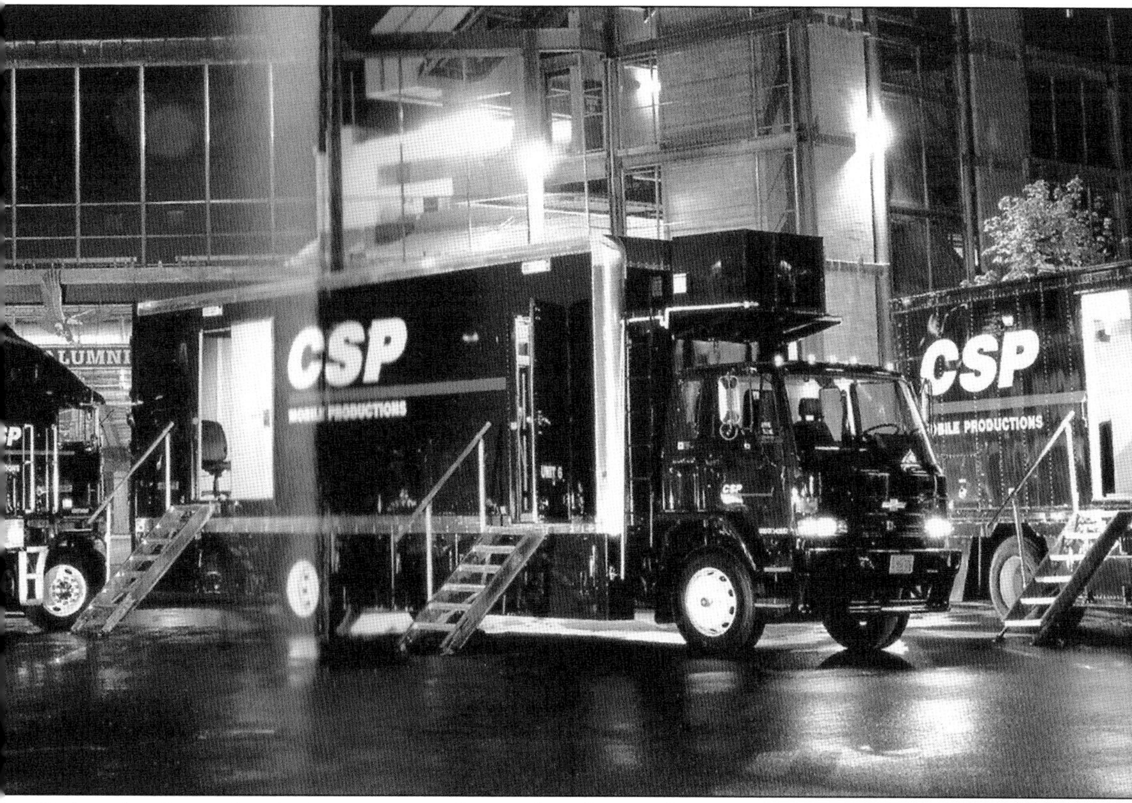

Today the Rines family business is video and audio production services. Congress Square Productions, CSP, is a fleet of mobile television and audio production trucks which travel to every part of North America where live sporting events, music concerts, or remote conference venues need to be broadcast or recorded. Nat Thompson, Lew Colby, and Lenny Chase run the operation from Saco, Maine. The trucks have been used for Celtics, Bruins, and Red Sox games, the Olympics, many music concerts, and a variety of college and semi-professional sports events.

In January 1998, WCSH6 and WLBZ2 were sold to the Gannett Corporation. Longtime broadcasters like the Rines family, Gannett still maintains the same integrity, high quality, and commitment to news, entertainment, and public service as the Rines family did.

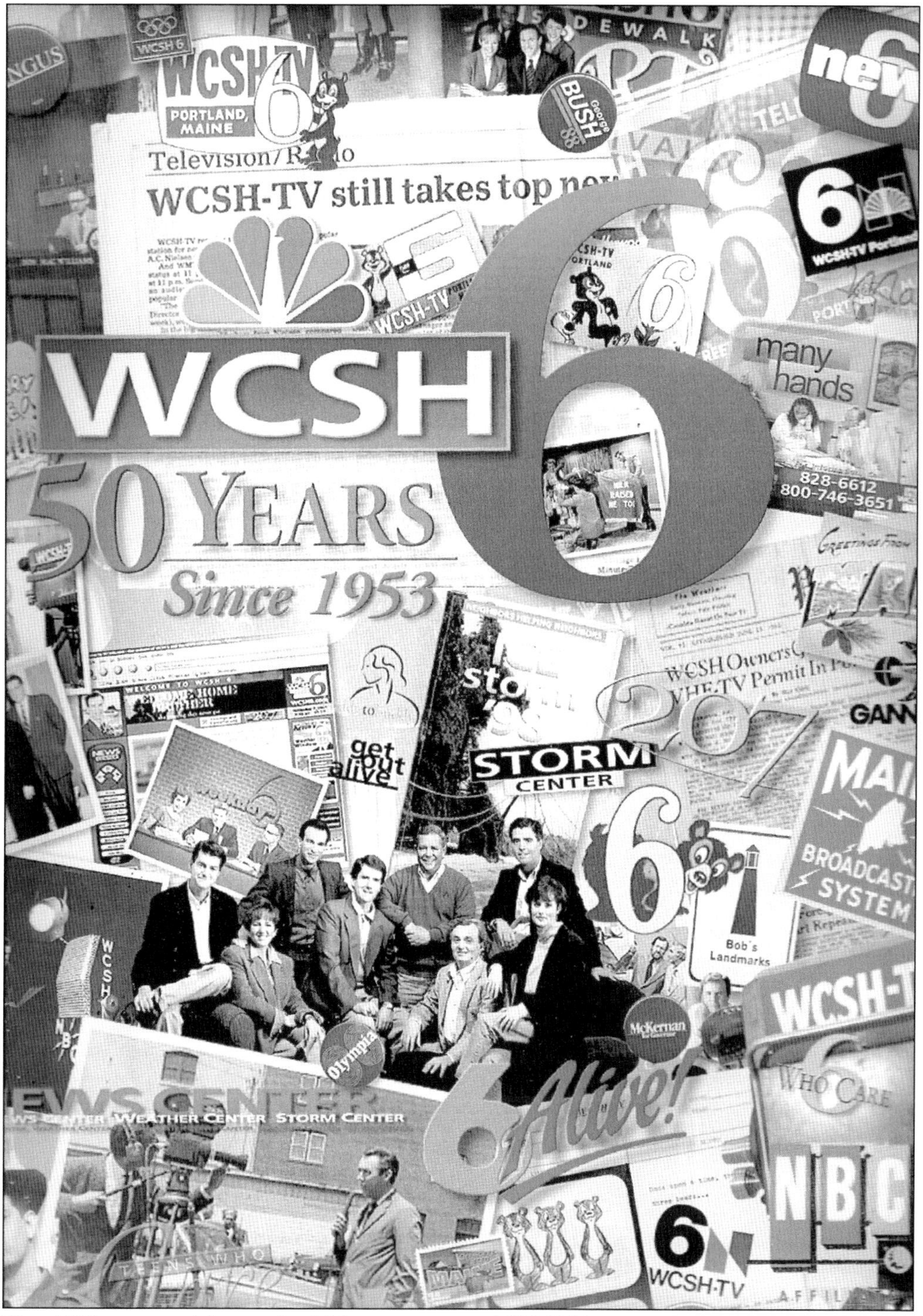

This 2003 poster celebrates the 50th anniversary of WCSH6.

Employee Acknowledgments

The Rines family members could not have done what they did without the help of many talented and dedicated people. George Kelly, the general manager of the hotels in the 1940s and 1950s, assisted William Rines, who was in his early twenties when his father died, and Adeline, who was drawn in by her husband's death and was not accustomed to running a business. George was a cook at the Eastland as a young man. Henry Rines recognized his sharp mind and quick intelligence. He financed George's education and was rewarded with a strong and devoted manager.

The creative talent of Jack Atwood cannot be over emphasized. He started his career at WLBZ Radio in the 1930s and was a quick study in all aspects of the business. He quickly rose through the ranks and, by the 1960s, he became general manager of both the radio and television businesses. His innovative television program ideas and ability to recognize talent were genius. Among the talented chief executive officers of the company whose careers he nurtured were Don Powers, Bruce McGorrill, and Lew Colby. The radio and television industry, like many other businesses, is based on inspirational and creative people. The ideas brought to the Rines family businesses were manifold. The imaginative talents of longtime production employees like Bun Pool, Dave Serette, Paul Doughty, Mike Marshall, Debbie Mundee, Bill Taylor, and Dave Plummer are without equal in the television production community. Margo Cobb, Jeff Marks, Ed and Thompson Guernsey, Ben Hubley, Bruce Lewis, and Judy Horan were station managers whose talents could be matched against any in the industry. And the sales abilities of Lila Saindon and Jim Doyle are well known throughout the broadcasting world. News directors like Michael Curry have left their indelible imprints on the "NewsCenter" product. Chief engineers like Clem Payeur and Jim Boutin applied their expertise during extremely complicated technical transitions. Bessie Blake, Ken Peterson, Bob McLain, and Dale Eichorn ably handled the financial details.

But not enough can be said about the on-air talents that have graced the airwaves of the Rines family television and radio stations. Gifted on-air personalities like Linwood Pitman, Clif Reynolds, Agnes Gibbs, Olga Lemke, Dave Astor, Don MacWilliams, Lee Quimby, Fred Nutter, Eddy Driscoll, Jake Broffee, and all the ministers of the First Radio Parish Church are only a few of the memorable and creative people who shared their flair with the audiences of Maine and New Hampshire. But, the best and brightest that the industry has to offer is the present news team of the Gannett Corporation in Maine, the former Maine Broadcasting System. For those of you who have traveled around the country and sampled other local television news programs, most would agree that the news talent seen in Maine is second to none, anywhere. There are many reasons for this, but not the least is the nurturing nature of the environments created by the WCSH and WLBZ station management, originally starting with the Rines family and today continued through the management of the Gannett Corporation. A successful business can be measured in many different ways, but it never took long for most outsiders visiting the Rines family business to see the warm environment and friendly nature of the staff. "It's like one big happy family here . . . . It's immediately recognizable," were words spoken at least once a week by guests and business associates. That environment, established by the family and management, shows through in the product. The talent that we see in local news every day and night may be some of the last true craftsmen and women in America. Surely audiences would agree that WCSH and WLBZ television presently have the best local news programs anywhere.